WHAT AGENTS ARE SAYING ABOUT
The Millionaire Real Estate Agent!

"The Millionaire Real Estate Agent changed my life! The concepts were very awakening and enlightening to me. The systems already mapped out for me to follow are priceless. Just take the book and carry it with you at all times as a road map to get you where you want to go."

Leith Seegers-McKahan
Arlington, TX

"The concept 'Millionaire Real Estate Agent' is a lofty goal for anyone to strive for. The models provided in this book identify the pathways and the pitfalls. From the outset, Gary makes it clear that 'the money' is not the issue, but merely a marker. The ultimate goal is making a business worth having in order to have a life worth living."

Kathy Auerbach
Bellingham, WA

"This material was much more than an eye-opener. It was a door-opener, taking me to the next level. Gary has a way of communicating directly to you as if you were the only person he is talking to."

Paul Andres
San Francisco, CA

"Wow! What a concept! It's about time real estate agents looked at their work as a business and not as a job."

Randy Selby
Houston, TX

"Why not me? I have literally 'crossed over' from being a real estate agent with limitations to being a real estate consultant without any limitations on what I can achieve."

Jo-Anne LaBuda
Worthington, OH

"Everyone wonders why some agents clearly outmaneuver the majority of their competitors. For the first time in my thirty-year career, someone has shown us the way! Gary Keller has agreed not only to give us the map for the road to success, but more importantly, to teach us to stay on that road, find new routes, and go further with every new course adjustment."

Shirley Olea
San Francisco, CA

"If any agent currently in real estate wants to make more money, net more money, work less and succeed at the highest level possible in their professional and personal lives, then The Millionaire Real Estate Agent *was designed for them. Our business, our net worth, and our lives have all been greatly enhanced because of this incredible education."*

Jan Richey
Plano, TX

"The concepts taught by Gary Keller can and will make you rich if followed."

Jim Buff
Asheville, NC

"This material is laid out with straightforward techniques that make it possible for any agent to truly achieve the 7th Level of ownership, and having the business run itself."

Tim Burroughs
Boise, ID

"Prior to real estate, I worked for IBM, Toshiba, and Dell. Never have I experienced such valuable training. It is the most exhilarating real estate training that I have ever received. Thanks so much for teaching me to take my business to the next level."

J. Rene Ward
Round Rock, TX

"It is NOT a pipe dream! The Millionaire Real Estate Agent concept and model is simple, straightforward, and very doable. Gary Keller has developed the blueprint for success. If you can get out of bed in the morning and be disciplined, there is no reason not to succeed."

Peggy Devoney
Atlanta, GA

"It is the most thought-out real estate business model ever. The concept is not pie in the sky. It is not even a concept because it is being done every day. Think big! Lead generate! Add systems! Hire three great people. You're a millionaire! Many thanks to Gary and Dave for sharing their vision."

Gene Arant
Austin, TX

"The Millionaire Real Estate Agent is a blueprint that takes away any guesswork. Now there's no excuse for not knowing what you need to do for great success or even how much it will cost. I strongly recommend this material to anyone who wants to achieve millionaire status."

Elaine Sans Souci
Phoenix, AZ

"This material is another giant step to the top. It helped me remove my limited thinking, and I have already implemented the material. I appreciate not having to invent something new—all I have to do is put it in practice."

Steve Chader
Mesa, AZ

"Why not think big when you have the resources provided in this book? The tools have been handed to us and the path to enriching our life and career is just waiting for us to jump in and go for it!"

Beth Schneider
Edmund, OK

"Finally, a clear path to realize my full potential in real estate. My team will never look back."

Andy Allen
Austin, TX

"This gives me the cutting edge above my competition. It has completely changed the way I run my business!"

Deone Smith
Ogden, UT

"When broken down into systems, models, and concepts, I can see that this is an absolutely achievable model and not just wishful thinking!! I have written out my plan, and now it's all about execution. Thanks so much to Gary and Dave for all the research and development they've done."

Sherrie Puffer
Asheville, NC

"I feel as though my windshield had been dirty for the past several years and it was unclear as to what direction I was going in the real estate industry. Now it is CRYSTAL CLEAR! I am three hires away from becoming the millionaire agent. I'm about to hire the first. I will get there soon!"

David Fitzgerald
Phoenix, AZ

"The Millionaire Real Estate Agent is absolutely eye-opening! A virtual 'cookbook,' the Millionaire Model was laid out for those agents who desire to turn their 'job' into a true business. This material offered me an essential key to bridge my 'Work Life' to my 'Life's Work.'"

Michael Hodson
Tacoma, WA

"Somewhere along my path I was taught not to dream too large lest I face the certain pain of disillusionment. Gary challenged me to move past fear, starting with a Big Why, and he laid out the steps I need to take for daily progress."

Marc Nicholson
Atlanta, GA

"Gary and Dave have shown me how to get out of the 'ugly zone' of trying to do everything myself and into the 'prosperity zone,' whereby I can grow my business substantially, work fewer hours, and make more money."

Charles Sullivan
Gaithersburg, MD

THE
MILLIONAIRE
Real Estate Agent

THE
MILLIONAIRE
Real Estate Agent

It's not about the money

Gary Keller
with Dave Jenks and Jay Papasan

McGraw-Hill

New York   Chicago   San Francisco   Lisbon   London   Madrid   Mexico City
Milan   New Delhi   San Juan   Seoul   Singapore   Sydney   Toronto

33   34   35   36   37   38   39   40   QFR/QFR   1   5   4   3

ISBN 0-07-144404-1

McGraw-Hill books are available at special quantity discounts to use as premiums and sales promotions, or for use in corporate training programs. For more information, please write to the Director of Special Sales, Professional Publishing, McGraw-Hill, Two Penn Plaza, New York, NY 10121-2298. Or contact your local bookstore.

Grateful acknowledgment is made for the following previously published material: Selections excerpted from "The Difference That Makes the Difference" reprinted with the permission of Simon & Schuster Adult Publishing Group from *Unlimited Power* by Anthony Robbins. Copyright © 1986 by Robbins Research Institute.

* Photo of Don Zeleznak on page 346
  Copyright© 2002 David Schmidt

The Millionaire Real Estate Agent *is dedicated to the men and women whose hard work and entrepreneurial spirit place them squarely on the front lines of free enterprise— this book is dedicated to real estate agents everywhere.*

Acknowledgments

Although the writing team for this book only convened in the summer of 2002, the genesis for *The Millionaire Real Estate Agent* can, in fact, be traced back to the mid-1980s when I began actively searching for proven models for excellence in the real estate sales industry. Those ideas were tested and refined while working one-on-one with hundreds and hundreds of top agents. To these hardworking agents (far too numerous to name here), I offer my sincere gratitude for their feedback, vision, and insight. Later, when we formed Keller Williams University, my coauthor Dave Jenks helped me to craft and crystallize these concepts while writing the manuals and class materials for our "Mega Agent Boot Camps."

In June 2002 the idea of *The Millionaire Real Estate Agent* was truly born. At a Mega Agent Mastermind session, we brought together some of our top agents from across the country and raised the question "What would it take to net a million in personal income?" We spent the rest of the afternoon brainstorming, sharing ideas, and collaborating models that would later serve as the rough draft for this book. So while no book this long in the making can easily be credited to all the people who have helped shape it, I'd be remiss not to begin by acknowledging the contributions of those exceptional Mastermind attendees.

Their input was so valuable, in fact, that we went back to the well and reconvened the group in August 2002 to have them provide feedback on the working ideas for the book. Many thanks to all these high achievers pictured here:

Figure 1: Mega Agent Mastermind Group, Day One

Front Row: Patty Ancona, Judy Johns, Betsy Scheffe, Chris Cormack, Mary Charters, Krisstina Wise Anderson, and Terri Brenkus. Second Row: Melissa King, Terri Pescatore, Rae Wayne, Steve Scheffe, Peggy Richey, Jo-Ann LaBuda, Nikki Ubaldini, Linda McKissack, Jim McKissack, and Marie Zic. Back Row: Steve Johns, Aaron Lancaster, Dave Johns, Jeff Pantanella, Marc Nicholson, Andy Allen, Mike Mendoza, Martin Bouma, Kathy Courtney, Gary Ubaldini, Gary Keller, Brad McKissack, Sean Healey, Rick Geha, and Debbie Zois.

Figure 2: Mega Agent Mastermind Group, Day Two

Front Row: David Raesz, Lisa Pinson, Audrey Bienz, Pam O'Bryant, Holly Neal, Shirley Meyners, Carol Royse, Sherrie Puffer, Marybeth Tiemeyer, Brad Puffer, and Laurie Wall. Back Row: Gene Arant, Zac Sestina, Dan Harker, Rick Dittemore, Tom Brandt, Gary Keller, Rich O'Bryant, Peg Braxton, and Larry Wall.

And for their direct contributions to this book, I'd like to make special note of the "Millionaire Agents" who agreed to be interviewed for this book. These agents represent some of the best in our business, and their experience and wisdom are as inspirational as their incredible success in real estate sales. For sharing that experience, wisdom, and success with us, I'd like to thank the following real-life Millionaire Real Estate Agents: William Barnes, Glen Calderon, Chris Cormack, David and Judie Crockett, Rachel DeHanas, Allan Domb, Valerie Fitzgerald, Jack Gross, Mary Harker, Jerry Mahan, Cristina Martinez, Ronnie and Cathy Matthews, Mike Mendoza, Gregg Neuman, Elaine Northrop, Joe Rothchild, Jill Rudler, Bill Ryan, Russell Shaw, John Toye, Barbara Wilson, Sherry Wilson, Tim Wood, and Don Zeleznak. Integral to the success of the interviews were Roland Castillo, who coordinated the technical details of capturing all the interviews on audio files; Michelle Lorino, who with Mo Anderson managed to schedule interviews with some of the busiest people in our industry; Olivia L. Fagerberg, who painstakingly transcribed the bulk of the interviews; and Linda Henderson, who pinch-hit for Olivia when we were in a bind.

Special thanks go to the extraordinary writers and teachers who work so hard to help so many: Bill Barrett, Dave Beson, Howard Brinton, Brian Buffini, Carla Cross, Charlie Dahlheimer, Darryl Davis, Mike Ferry, Michael Gerber, Allen F. Hainge, Mark Victor Hansen, Gregg Herder, Don Hobbs, Tommy Hopkins, Carol Johnson, Danielle Kennedy, Robert T. Kiyosaki, David Knox, Laurie Moore-Moore, Steve Murray, Jerry Rossi, Joe Stumpf, Floyd Wickman, Rick Willis, and Pat Zaby. Their amazing work helped inspire and inform the writing of this book.

I'd also like to thank my colleagues Mo Anderson, Darren Bien, Pat Flanary, Sharon Gibbons, Steve Schlueter, Mary Tennant, Joe Williams, and Mark Willis for their continual guidance and leadership; our Keller Williams University crew of Kelly Parham, Molly Brown, Tammy Kroop, Xina Seaton, Jody Gay, and Kris Malejko, whose tireless work on the manuals and events for this book provided invaluable insight for us during the writing process; our design team of Shannon Cooper, Ryan Kucera, and Justine Smith, who provided feedback and direction for the jacket and interior design; Steve Simon and Christine Martin for their PR and marketing work and wisdom; Cathy Pham, who helped us get invaluable feedback from some of the visionaries in our industry; Valerie Vogler-Stipe for protecting my "book time" and for her invaluable help revising diagrams and entering our edits through multiple drafts of the manuscript; Gary Gentry and Althea Osborn, two of the finest real estate agents ever to associate with me, for their faith, influence, and commitment; Mark Victor Hansen for his personal support and inspirational leadership for more than twenty-five years; Kim Kiyosaki, who, despite being down with the flu, kept the communications lines open; Lynn Morgan, my first real estate sales manager, for her early guidance and faith in me; the National Association of Realtors and the Canadian Real Estate Association for their tireless work on behalf of agents, home buyers, and sellers; and the members of all local Boards of Realtors, State Associations of Realtors, and Provincial Associations of Realtors, who provide the grassroots leadership for our industry.

To my coauthors, Dave Jenks and Jay Papasan, I'd like to express my gratitude for their willingness to pursue this mammoth project to the end, to make sacrifices and to give 100 percent every day. Dave's exceptional ability to express the complex ideas in a simple, memorable way proved as invaluable to our efforts as his extensive experience in the real estate sales business and his gift for "finding the truth" in the numbers. Jay's publishing and writing experience was a boon to our newly founded publishing enterprise. His day-to-day work on the writing and editing helped provide continuity and consistency to our process. My appreciation goes to them both.

I'd also like to extend special thanks to our publisher, McGraw-Hill Trade, and our editor, Richard Narramore, for picking us up and expanding our publishing horizons. The fine folks at The Philip Lief Group also deserve our thanks. In particular, Philip Lief, Judy Linden, Lynne Kirk, Marybeth Fedele, Jill Korot, and Annie Jeon warrant our gratitude for their fine work on and in support of this project.

So much credit goes to my parents for making sure I was given a great education in life and for guiding me into the real estate industry. For my wife, Mary, and son, John, words cannot express what they have brought to this project—they are the true loves of my life. And thanks to God from whom all things come.

Lastly, I'd like to thank you, the reader. It has been my experience that the best ideas are always those shaped by many. I openly invite you to share your suggestions for improvement and your experiences working with these models. Without a doubt, your feedback will form the basis for future editions of *The Millionaire Real Estate Agent*.

Gary Keller
807 Las Cimas Parkway
Suite 200
Austin, Texas 78746
gary@millionaireagent.com
(512) 327-3070
www.millionaireagent.com

CONTENTS

Preface 21

Introduction 25

Part One: Charting the Course

Overview 31

Six MythUnderstandings Between You and
  High Achievement 47
    Myth One: "I can't do it." 49
    Myth Two: "It can't be done in my market." .53
    Myth Three: "It would take too much time and effort—
           I would lose my freedom." 55
    Myth Four: "It's too risky. I'll lose money." .57
    Myth Five: "My clients will only work with me—
           only I can deliver quality service." 59
    Myth Six: "Having a goal and not fully realizing it
           is a negative thing." 61

Part Two: The Four Stages

Think a Million—Stage 1 67
  The Nine Ways the Millionaire Real Estate Agent Thinks 71
    1. Think Powered by a Big Why 72
    2. Think Big Goals and Big Models 78
    3. Think Possibilities 81
    4. Think Action 84
    5. Think Without Fear 85
    6. Think Progress 87
    7. Think Competitively and Strategically 89
    8. Think Standards 92
    9. Think Service 93

The Three L's of the Millionaire Real Estate Agent 97
   Leads—Lead Generation vs Lead Receiving 99
   Listings—The High-Leverage, Maximum-Earning
       Opportunity 101
   Leverage—The Who, How, and What of Real Estate 103

The Eight Goal Categories of the
Millionaire Real Estate Agent 107

Earn a Million—Stage 2 119

The Four Fundamental Models of Real Estate Sales Success . 128
   Model One: Your Economic Model 129
     The Three Key Areas of Your Economic Model 130
       1. Focus on the Numbers You Must Hit 130
       2. Focus on Appointments 131
       3. Focus on Conversion Rates 132
   Model Two: Your Lead-Generation Model 133
     The Three Key Areas of Your Lead-Generation Model 136
       1. Prospect and Market 136
       2. Set Up a Database and Feed It 142
       3. Systematically Market to Your Database 145
   Model Three: Your Budget Model 152
     The Three Key Areas of Your Budget Model 153
       1. Lead with Revenue 154
       2. Play Red Light, Green Light 155
       3. Stick to the Budget 156
   Model Four: Your Organizational Model 158
     The Three Key Areas of Your Organizational Model 159
       1. When Doing All You Can Do,
          Hire Administrative Help 159
       2. Hire Talent 161
       3. Train and Consult 164

The Millionaire Real Estate Agent Models 172

Model One: The Millionaire Real Estate Agent
  Economic Model 175
The Fundamentals 175
Doing the Math 177
Model Two: The Millionaire Real Estate Agent Lead-
  Generation Model 185
Marketing Based—Prospecting Enhanced 185
The Costs of Massive Lead-Generation Success 189
Focus on Listings 191
Model Three: The Millionaire Real Estate Agent
  Budget Model 192
Model Four: The Millionaire Real Estate Agent Organizational
  Model 196
The Hiring Path of the Millionaire Real Estate Agent 198
Seven Recruiting Sources 203
The Nine Major Compensation Options 205

Net a Million—Stage 3 217
Leads 220
  1. Sustaining a Solid Lead-Generation Program
     That Emphasizes Marketing and Consistently Increases
     the Number of Leads 220
  2. Tracking and Converting Leads Through Others 222
  3. Protecting Your Lead-Generation Focus Time 224
  4. Weighing Your Options—The Process of Discovering
     What Works and Doesn't Work for You 226
Listings 228
  5. Knowing the Minimum Number of Seller Listings
     You Must List Each Month 228
  6. Listing the Minimum Number Each Month 229
  7. Getting Sellers to Accept the Team Concept 231
  8. Consistently Marketing Your Seller Listings for
     More Leads 232

Leverage 234

    9. Making the Time to Learn and Implement the
       R/T/C/K Process 234

    10. Hiring "Capacity" Talent vs "Cul-de-sac" Talent 237

    11. Achieving Accountability to the Right Standards 240

    12. Creating Teamwork with "Rock and Role" 245

    13. Combining Quality Service and Quantity Service 248

Money 249

    14. Sticking to the Budget Model and Controlling Your
       Costs 250

You 253

    15. Staying Focused on the 20 Percent 253

    16. Counterbalancing Your Life to Maintain Your
       Energy at a High Level 259

Receive a Million—Stage 4 263

    1. Active vs Passive Income 269

    2. The Opportunity of the 7th Level 272

    3. The Three Key Hires of a Millionaire Business 275

    4. Your Role and Responsibilities 278

Part Three: Staying on Top

Putting It All Together with Focus 289

    1. Create a Personal Plan and Then Make Process Your Focus .292

    2. Time Block for Focus 294

    3. Get Accountability to Keep Your Focus 297

    4. Make Sure Your Environment Supports Your Focus 302

    5. Keep Your Energy to Maintain Your Focus 306

Real-Life Millionaire Real Estate Agents 313

Appendix A: Sample Profit and Loss Report 349

Appendix B: Sample Balance Sheet 357

About the Authors 361

"Don't be afraid to take a big step if one is indicated. You can't cross a chasm in two small steps."

David Lloyd George
Former Prime Minister of England

PREFACE

*"If I have seen farther than others, it is because
I was standing on the shoulders of giants."*

Isaac Newton

HUNTING WOLVES AND AIMING HIGH

Several years ago my son, John, and I were driving and listening to a book on tape. In the story, a shepherd's son has come of age and goes out to spend his first summer alone tending the sheep in the hills above the village. One night, he awakens to the sound of a wolf howling nearby. The night is black and he is seized by fear, but he dutifully grabs his rifle and races out into the darkness to protect his livestock. Across the way he sees a wolf at the throat of one of the sheep. As he puts his rifle to his shoulder and takes aim, he remembers the advice of his father: "At night, it is very difficult to judge the distance to your target, and, more than likely, you'll underestimate the distance and miss low. To have a better chance of hitting the target, *aim high*." The shepherd's son adjusts his aim, raising the sights ever so slightly, and hits the mark.

What struck me about this scene was not the bravery of the boy, which shouldn't be doubted, or the drama of the moment, which had John and me on the edge of our seats. For me, it held all the elements of a great fable and perfectly illustrated something I've come to believe to be true in life. No one can accurately judge what the future holds. Tomorrow is as dark and

21

as difficult to judge as the gap between the shepherd boy and his target. Yet so often we set our goals as if the next day, month, year, or decade were as clear as an August afternoon. Is it any wonder most plans fall short of the mark? *Aim high*. That's the moral of the story. Whether you are hunting wolves at night or setting your life's goals, *aim high*.

This book is about *aiming high*. It's not about the money. It's really about the fact that most great achievements in life are the result of thinking big and aiming high. The word *millionaire* is just a placeholder for that idea. It also makes for a snappier title. Obviously, you've read this far. Honestly, would you have picked up *The Real Estate Agent Who Thinks Big*? I rest my case.

This book is for you. We believe that no matter where you are in your real estate career, thinking big will take you to a higher place; in fact, it may help you become the very best you can possibly be. To be your best, think big and aim high.

Big Questions and the Top of the World

With relatively low start-up costs and no hard ceilings, a real estate career seems perfectly tailored for any ambitious entrepreneur. In this industry, your limits are truly self-defined. Your approach, your ability, and your willingness to do the work of real estate sales will be the greatest determining factors for your success. In his book *The Aladdin Factor*, Mark Victor Hansen teaches us that in life the size of our answers is determined by the size of our questions. With *The Millionaire Real Estate Agent*, we will ask, explore, and answer the most important question anyone in real estate sales could ever ask of themselves, "How do I, as a real estate salesperson, take my sales income to the highest level possible?" Believe it or not, it is a simple question with a simple answer. In this book, we will lay out for you how to think like a Millionaire Real Estate Agent. Then, we will show you, step by step, how to earn and net a million in annual income. Finally, we'll point out the path to receiving a million in passive income.

Truthfully, I believe that the key to becoming your very best is to think at a very high level. If, by reading this book, you can get your mind around the concepts in the chapter entitled, Think a Million, and learn to think like a Millionaire Real Estate Agent, you'll discover that earning, netting, and receiving the most money possible from your real estate career will seem much more attainable to you.

If there is one thing that I've learned in life, it is that small goals tend to place limits on our potential, and that Big Goals have a tendency to pull us right through the small goals on the way to attaining the big ones. Why? It's all about what you are focused on. What happens is that we tend to slow down once our goals are within reach. Small goals, by definition, are almost always within our reach, so we end up achieving them quickly, but we never get the chance to build up a head of steam. On the other hand, when we pursue big, ambitious goals, we have the chance to build up so much momentum that it carries us right past those small goals in the pursuit of bigger game. James Allen once wrote, "You will become as small as your controlling desire; as great as your dominant aspiration." In the end your business and your life ultimately reflect the goals you pursue. It all comes down to the difference between goals that just satisfy you and goals that truly maximize you.

The formula is straightforward—think big, act bold, and you'll live a larger life. To be totally honest, the end goal of this book is not necessarily to teach you how to put a million dollars in the bank every year. Even though we do offer a complete and accurate analysis of that pursuit, the real purpose of *The Millionaire Real Estate Agent* is to encourage you to live large. Throughout history, we have seen that Big Goals pull us beyond our known potential, push us to live lives bigger than we'd imagined. I earnestly believe that the gifts you will receive from this kind of approach are far greater than any monetary reward you might achieve. Maybe Oliver Wendell Holmes put it best when he wrote, "The greatest thing in this world is not so much where we are, but in what direction we are moving."

I think we can all agree that the future is largely unpredictable. Asking the big questions and seeking the big answers also tend to lead us to achieve our very best level of preparedness. That preparedness allows us to act more effectively, in the moment. You're less likely to be caught off guard by an unexpected turn of events. Remember, the shepherd boy could not have predicted when a danger might arrive or in what shape it might manifest itself, but he knew enough to pack his rifle, keep it close, and aim high.

Let me put it to you a different way. For most of us, climbing Mount Everest is a symbol of exceptional achievement. Now, stop and think about this for just a moment. Those individuals who intend to climb Everest successfully don't think in terms of just getting to Base Camp and then figuring out the rest from there. Before they even set foot in Nepal, they have already meticulously imagined and thoroughly prepared themselves for the entire journey from Kathmandu to Base Camp and beyond that to the top of the world. If they are really smart and want an even greater measure of readiness, they've also studied the experiences of others and, using that knowledge, have properly prepared themselves for a most challenging adventure. People who are planning to reach the summit of Everest are asking very big questions and finding very big answers. They've learned that only those who dare to think greatly can ever achieve greatness.

If you're interested in getting the most from yourself and are willing to ask the question, "How do I take my real estate business to the highest point possible?," then strap on your climbing boots and take a deep breath. This book can be your road map, even your guide. The journey won't necessarily be easy, but it will change your life. It begins by thinking big and aiming high.

INTRODUCTION

*"The greatest truths are the simplest,
and so are the greatest men."*

Augustus and Julius Hare

YOU'RE NOT METHUSELAH!

Everyone is on track to be a millionaire. I'm certain that given a long enough time line, everyone would reach the million-dollar-income mark. This approach is called the Methuselah Method. According to tradition, Methuselah was the oldest man who ever lived. It is believed he lived 969 years. Now, I'm convinced that—even if he were the worst money manager of all time—at some point he was considered a "millionaire" by the standards of his era. Unfortunately, barring evolutionary leaps or medical miracles, if you're a follower of the Methuselah Method, you probably won't live to see your millions.

Of course, there are those who want to get there a little faster. They are on a thirty-year, fifteen-year, or five-year plan. What distinguishes them from others is they understand that to be really successful in this game called real estate sales, they can't go about it haphazardly. Only those with as much gas in their tank as Methuselah can afford to explore the trial-and-error route. Those who want to get there more quickly know they will need a big plan, preferably a simple, straightforward one. Our goal with this book is to share that big plan.

One of the greatest stumbling blocks to achieving great success for most people is that they cannot get their heads around how obvious and uncomplicated success can be. One of the greatest myths in life is that the road to success is hidden away, and if you could find it, it would be twisting, uphill, covered in fog, and full of pitfalls. Blame the bards who created our original success stories—the path to the princess was always hidden away, and to get there you had to pass through the dragon's lair. As a result, we tend to distrust obvious and straightforward ideas, or, at best, we patronize them saying they are "common sense" and that "everybody should know that." It almost seems as if, by some flaw of human nature, we simply tend to favor secretive and complex ideas over obvious and simple ones.

In his book *Acres of Diamonds*, Russell H. Conwell tells the tale of two farmers. The first farmer sells his farm to the other so he can go in search of diamonds. The story ends with the first farmer never finding his precious diamonds and the new farmer finding "acres of diamonds" out in the very fields he had purchased from the first. The moral: You probably already have or know everything you need to be successful. So instead of looking for the "new-new" you might want to work on the "old-old" a little more. The opportunity for your success might be right under your very nose.

And it is not a question of validity, either. Complex solutions may be perfectly valid. The problem is, complex plans are just that, complex, which makes them hard to implement and sustain. Jazz legend Charles Mingus once said, "Making the simple complicated is commonplace; making the complicated simple, awesomely simple, that's creativity." I agree. Life and business are complex, but the road to success in life and in business is paved with simplicity. The truth is that all plans must be reduced to simplicity in order for us to be able to implement them. No one can live or operate in complexity for very long—lasting success always lies in our ability to reduce things to their simplest level.

The Millionaire Real Estate Agent

THE "BIG SECRET" AND AN INVITATION

In our research over the years, we've found people often imagine that success in business is much more complicated than it really is. This point of view turns simple accountability for results into a blame game where the catch phrase is "I didn't know!" It allows us to blame our failures on things we did not know or understand. If you play that game, you may be looking for the "Big Secret." More than likely, you're probably not being completely truthful with yourself. You may be looking for the "Big Secret" because you want success to come easier, and you're not alone.

Here's the truth about the "Big Secret" and about how you can make it come easier: *Success is less complicated than most people make it*. Many, many answers can be complicated, but the answers that matter most almost never are. What we now know is that if you seek complex solutions to complex questions, you'll end up chasing complexity your whole life. On the other hand, if you can decide to seek simple answers to complex questions, you will find good, simple answers and spend your life taking action. It is the difference between seeking truth and living it.

Try this. Call up an acquaintance who is about eighteen years old and ask him or her to share with you the meaning of life. You're liable to get a very long, convoluted answer that may or may not make reference to melting ice caps. Now call an acquaintance who has lived a long, full life and pose the same question to that person. Odds are you'll get a very simple one-word answer—love. The young person's answer may not necessarily be wrong. The older person will just get to the point faster and much more succinctly. The reason? They have confronted life's complexities and discovered that while life is truly complex, the joy-filled path to real meaning and true happiness is quite simple.

I believe that if you're prepared to acknowledge where you are on the continuum of accomplishment and to recognize the shortcomings that have kept you from going further, you've mentally positioned yourself well to pursue the highest of possibilities. Rest assured that substantial elbow grease is required. The path may be simple and clear-cut; however, it is not without effort. As Peter Drucker says, "Plans are only good intentions unless they immediately degenerate into hard work."

The ideas we present in this book bear no comparison to rocket science or brain surgery. Nevertheless, when taken as a whole, they may appear overwhelming. What then looks like complexity is really just the accumulation of simple ideas added together over time. So, I encourage you to take a step back, look at the big picture, pick a place to get started, and dive in!

What follows is a series of ideas that our research and experience have proven to be true. While our primary intent was to share these ideas, we hope you will also find some inspiration. I've found that those who are shown the truth and are also inspired by it are those who are most likely to take effective action. But, regardless of whether or not you find these ideas inspirational, you may still see benefit in adopting them and choose to accept and act on them. Just like dieting, exercising, or saving money, any fundamental change in our habits begins with a personal choice, an act of volition. In this case it is choosing to think big and aim high.

It's my sincerest hope that this book will prod you to think outside the box regarding your career. It's why I wrote this book. You see, for many years the real estate agent has been perceived and positioned as a nonbusiness person with a sales job. It's been said many times that choice not chance determines destiny. I believe you, the real estate agent, can determine your own destiny because you have a choice to either:

1. Practice real estate as a job
2. Run your real estate practice as a business

Would you rather have a business than a job? Would you like to take that business to the highest possible level? If so, I invite you to turn the page.

Part One:

CHARTING THE COURSE

OVERVIEW

"I must create a system or
be enslaved by another man's."

William Blake

WHY ARE YOU HERE? YOU'RE IN MANAGEMENT AND WE'RE ALL IN SALES

Several years ago at a real estate sales seminar, I had an interesting conversation with another real estate agent. The revelations that emerged from that conversation have since proven essential to my ability to consult with salespeople. Here is my best recollection of how that conversation went:

AGENT: Gary Keller, right? I noticed you from across the room and just wanted to introduce myself and let you know I've heard a lot about your company.

ME: Well, thanks. We've worked hard to get where we are.

AGENT: Excuse me for asking this, but why are you here?

ME: I'm sorry? What?

AGENT: Why are you here? You're in management, and we're all in sales. I was just curious to know what you're doing at a sales seminar.

Honestly, I was a little taken aback by the question. Sure, I was in management, but I'd been a successful real estate agent before our company was formed, and, frankly, I really still thought like one. In life, one of the toughest obstacles we can face is the difference between how we see ourselves and how others see us. What lies in between the two perspectives can be an obstacle to effective communication and a source of misunderstandings. A big part of my job has been working with top real estate salespeople, and I'd been doing this for more than twenty years. It had never occurred to me that someone might not see me as a real estate agent myself, so I decided to ask a few probing questions.

ME: Let me ask you a few questions. Do you go on buying appointments?

AGENT: Actually, I have buyer specialists that do that for me.

ME: Me too. Do you go on listing appointments?

AGENT: (*Shakes his head.*) No. I have listing specialists that handle all the listings for my team.

ME: How about that! I have listing specialists too. I bet you have a support staff to help with marketing, bookkeeping, and paperwork, right?

AGENT: Sure.

ME: We both have buyer specialists. We both have listing specialists. And we both have a support staff. Interesting. If you don't mind my asking, what was your sales volume last year?

AGENT: Hmm. Actually, I did a little over $50 million in sales last year.

ME: Wow! Congratulations! That's really awesome! Now, if it would better help you understand why I'm here, just think of me as a multi*billion*-dollar producer.

You see, if you really look at the organizational structure and the systems, there is not a lot of difference between a well-run real estate office and a mega agent's real estate sales team. Both have buyers and sellers who drive the bottom line. They have administration and infrastructure. And they have what is essentially a CEO coordinating the team's activities to increase productivity and profits.

I point out these parallels when I work with agents, and what they ultimately discover is that I do the same things they do. I am just highly leveraged through association with great talent and have thoroughly documented my systems. I'm a real estate agent living large.

Let me define "living large." Since the late eighties no other real estate broker has had more houses sold under his or her license in Austin, Texas. In fact, my two Austin real estate offices ranked first and fourth in the country in closed real estate transactions (according to the 2001 REAL Trends ranking of single office companies). Thanks to an average annual growth rate of more than 40 percent between 1998 and 2001, Keller Williams Realty International catapulted out of regional obscurity to become the seventh largest real estate company in the country. And Inman News tagged Keller Williams as the industry's Most Innovative Company in 2001.

So if you see me at a real estate agent event, I sincerely hope you'll say hello. I also hope you'll understand why I'm there. I'm a real estate agent too.

MASTERING THE "GAME"

When we started our company in 1983, we had no idea what amazing people we would associate with in the years to come or how much we'd learn from those associations. We have had the opportunity to work with and learn from top sales associates from every corner of North America:

industry leaders such as Brian Buffini, Tom Hopkins, Floyd Wickman, Bill Barrett, Mike Ferry, and Howard Brinton; and even business visionaries such as Robert Kiyosaki, Michael Gerber, and Mark Victor Hansen. Every one of these people helped shape our successes and the message of *The Millionaire Real Estate Agent*.

Through our shadowing, consulting, masterminding, and mega agent programs, we've had the opportunity to work one-on-one with hundreds and hundreds of top agents. Their contribution to this book and our overall success cannot be overstated. However, we knew that for the purposes of *The Millionaire Real Estate Agent* we would also have to draw on the experiences of top producers with whom we had not yet worked personally. So we picked up the phone and started calling. We worked our way through the top fifty real estate agents in the country as ranked by REAL Trends and set up as many interviews as we possibly could. We listened. We listened hard. We took notes and bounced our ideas off the very best in our industry.

Without a doubt, these high achievers are masters of their game. What became very clear very quickly is that they are experts on their markets and often have developed successful systems that perfectly complement their markets and their own mix of personal strengths and weaknesses. They had a lot to share. They were also very curious about what we'd find. While many would freely admit to having mastered "their game"—their personal approach to real estate—few would lay claim to having mastered the "Game" in the broader sense.

We took all that we learned, passed it through the filter of our own experience, and combined it into simple, effective models anyone can follow to take their real estate sales practice to the highest possible level. As a result, this book is not about "our game" or even a collection of theirs. It is about the "Game." We feel personal mastery is best pursued through a thoughtful analysis of the "Game" and then relating that new understanding to personal circumstances (your market, your strengths, and your weaknesses). It is an ongoing process. This book may represent the first step for some, but for many it will be yet another checkpoint in their continual pursuit of personal mastery in the "Real Estate Sales Game." Our hope is that you will take this book, reflect on it, apply the models from it, and then personalize it over time to master your game at the highest levels possible.

MODELING—
THE CORNERSTONE OF SUCCESS

Two events in my life forever changed my thinking on what I believe a person is capable of achieving through God-given talents alone. The first was when a Baylor professor chided a certain cavalier young student who thought he might have all the answers. (That would be me, of course.) He said, "Son, you're not the first person to want to have a successful career. You're not the first person to have dreams you want to fulfill. You're not the first person to want to be the very best you can be in life. You need to realize that people have lived before you. And you might be wise to slow down for just a second and figure out what they learned on their journey before you start your own." I listened attentively and thought I understood what he was saying, but I wouldn't really *hear* him for almost a decade.

The second event happened in 1987 when our young company was faced with a collapsed economy. Up to that point we had been successful on certain levels, but there were now some big challenges that were holding us back. In the end, I found that I didn't have all the answers. In my opinion, our growth till then had been sustained through sheer hard work. Then the market turned sour, and we were faced with a new and very real ceiling of achievement. That was the year I read *Unlimited Power* by Anthony Robbins and finally heard my professor: "People have lived before you." Robbins' book made that point in a very powerful way. Here are some of the passages that I underlined and that I'd like to share with you:

Passage #1:

Long ago, I realized that success leaves clues, that people who produce outstanding results do specific things to create those results.

Passage #2:

Actions are the source of all results. . . . This process of discovering exactly and specifically what people do to produce a specific result is called modeling.

Passage #3:

To me, modeling is the pathway to excellence. . . . The movers and shakers of the world are often professional modelers—people who have mastered the art of learning everything they can by following other people's experience rather than their own.

Passage #4:

To model excellence you should be a detective, an investigator, someone who asks lots of questions and tracks down all the clues to what produces excellence. . . . Building from the successes of others is one of the fundamental aspects of most learning.

Epiphany! A lightbulb went off in my head, and I had an "aha." I then slowed down just long enough to start looking in much greater detail at what successful people were doing. I also systematically involved my team in the modeling process. The models we discovered and implemented that year helped us break through the challenges of the lagging economy and laid the groundwork for our later accomplishments. Ever since this breakthrough, it has been my goal to actively, aggressively, and continuously model the real estate business for its owners and agents.

At the same time, I do think that it would be a mistake to discard creativity. Without a doubt, we have been innovative in our real estate business. The trick to getting the most out of our creativity is always to start with a set of proven foundational models for success. Once we find success with our initial models, we can then allow for creative thinking. But only after we've followed the models do we allow ourselves to tweak, innovate, refine, and fiddle until the models work to the level of our expectations. The key to taking this approach is to avoid placing creative innovation ahead of the effective implementation of proven foundational models.

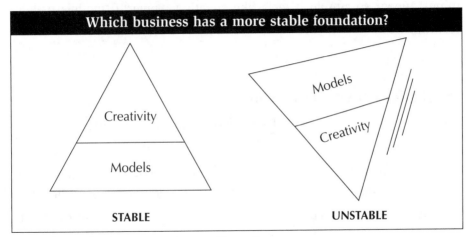

Figure 1

The reality about using models is that if you begin with creativity and then try to add a model, or if you try to add creativity to a model you haven't fully implemented, you risk rendering the model completely ineffective. Many people don't fully realize this. More than likely, they will try to use creativity as a shortcut or as a way to cover up for their lack of properly or fully implementing the model. The truth is that when you add creativity to a practiced and proven model, you will always have a much greater chance of achieving your highest possible results.

In *The Millionaire Real Estate Agent* I will present to you a set of models. They are based on the actual experiences of the very best in our industry. I strongly encourage you to accept what they have learned to be true and then, by applying these models, use their successes as your own launching pad. Once you've implemented these models and feel you have a thorough understanding of them, I encourage you to innovate around them to see if you can improve the results. That's implementation before innovation.

Reinventing the wheel every time is just plain exhausting work. And it leads to breakdowns and burnouts. On the other hand, I think you'll discover that modeling will be very empowering. In fact, it may make things appear so simple it feels like cheating. Powerful models usually feel that way.

NATURAL ABILITY AND ACHIEVEMENT CEILINGS

In my experience, people tend to predict success based largely on a person's natural abilities. This can truly be problematic no matter where you see yourself in this spectrum. Lots of natural ability can lead to overconfidence. Likewise, lack of natural ability contributes to low confidence, so much so that many never even attempt tasks that appear to be outside the realm of their natural abilities. The truth about ability is that it is neither set nor predetermined. However, it can be developed or it can be wasted.

Now here is the simple truth we must all deal with: Natural ability can take us only so far. No matter how gifted we may be, each of us will eventually hit our own ceiling of achievement. There is no "if" to that assertion, just a "when." So the most important achievement question you may ever have to ask yourself becomes: "When I hit that ceiling of achievement—whether it is low or high—how will I break through?"

What I've discovered is that by starting with models you can push your ceilings higher and, eventually, break through them. But even great models will have limitations, so eventually you'll hit a new ceiling. This is when I encourage creativity. This is when I encourage you to start adapting the model. Don't abandon it—adapt it. Once the right amount of innovation is added, you will more than likely experience another breakthrough and move forward. That is the cycle. Each improvement will have its limitations, and, sooner or later, you'll have to tweak your model to ensure continued progress.

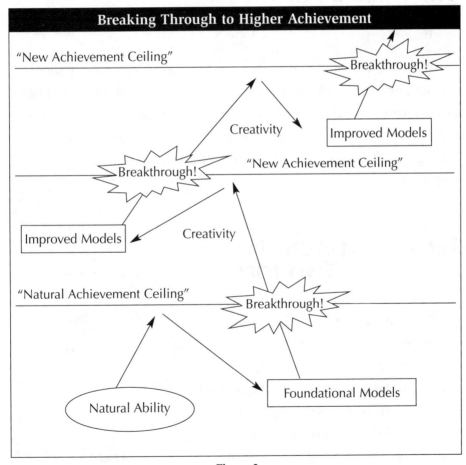

Figure 2

So the trick to having breakthroughs in your life is to adopt the right foundational models. In our experience, these models need to be as big and ambitious as you can possibly find. Typically, the bigger the model the further you can ride it before hitting a ceiling. And that is one of the most exciting advantages big models offer. The foundational models we present in *The Millionaire Real Estate Agent* are founded on three cornerstones, which we call the Three L's of the Millionaire Real Estate Agent.

THE THREE L'S OF THE MILLIONAIRE REAL ESTATE AGENT

When we first started grouping our findings by category, it appeared that we might have eight core issues. On closer examination, we were able to eliminate three and narrow the list to five. Ultimately, we discovered the finish line lay at three core issues that support our model—Leads, Listings, and Leverage. We call them the Three L's of the Millionaire Real Estate Agent.

LEADS—EVERYONE HAS TWO JOBS

You can have a doctorate in real estate, outfox a professional litigator in a contract negotiation, appraise property better than anyone in your market, and have more financing knowledge packed in your head than a mortgage guru, and it won't do you a lick of good without clients. To succeed in real estate, you

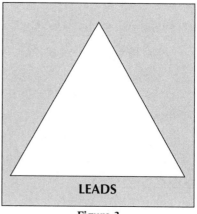

Figure 3

must have client leads. It's that simple. Until you have enough leads (to meet or exceed your goals), there is no other issue. No matter if you are a doctor, lawyer, or entrepreneur, everyone has two jobs—their chosen profession and lead generation.

I remember reading an article written by a fellow real estate agent who was distressed to learn he was also in the lead-generation business. His article was a lament. He was personally distressed. He somehow thought that with his professional certification, he could sit back and the world would find him. It was easy to identify with this guy. I earned a four-year degree in real estate and never once did a professor mention lead generation. No one told me. Later, to my horror, it became clear that if I wasn't any good at lead generation, no one would ever know what an educated and knowledgeable real estate professional I was. It was time to face the facts. To succeed as a real estate professional, I had to learn to generate client leads.

LISTINGS—THE "GIFT OF THE REAL ESTATE GODS"

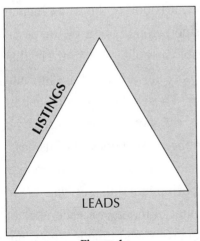

Figure 4

Listings are the high-leverage, maximum-earning opportunity in our industry. Conventionally, your income from having a listing sell is no different than closing on a similarly priced home for a buyer. What separates the two is the amount of time necessary to work them. In our experience, a highly productive individual can personally obtain fifteen to twenty-five seller listings per month. The same agent would be hard-pressed to sell homes to seven or eight buyers a month for any prolonged period of time. With the right approach over time, you should be able to secure and sell as many as two to three listings for every buyer you could sell.

So from the very start, by concentrating on listings first and foremost, you could potentially double or triple your gross income on the same amount of work. If this isn't incentive enough, then consider how listings provide a lead-generation platform through direct mail, ads, signage, and open houses. It is a fact that being in the listings business begets more business. Our research shows that one listing properly marketed should generate enough leads to produce a minimum of one closed buyer.

At the end of the day, listings give you better control. They give you better control of your time, your marketplace, and your future. That's why we affectionately call them the "Gift of the Real Estate Gods."

LEVERAGE—
TIME VS MONEY

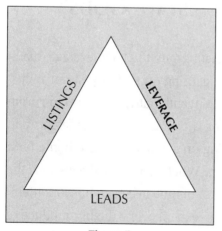

Figure 5

We've all heard that time is money. Well, that simply isn't true. In fact, it is one of the worst mental maps perpetrated on us by unknowledgeable people. The truth is that time does not always translate into money. Those who work the longest hours are not always those who make the most money. As businesspeople, we look at the time-money relationship in a different way. We're continually trying to net the maximum amount of money for each hour of time invested. In the beginning of our careers we spend time to earn more money. Then we learn to work smarter and begin to earn more in the same amount of time.

Just like in our discussion of ceilings of achievement, we've discovered that there are limits to our personal efficiency. The ultimate key to tilting the money/time ratio in your favor will be leverage. Leverage can be divided into three categories: people, systems, and tools.

Leverage Answers Three Important Questions

Who is going to do it?

How will they do it?

What will they do it with?

The Answers: People, Systems, and Tools

Figure 6

By far, the most important of these is people. While good systems and tools can help average performers consistently contribute more to the bottom line, nothing comes before hiring and keeping talent. If you're like most salespeople, then designing and implementing systems and tools may not be your strong suit. The best way around this is to hire someone who is proficient at details and systems. That's why we recommend hiring administrative support talent first. When you've put in all the time you have or are willing to give and still want to increase your income, add leverage.

The Three L's of the Millionaire Real Estate Agent—Leads, Listings, and Leverage—are the pillars of any successful real estate sales business. I believe these are the core issues that drive massive sales volume. In fact, we made them the framework for our foundational model of *The Millionaire Real Estate Agent.*

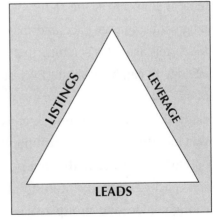

Figure 7

Now that we've established the three cornerstones for your achievement model, it's time to set out on the path to becoming a Millionaire Real Estate Agent. We've discovered there are four natural stages you'll go through on your journey.

THE FOUR STAGES OF GROWTH ON THE PATH TO A MILLION

The Millionaire Real Estate Agent should progress through these four stages: Think a Million, Earn a Million, Net a Million, and Receive a Million. From our experience, most real estate professionals do not even begin, if ever, to Think a Million until they are well into their careers. The failure to see this much potential from the beginning can lead to the inevitable and devastating work of reinventions, take backs, and do overs. But even more important than avoiding massive reinvention is the fact that this kind of short-term thinking does not position you for big long-term success.

There is a big advantage to studying and understanding all four stages before you begin. If you can Think a Million, you have cleared the path to Earn a Million. Our hope is that by examining the process at the start, you'll progress at a faster pace and make fewer mistakes. Let's return to the analogy of climbing Mount Everest. More than one hundred years elapsed between the time Everest was identified as the highest point on Earth and the day the first person reached the top. Interestingly enough, a second group reached the summit just one year later.

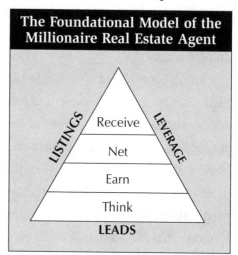

The Foundational Model of the Millionaire Real Estate Agent

LISTINGS — Receive — Net — Earn — Think — LEVERAGE — LEADS

Figure 8

The Millionaire Real Estate Agent

Today, dozens of people reach the top every year. Once the path was identified, the journey became more accessible to others. It is our intention that this book will have the same effect on your real estate career.

The truth we discovered is that if you don't achieve the goals of one level, you'll find your sales career probably won't progress to the next. You have to Think a Million in order to Earn a Million. Earn a Million is the platform that supports the ideas of Net a Million. Successful progression through all three is a definite prerequisite before advancing to Receive a Million.

Commit the Foundational Model of the Millionaire Real Estate Agent to memory. Draw it on the back of a business card and stick it in your wallet. Tattoo it on your forearm. Frame it and put it above your desk. Share it with your staff, and enlist the support of the key people in your life. Just don't forget it no matter where you are in your real estate journey—it will keep you focused.

Moving Forward

I want you to be your best. Some people dream of doing their best, while others just go out and do it. You may choose to think big and aim high but never reach the kind of production described in this book. And that's okay, because by thinking big and aiming high, you will certainly reach a higher place. In fact, you will probably reach your highest potential possible, which is magnificent. Here is an inescapable truth: People who push themselves to their limits make peace with their limitations and avoid regrets at the end of the day and at the end of their life. They give it their all. It's the difference between being able to say, "I'm glad I did" versus "I wish I had." And there is a big difference.

Many have pointed out that we work in a recognition-seeking, awards-driven industry. We believe that awards and recognition, though important, can devalue the true rewards of giving it our all. In the end, it's not a race or a competition. Maybe it is not even about achieving the summit. The true joy is in the journey. If achievements and experiences define your life, then it follows that maximizing your experiences maximizes your life.

POINTS TO REMEMBER: Overview

- People have lived before us and success leaves clues, so it would be wise for us to learn from their journey before starting on our own.

- Big Models lead to Big Success. With proven models, avoid placing creative innovation ahead of effective implementation. Know your models before you personalize them.

- Everyone will hit a personal ceiling of achievement. Adopting the right foundational models will enable you to break through that ceiling.

- Focus on the Three L's of the Millionaire Real Estate Agent: Leads, Listings, and Leverage.

- Remember, everyone has two jobs—their chosen profession and lead generation.

- Listings give you control of your time, control of your marketplace, and control of your future.

- Leverage is about people, systems, and tools. It answers three important questions:

    - Who is going to do it?

    - How will they do it?

    - What will they do it with?

- Lastly, the path of the Millionaire Real Estate Agent goes through four stages—Think a Million, Earn a Million, Net a Million, and Receive a Million—and they are best pursued in that order.

MYTHUNDERSTANDINGS

*"Whether you think you can or
think you can't, you're right."*

Henry Ford

SIX MYTHUNDERSTANDINGS BETWEEN YOU AND HIGH ACHIEVEMENT

Over the course of my life, I've come to believe in the wisdom of Dr. Karl Menninger, who pointed out that in his experience "fears are educated into us, and can, if we wish, be educated out." The Millionaire Real Estate Agent models we reveal in this book embody basic principles that we believe are fundamental to real estate sales success at a high level. They represent the core activities that must be successfully and consistently done before massive sales achievement can be attained. But before we tackle these concepts, I believe you need to examine some of your core beliefs about success. How real or unreal they truly are, and how they may impact your chances for success. At best, your beliefs can lead to great confidence, and, at worst, they can lead to extreme doubt. If I've learned anything, it's that if allowed to exist, doubts can truly undermine your confidence, your actions, and ultimately your dreams.

Mark Twain's familiar story about cats and hot stoves is a great example of the power of beliefs and fears. Twain famously remarked, "We should be careful to get out of an experience all the wisdom that is in it—

not like the cat that sits on a hot stove lid. She will never sit down on a hot lid again—and that is well; but also she will never sit down on a cold one anymore." I've noticed that, like Twain's cat, we tend to base our actions on what we believe to be true. Unfortunately, what we believe to be the truth may actually be myth. When beliefs are based on truth, and not myth, our actions have foundation and are more likely to produce satisfying results. However, beliefs grounded in myths tend to lead to unfounded fears and a life of limitations.

The history books we all read growing up are filled with examples of myths leading to fears that hold us back. Galileo was imprisoned for daring to prove that the sun (not the Earth) was the center of our solar system. And how long did the belief that the Earth was flat hold back the discovery of the New World? Galileo and Columbus are just two obvious examples of how myths may hold us back and truths can set us free.

This chapter is really about fear. And the source of most of our fears is myth. I find it extremely helpful to think of fears in terms of what generally creates them—myths—and what sets us free from them—truths. It's about learning to look past your fears to the truth of a situation, investigating the myths, and avoiding the misunderstandings that hold us back. In our work with real estate agents, we've identified six common myths that tend to get in the way of success. So in order truly to set a stage for achieving the highest possible potential in your career, we believe you should pause, take a closer look at, and even confront what may be your own MythUnderstandings.

The Six MythUnderstandings Between You and High Achievement

1   **Myth**: I can't do it.
      Truth: Until you try, you can't possibly know what you can or can't do.

2   **Myth**: It can't be done in my market.
      Truth: Yes it can, but you may need a new approach.

3   **Myth**: It would take too much time and effort—
                I would lose my freedom.
      Truth: Time and effort are not the deciding factors in success.

4   **Myth**: It's too risky. I'll lose money.
      Truth: Risk is in direct proportion to how well you hold your incremental costs accountable to producing incremental results.

5   **Myth**: My clients will only work with me—only I can deliver quality service.
      Truth: Your clients aren't loyal to you; they are loyal to the standards you represent.

6   **Myth**: Having a goal and not fully realizing it is a negative thing.
      Truth: Having a goal and not trying to achieve it is a negative thing.

Figure 1

THE FIRST COMMON MYTHUNDERSTANDING

MYTH: I CAN'T DO IT.

TRUTH: UNTIL YOU TRY, YOU CAN'T POSSIBLY KNOW WHAT YOU CAN OR CAN'T DO.

What exactly is your ultimate potential? What are your limitations? Do you realize that whenever you say, "I can't do it," you are assigning limits to your potential? Upon reflection, do you think it is wise or even fair to do that to yourself? Let me share with you an interesting dialogue I once had with one of my students:

STUDENT: Okay, Gary. Do you really think it's realistic to talk to all of us about achieving those levels of success? It doesn't seem very realistic to me.

ME: That's a fair question. Do you mind if I ask you a question before I answer?

STUDENT: Sure.

ME: What's your ultimate potential?

STUDENT: I'm sorry? I don't follow you.

ME: What are your limitations? What are you capable of achieving? What is your ceiling? In other words, do you know what your ultimate potential is?

STUDENT: Hmm. I never really thought about it. I guess I have no idea.

ME: That's an honest answer, and I appreciate that. So here's the point: Nobody knows. And if you don't know what your ultimate potential is, then how can you possibly judge what is realistic? Honestly, what good does it do us to talk about what is realistic when, in the end, we don't even know what we're truly capable of achieving?

Unless you absolutely know your capabilities and limitations, why would you entertain this kind of inner dialogue! Short of a personal visitation from the Creator, you're unlikely ever to know the limits of your potential. So the question of whether you can or can't do something someday should probably never be considered.

Our dialogue actually continued, but with the whole class. Here is the rest:

ME: Let's just pretend for a second that I actually did believe in the "need to be realistic about your potential." Are you telling me that you would willingly turn your kids over to me to be taught that doctrine?

The Millionaire Real Estate Agent

CLASS:	No.
ME:	No, really. I'll take your thirteen- and sixteen-year-olds and sit them down and say, "Your mom and dad have hired me to teach you your limitations. You're not going to be all you hoped you could be. You have limits; you don't need to dream big because that is just unrealistic." Now, if that was what I was going to teach your children, are you going to turn me loose with your kids?
CLASS:	No!
ME:	Okay, then. Take your own advice. If you wouldn't talk to a child that way, why would you talk to yourself that way? You don't need that kind of nonproductive self-talk going on in your head. So are you going to think big or think small? Are you going to think limits or no limits?

Interesting, isn't it? Clearly, as loving parents, the last thing we want our children to fixate on is their perceived limitations. We want to encourage them. We want to nurture their self-confidence and reward effort over results. The last thing we want to engrain in our children is fear and the belief that they should limit the size of their dreams. So let's just take our own advice. Let's not have this dialogue with our children and let's avoid that sort of self-defeating inner dialogue with ourselves. In my opinion, this kind of negative self-talk is as pointless as it is unproductive. And here is an even greater truth that high achievers have long since discovered: Once you try and achieve one thing you thought might not be possible, it becomes easier and easier for you to "see the impossible" and then achieve it.

> "*I had no people skills, no sales skills, and no business experience, but I was determined to make it.*"
> Valerie Fitzgerald
> Millionaire Real Estate Agent
> Los Angeles, CA
> Sales volume—$60 million

Remember the four-minute mile? The four-minute mile was long considered impossible. Sportscasters and experts all deemed it outside the realm of human ability. One of the greatest milers of the era, Australian John Landy, made numerous high-profile attempts to break the four-minute mark but fell short each time. His efforts served to reinforce the widely held myth of the times, and for nine years all efforts to break the barrier proved unsuccessful. Then a British medical student named Roger Bannister decided he might be able to break the record and began training. He took his goal and broke it into manageable pieces—a quarter of a mile in less than a minute. Each day, during his thirty-minute lunch break at Oxford, Bannister worked on running ten consecutive fifty-nine-second quarter miles with two minutes of rest in between. By continually achieving one-fourth of his goal, Bannister began to believe. On May 6, 1954, a triumphant Roger Bannister ran the "miracle mile" in 3 minutes and 59.4 seconds.

Bannister's "miracle mile" is widely used to illustrate the power of positive attitude, of believing in possibilities. What is often missed is the subplot about the equal but opposite power of myth. John Landy, who had famously tried to achieve the four-minute mile for years, would go on to break Bannister's new record in less than two months. Two months. This doesn't appear to be a matter of simple coincidence. What had held Landy back was a myth, the myth that no one could break the four-minute mile. Bannister broke the record and, in doing so, tore down the psychological wall that was keeping Landy from success.

"I really didn't have management ability. I was a worker and a people pleaser. I had difficulty with delegation, but I learned I could do it. I just had to let things go—just show people what to do and why."

Barbara Wilson
Millionaire Real Estate Agent
Medina, OH
Sales volume—$57.3 million

No matter what your circumstances may be at the time, when you set out to achieve something, always begin with the belief that you just might do it. Real estate agents who succeed at high levels understand how debilitating thinking "I can't do it" can be. They understand that the very first step to discovering their potential is trying. You can't know what you're really capable of doing until you try and never give up. In fact, many people have said that they believe that failure is not the worst thing in the world. They believe the very worst is not to try at all. It's been observed that many of life's failures are people who did not realize how close they were to success when they gave up.

It's funny, but a person once pointed out to me that "ultimate potential" is a goal-less pursuit. I had to think about it for a bit before realizing it's true. We can never reach our ultimate potential. There is no goal, no finish line. So your focus must be on continual pursuit. Maximizing your potential is simply about trying and trying and never giving up.

THE SECOND COMMON MYTHUNDERSTANDING

MYTH: IT CAN'T BE DONE IN MY MARKET.

TRUTH: YES IT CAN, BUT YOU MAY NEED A NEW APPROACH.

The second MythUnderstanding we've encountered is closely related to the first. It seems that even when people are able to see that something is possible, they tend to fall prey to another unknowable assumption. They say, "It may be possible elsewhere, but it will never work in my market." And then comes the justification: "To do that in my market, I'd have to have an X percent market share, and that has never been done before." "To do that in my market, I'd have to have X number of buyers, and no one has ever done that before." "To do that in my market, I'd have to list X or more properties a month, and it's never been done here." . . . and so forth. Here's the truth: If it has been done in another market, it can be done in your market. What I want you to realize is that once it has been done, no matter where, it's just a matter of finding out how that can be possible in your world.

> *"You must seek ideas, training, and consulting outside your own area."*
>
> Tim Wood
> Millionaire Real Estate Agent
> Big Bear Lake, CA
> Sales volume—$38 million

What you're really saying when you say "It can't be done in my market" is "I haven't found the right way to make it work in my market." Frankly, you'll need to start by trying approaches that have proven successful elsewhere. Similar to the point we just made with the first MythUnderstanding, until you try an approach that worked in another market, you will never know whether it can or can't be done in yours. While your marketplace will certainly determine what some of the variables are, your plan of attack and your implementation of it will always be the key determining factors.

I know a lot of tremendously talented real estate agents who will achieve far less than they are capable of because they are stuck on a two- or three-listings-per-month business plan. It distresses me. They are perfectly capable of great success but become victims of the wrong plan. If you go to the back of this book, you'll find lots of real-life examples of Millionaire Real Estate Agents. They have done it in widely varying marketplaces. But they are doing it. If you're willing to adopt a million-dollar plan, you may find you are able to do it as well.

And here is a great truth I have personally experienced: The first one to overcome this MythUnderstanding enjoys a distinct advantage in his marketplace. If you believe and your competition does not, there is one less obstacle between you and your goals! And it's a big one!

The Third Common
MythUnderstanding

Myth: It Would Take Too Much Time and Effort—I Would Lose My Freedom.

Truth: Time and Effort Are Not the Deciding Factors in Success.

This is probably one of the greatest MythUnderstandings of all. And it seems to be the one most people fall prey to. They truly believe that the more successful you become, the more time and effort you will have to invest and the more freedom you'll lose. They say things like, "I'm not willing to make the sacrifices you'd have to make to have that level of success." People have lived before us and I believe the highly successful ones have proven this to be a complete and total myth. They understand that you can put in fifty-hour workweeks and make $50,000 a year or you can put in fifty-hour workweeks and make a million dollars a year. Still others understand that they can put in a fifty-hour workweek and experience no limits to their income earning potential.

Try looking at it this way. Any given approach to working will correspondingly create a limit to the amount of sales production that can be accomplished by a single individual in a given workweek. Some people then believe that this means they have hit the limits of their success! Then they try to get around this problem by simply working more hours, and that is what costs them their freedom. The key to success at this point is not to apply more time or effort to the equation but to think of time and effort differently. Try to see time and effort first as an efficiency and effectiveness issue. Do the best you can with the time you devote to your business, and when that takes you as far as it can, you then have a leverage issue. When time and effort take you as far as they can, then you add leverage to progress to the next level.

When you look at this closely, you will uncover a series of related myths about time and effort. Here are just a few:

MYTH: Activity means productivity.
TRUTH: You can be active without being productive.

MYTH: Efficiency equals effectiveness.
TRUTH: You can do something very efficiently and still be ineffective.

MYTH: More discipline means less freedom.
TRUTH: Discipline translates to effectiveness, which leads to accomplishment, and that creates more freedom—not less.

MYTH: "Justice for all." Equal time should mean equal reward.
TRUTH: Reward always comes down to who does the best job.

MYTH: We perform best under pressure.
TRUTH: You perform best when you focus, and pressure is a poor means to continually gain focus.

MYTH: I have time.
TRUTH: You have no idea how much time you have, so make every minute count!

Almost every one of the Millionaire Real Estate Agents we interviewed for this book understood how to be purposeful, focused, and extremely effective with their time. Then by maintaining their focus on what was important and applying leverage, they earned back their time. We spoke to agents who could work as little as three days a week and still have a highly successful business; others could expect multiple homes to close while they were away on vacation. These agents are living proof that the more successful you become, the more (not less) freedom you enjoy.

THE FOURTH COMMON MYTHUNDERSTANDING

MYTH: IT'S TOO RISKY. I'LL LOSE MONEY.

TRUTH: RISK IS IN DIRECT PROPORTION TO HOW WELL YOU HOLD YOUR INCREMENTAL COSTS ACCOUNTABLE TO PRODUCING INCREMENTAL RESULTS.

Anyone who has ever spent any time in a boardroom knows that when it comes to expenses, there are basically two kinds of people. There are those who cry, "It costs too much!" and there are those who counter, "We can't afford not to do it." Most people react one way or the other out of habit or nature. Most of the time, you can examine the numbers and make a sound, dispassionate decision. However, there are times when this won't work because you simply can't reliably assess the risks. Millionaire Real Estate Agents know how to operate when the end result is unclear. They understand that if you hold your costs accountable for corresponding incremental results—if you stay engaged after you write the check and evaluate the direct results of writing that check before writing more—you can greatly minimize your risks.

It's just like the childhood game Red Light, Green Light. However, instead of playing the traffic light for fun and games, you must be a traffic light for your expenses. Here is how it works: Once you have a green light, you increase your expenses by an appropriate amount to accomplish a corresponding goal. Now that you've increased your expenses, you must hold that incremental increase accountable to deliver an incremental increase in income! You're now sitting at a red light. And you'll continue to sit there with no increase in your spending until you see the appropriate incremental increase in your income. Once an acceptable incremental increase shows up for that level of spending, the light turns from red to green, and you are now free to add another incremental increase in spending.

This isn't so complicated, yet too many people act as if it is a green-light world and run red light after red light without so much as tapping the "expense brakes." This process is about scrutinizing your results hard and understanding exactly where they come from. Don't pay for a second of anything until you're sure the first one is producing great results! Red Light, Green Light is how you can greatly reduce the risks of increased spending.

Early in my career, I remember fretting over what seemed to be an extraordinary monetary risk involving a new hire. This was at a juncture when one of my businesses needed a new manager. I had interviewed a superb candidate but knew she would command twice the salary I'd ever paid anyone in that position. My initial mistake was in assessing my exposure in terms of her annual salary, which for the purposes of this discussion we'll say was $60,000. In that business, $60,000 would have been a lot of money to guarantee someone for that position. I was very nervous and afraid of the apparent increased risk this guarantee represented. Then it dawned on me that my actual risk was really only the difference between what I had previously paid for the position and the new person's salary. So, in essence, I was risking only about $30,000 a year on this new person. This was a better and truer perspective, but $30,000 still felt like a substantial risk to me. Then it occurred to me that if this person was not performing, I wouldn't be paying the salary for an entire year. The truth was, I would be at risk only for about $2,500 for every month the individual was with the company.

I realized that if I paid close attention to her performance, I'd quickly be able to determine if she was right for the job. I knew I would have to hold her accountable to bring in significant results to justify that kind of guarantee. I finally determined that if after three months performance had fallen or remained the same, I would need to be prepared to part ways and move to another candidate. So my actual risk would only be $7,500 ($2,500 times three months). Once I thought of it that way, I decided

I could afford that risk. What happened was by the end of three months profits had increased more than enough to cover the additional $2,500

> *"When I hired an assistant, my business took off. My advice is don't try to do it all yourself. Go get people."*
>
> Jill Rudler
> Millionaire Real Estate Agent
> Westerville, OH
> Sales volume—$58 million

a month in increased costs. By the end of the year, even after the additional $30,000 I'd invested in wages, our net profits were still markedly higher than the previous year.

Any dollar you spend that increases your net profits is ultimately a dollar well invested. For one person that dollar represents cost. For another it represents an investment. Millionaire Real Estate Agents understand the difference between costs and investments. They play Red Light, Green Light and add costs incrementally, hold them accountable to incremental gains, and then and only then, move forward. Overcoming the "It's too risky" MythUnderstanding is about evaluation, engagement, and patience.

THE FIFTH COMMON MYTHUNDERSTANDING

MYTH: MY CLIENTS WILL ONLY WORK WITH ME— ONLY I CAN DELIVER QUALITY SERVICE.

TRUTH: YOUR CLIENTS AREN'T LOYAL TO YOU; THEY ARE LOYAL TO THE STANDARDS YOU REPRESENT.

To tell you the truth, this is probably the number one reason great real estate agents don't succeed to their highest potential. To become a Millionaire Real Estate Agent you will have to hire additional help. Some Millionaire Real Estate Agents have small staffs. Others have six or more people helping them with the work involved with producing spectacular sales volume. Eventually, to reach your highest sales potential, you will have to learn to delegate responsibilities and authority to others.

Please hear me and hear me well. If you get nothing else out of this book, please consider this important point: Whatever services you provide, as specialized as they may be, can be duplicated through the right people implementing systems to achieve standards you approve.

What's all this talk about standards, you ask? Your unique services are a by-product of your standards. Whether you realize it or not, you have set beliefs on how quickly you should respond to a buyer inquiry, how a listing interview should be conducted, or how a difficult contract negotiation should be handled. Most successful real estate agents hold themselves to unwritten personal standards in these areas without always being able to articulate them quickly. Yet they all seem to be able instantly to recognize the moment their standards have been breached.

The right approach to delegating tasks is to determine, clearly, what experience your clients (and you) expect your services to deliver and then articulate that to your staff so they, too, can deliver that experience. Any task can be defined. And if it can be defined and have standards attached to it, it can also be delegated. Systems are simply road maps, instructions that allow these standards to be repeated and duplicated easily.

If systems and standards could not ensure the duplication of a particular level of service, then all companies would be made up of one person. When you think about quality standards in the service industry, what companies do you think of? Nordstrom, the Ritz Carlton, Tavern on the Green, and all the other companies that place a premium on the quality of their customers' experience. These companies stake their reputation on their standards, and they teach their employees how to duplicate them.

> *"We sell the team concept. We say meet the CC Sells specialists."*
> Chris Cormack
> Millionaire Real Estate Agent
> Ashburn, VA
> Sales volume—$70 million

To work at Disney, employees have to attend Disney University, an intense crash course in their service systems. Employees are taught all the essential facts, memorize park layouts, and are instructed on how to keep their energy high and attitude right. The Disney philosophy is: "The front line is the bottom line." They understand that the average visitor saves for two and a half years before making the journey, which makes for some lofty expectations. The average homeowner waits as much as four times as long to make a home purchase. What are their expectations? How can you ensure that your staff can meet those expectations the way you do? Standards and systems. The interesting truth is when you systematize services to a defined standard so others can deliver them, your clients actually get better service. And isn't that what you're after?

THE SIXTH COMMON MYTHUNDERSTANDING

MYTH: HAVING A GOAL AND NOT FULLY REALIZING IT IS A NEGATIVE THING.

TRUTH: *HAVING A GOAL AND NOT TRYING TO ACHIEVE IT IS A NEGATIVE THING.*

Fear of failure is so common it even has its own phobia— Kakorrhaphiophobia. ("Kak-or-rhaph-io-pho-bia." Try saying that three times fast!) The problem, for some of us, is that overcoming our fear of failure, especially public failure, is very difficult to accomplish.

When I was a child, my parents had a framed print across from my bedroom called *Portrait of an Achiever*. Below that title was this list:

- 1832 Failed in business—bankruptcy
- 1832 Defeated for legislature
- 1834 Failed in business—bankruptcy

- 1835 Fiancée died
- 1836 Nervous breakdown
- 1838 Defeated in election
- 1843 Defeated for U.S. Congress
- 1848 Defeated for U.S. Congress
- 1855 Defeated for U.S. Senate
- 1856 Defeated for Vice President
- 1858 Defeated for U.S. Senate

Had you stopped there, you would have missed the final point:

- 1860 Elected President of the United States of America

The subject, of course, was Abraham Lincoln. God bless my mom and dad for hanging that in the hallway. What a great message: You cannot fail unless you quit. If Lincoln had quit in 1858, he would have been dismissed as a footnote in American history rather than be remembered as the honored statesman he became. He kept trying, he didn't quit, and the rest, as they say, is history.

If there is anything that history bears out, it is that failure almost always precedes success. There are so many similar examples. Probably the most famous is Thomas Edison, who claimed to have failed a thousand times before successfully designing the lightbulb. What if he had stopped at 999? Theodore Geisel (a.k.a Dr. Seuss) was rejected twenty-seven times before finding a publisher. Mark Victor Hansen's *Chicken Soup for the Soul* was rejected by more than thirty publishers before going on to sell more than 70 million copies worldwide. Henry Ford failed and went broke five times. Tom Landry, Chuck Noll, Bill Walsh, and Jimmy Johnson share the record for having the worst first-season records in NFL

> *"People need to stop wasting focus on what they could have done and focus on what they can change, now."*
>
> Russell Shaw
> Millionaire Real Estate Agent
> Phoenix, AZ
> Sales volume—$50.6 million

history—they won only a single game. They also account for eleven of the nineteen Super Bowl victories from 1974 to 1993.

One of the secrets to great success is to change your perspective on failure. You see, everyone experiences failures before they ultimately succeed. Some let their failures stop them. Some keep trying. People like Edison, Ford, and Lincoln chose to view failure as a learning experience to build on and not as a permanent defeat. It may sound like double talk, but failure is progress. At the very least, in attempting to achieve a dream and failing, you've learned to eliminate that approach the next time you try. Use your failures as stepping-stones. The next time you try something, bear in mind that history has made it very clear that you will probably have to fail a few times before you get it right. Remember Lincoln.

Too many people live their lives under the mistaken assumption that success is a matter of avoiding failure. The problem with that approach to living is that when you actively avoid failure, you tend to avoid challenges as well. Success is not about avoiding failure. Failure is about avoiding failure. Success is about trying. Groundbreaking scientist Louis Pasteur once shared this: "Let me tell you the secret that has led me to my goal. My strength lies solely in my tenacity."

AFFIRMATION

A long time ago, someone taught me to say, "If it's to be, it's up to me." When I first heard it, I thought it was a great action affirmation. However, over the years, I've played with it a little bit and tried to center it more on personal faith than simple action. For a while I'd ask, "If it's to be, why not me?" But as I would say it to myself, I still felt there was still some doubt persistent in the message. Now, I simply say, "If it's to be, it will be me." We'd encourage you to adopt that as your personal affirmation. Faith leads to momentum. It's quite possible that the most important contributor to your ultimate success will be your ability to keep moving, to make progress, and to learn as you go. So jump out there and enter the real estate sales race with confidence. And remember, you can't get anywhere if you never start!

POINTS TO REMEMBER: MythUnderstandings

- You need to examine your beliefs, search for the truths, and abandon your myths.

- People are succeeding at high levels, and so can you.

- Just because it has never been done in your market doesn't mean it is impossible to achieve. Get a big plan that matches your market, and go for it!

- There is only so much time and effort you can give. A big dream doesn't necessitate more time and effort; you just have to focus and apply yourself differently.

- Growing your sales business is not inherently more risky than staying where you are. The risk of inaction is often greater than the risk of action. You must understand your costs, hold them accountable for results, and keep moving forward.

- If you have defined standards and can teach them to others, you can delegate work and gain the leverage you need to grow. Remember, customers are actually loyal to the service standards you represent—not just to you.

- Failure is nothing to be feared. The very best of us have used failures as stepping-stones on the path to ultimate success. The only true failure is in quitting or not trying at all.

Part Two:

THE FOUR STAGES

THINK A MILLION

Figure 1

BUILDING A TWENTY-LANE HIGHWAY FOR YOUR FUTURE

How you think matters. How you think in the beginning *really* matters. Having learned this early in my career when I faced an uncertain future brought on by the late 1980s shift in the real estate market, I vowed to make thinking my first action step. And I was immensely rewarded. One small example of how thinking first changed my actions was in how I started answering my telephone. I had the ambition of building a large real estate business but had only two local real estate offices and no immediate prospects for more. Nonetheless, I began answering my phone with the line "national office." I know this may have sounded brazen, but it was amazing how this simple act created incredible positive momentum, enthusiasm, and credibility for my long-term goals. There is no question that it contributed to our success.

At about the same time, by thinking first, we also saw the future need for and created right up front some basic operating infrastructures that could handle not hundreds, but tens of thousands of agents. In fact, many of those systems are still in place today! Because we could envision a big future for our company and took the appropriate measures on the front end, our vision was like a twenty-lane highway enabling the business to leap forward at a rapid pace with no need for massive restructuring or major reinventing. Thinking first can have these kinds of effects in your life and your business. It is that powerful.

> *"I learned to use creative visualization. I saw my success. I pictured my life getting much better. The more I made those pictures happen, the more I created a new life for myself."*
>
> Elaine Northrop
> Millionaire Real Estate Agent
> Ellicott City, MD
> Sales volume—$71 million

WORK TO LEARN
BEFORE YOU WORK TO EARN

Let's go back for just a second to our mountain-climbing analogy. If becoming a Millionaire Real Estate Agent is like climbing Mount Everest, then let's consider the first stage, Think a Million, as Base Camp. I can't emphasize enough that the quality of the preparations you make here will largely determine how high you will be able to climb.

How well you prepare can also save you from some unwanted and unintended consequences that could lead to real setbacks. Many top sales producers report that they did not really begin to think strategically until they were already well on their way. The mistakes they made had consequences and, in some cases, really held them back for a time. An agent I consulted with several years ago can attest to the dangers of starting your climb without first pausing to think big. Early in her career, she had created a compensation plan for her assistant in which the bonuses increased dramatically as production grew. Eventually, the agent found herself in a cul-de-sac where her sales volume kept increasing, as well as her cost of sales, but her net profits had unreasonably plateaued. In the end, she admitted that she had never imagined she would reach a place where her approach to a scaled compensation concept would become a liability. As a result, she was faced with an unpleasant "take-back" situation, in which she had to reduce compensation and risk losing a valued staff member. There is no doubt: To put ourselves in the best possible growth position, we must Think a Million from the start!

In this chapter we'll examine:

- The Nine Ways the Millionaire Real Estate Agent Thinks
- The Three L's of the Millionaire Real Estate Agent
- The Eight Goal Categories of the Millionaire Real Estate Agent

Think a Million is an attempt to help you capture not only the mind-set and attitude of the Millionaire Real Estate Agent, but also the focus. Through experience top agents have learned to differentiate between what is truly important, what can be delegated, and what can simply be ignored. One of the biggest challenges we have (and I continually face this, too) is overcoming the incredible urge to leapfrog the Work to Learn phase and go straight to the Work to Earn phase. But resist we must.

Have you ever thought about how many years medical students must work as interns and residents before being allowed to practice their trade independently? Besides laboring through four years of undergraduate studies and another four of medical school, doctors must typically practice as an intern for a year and then serve a minimum of two years as a resident. It is staggering to think about, but the Work to Learn process for an average surgeon can last as long as twelve years. Medical students invest a lot of money and time before they Work to Earn.

The real estate agent on the other hand . . . Well, we tend to pay for our training on a credit card and expect to start earning income immediately. It is amazing how many real estate agents I've met over the years who have "backed into" the profession. Many take up real estate as a second career or as a weekend moneymaker. And though there is absolutely nothing wrong with this, most face a real need to make money early on. Because they began their career with mortgages, college tuition for the kids, or a certain lifestyle to maintain, they are forced to dive in and learn as they earn. As a result, they don't get the chance to pause up front and work on how they think and act. How many agents do you know who truly study the business of real estate before they enter it? The truth is it would be far better for them if they said, "I need to wait just a little bit and Work to Learn. Before I get going too fast, I need to take a step back and gain some understanding." Napoleon Hill put it very well in the title of his famous book *Think and Grow Rich*.

Truly aggressive people might at first think this is a waste of good selling or listing time, but the fact of the matter is, "Ready, aim, fire!" always wins out in the long run over "Ready, fire, aim!" And if you're building a career, you're in it for the long run.

Think a Million is designed to be a crash course on Working to Learn. We hope that you're already thinking big like a high achiever and that you just need us to confirm you are on the right track and, maybe, to fill in a few blanks. Most, however, have never taken the time to examine what makes them successful or not. Content with their current possibilities or unaware of their potential, these agents pull their practice through the ups and downs of the market using a combination of personal charisma, work ethic, and determination. These are all absolutely admirable traits! Our hope is that, in the next few pages, you discover that if, in addition to those characteristics, you can maintain a certain frame of mind and concentrate on a handful of key issues, the path to a much higher place will open up before you. I've come to understand that if you don't think first, thinking later may not help you.

THE NINE WAYS THE MILLIONAIRE REAL ESTATE AGENT THINKS

About one-third of the Think a Million formula is attitude and perspective. Now, don't be mistaken. The Nine Ways is not just a rehashing of popular clichés about positive thinking and affirmations. We've learned that when you're looking to change your habits, you need to be more precise and a little more on purpose. A mechanic can't tune an engine based on a generic statement like, "The engine makes a funny sound." If you offer that up in the garage, a good mechanic will ask you whether it is it a grinding noise or a high-pitched whir, when the car makes the sounds, and when the vehicle first started showing signs of trouble. Just like the successful mechanic, if you want to improve the way you think about your real estate career, you'll have to start by zeroing in on some key specifics.

In breaking down the way the Millionaire Real Estate Agent thinks into nine specific categories, two categories—Think Powered by a Big Why and Think Big Goals and Big Models—clearly stood out from the rest as foundational mind-sets that almost all top real estate agents have in

The Nine Ways the Millionaire Real Estate Agent Thinks
1. Think Powered by a Big Why — **FOUNDATIONAL**
2. Think Big Goals and Big Models
3. *Think Possibilities*
4. *Think Action*
5. *Think Without Fear*
6. *Think Progress* — ***SUPPORTIVE***
7. *Think Competitively and Strategically*
8. *Think Standards*
9. *Think Service*

Figure 2

common. The final seven—Think Possibilities, Think Action, Think Without Fear, Think Progress, Think Competitively and Strategically, Think Standards, and Think Service—are no less important but tend, interestingly enough, to be supportive to the first two.

Over the years, whenever I consulted with agents, I always probed for the ways they thought. When they would tell me about their current production level, I wouldn't pronounce it as good or bad but simply asked how they felt about it. I asked them why they chose real estate and what kept them going. Before thirty minutes was up, I could usually identify at least one of the Nine Ways that had evaded them. Now, make no mistake about it, while some of the Nine Ways the Millionaire Real Estate Agent Thinks are more vital than others, all are essential to creating a high level of success that can weather storms and the test of time. The first and probably the most powerful way that the Millionaire Real Estate Agent thinks is to Think Powered by a Big Why.

1. THINK POWERED BY A BIG WHY

Above all else, we've discovered that one thing all high achievers have in common is they are working for a Big Why. The Big Why is about having a purpose, a mission, or a need, that in turn gives you focus. High achievers always have a Big Why powering their actions.

> *"If you have the right why, it kicks the tar out of any how. You can always figure out the how."*
> Tim Wood
> Millionaire Real Estate Agent
> Big Bear Lake, CA
> Sales volume—$38 million

A great example of how a Big Why works in our lives is the day-before-a-vacation miracle. Ever see anyone work the day before a vacation? It is truly amazing! No matter how they approached yesterday, today they have become a model for the entire world on how to get things done. Why? Because if they get it all done, they get to go play! That's a pretty Big Why! So the day before we leave for vacation, we're on a time-management mission! We don't sit around idly and surf the Internet or chitchat with fellow workers. We screen our calls, ignore trivial e-mails, and toss out junk mail with abandon. Maybe we even eat lunch at our desk or on the run, and by the end of the day we've accomplished more than we ever thought was possible in a single day and still have time to pack, drop the dog off at the kennel, and cancel the newspaper. It's simply incredible! How does this happen? **Because a Big Why brings big focus and big energy,** and a Little Why brings little focus and little energy. HIGH ACHIEVERS ALWAYS HAVE A BIG WHY!

Now imagine if you could live *every* day with such purpose. How far could you really go? Is your motivation to work every day the kind of motivation that can take you to your highest possible level? Okay, let's pause for just a moment. For the next couple of minutes, I'd like you just to think about what really motivates you, then write down your thoughts. Go ahead and stick your bookmark right here and close the book until you're done.

You're back. We hope you've got a good idea of what your Big Why is. Chances are you wrote down more than one source of

> *"At first my motivation was money. Now, God and family come first. I like my lifestyle."*
> Jack Gross
> Millionaire Real Estate Agent
> Bethlehem, PA
> Sales volume—$132.1 million

daily motivation. That's fine. Most people are driven by a number of reasons and a lot of Little Whys can add up to a very Big Why. At the end of this section, I'll ask you to organize those whys and place the most important to you at the top of the list. But before you start that process, let's consider a few of the dangers of working for the wrong Big Why.

A few years back, a dear friend and I were sharing our business goals for the upcoming year. Now, I don't really make New Year's resolutions like most people. Sure, I'd like to have more sales and take more to the bottom line, but that is just one aspect of my overall annual business goals. As we'll discuss later in this chapter, long ago, I discovered the magic of business goal categories. Each year I simply choose the next achievement targets in each category rather than re-creating the whole system. For me, business goals are part of a larger personal strategy designed to push me to my limits and make me grow. Unfortunately, to my friend, they seemed to be more about pure ambition and possible greed than about personal development. That misunderstanding was the source of the conversation I'd like to relate to you now. It was very telling and honest, and I think it may help shed some light on the difference between living with and without a Big Why:

FRIEND: When I look at your business goals, I have to ask, "Why do you want *all* that money?"

ME: What do you mean by "want all that money"? I don't.

FRIEND: Then why do you set all those goals to get it? It sure looks like you want it.

ME: Now, friend, no offense, but I don't work for money. You do.

FRIEND: That's not true.

ME: Sure it is. Because when you have enough, you stop working.

FRIEND: What do you mean?

ME: I mean that the amount of effort you put out at work is directly related to the amount of money you're getting paid. You appear to know exactly how much money you want to make and when you make it, you stop working. You work for money.

FRIEND: Hmm. I guess I never thought of it that way.

ME: Well, try thinking of it that way for a moment. Then, go a little further. Now, you say you have everything you need, but it appears to me that you feel maybe you could have accomplished a little more by this point in your career. Right?

FRIEND:	Gary, you know I hate it when you do the tough-love thing with me.
ME:	Well?
FRIEND:	You're right.
ME:	Why do you think that is? Maybe your focus on money is actually holding you back?
FRIEND:	But I do need a certain amount of money.
ME:	We all do. Try looking at it this way. I also need a certain amount of money, but the difference is, I've never worked for money. Never. Never even really thought about it. When I wake up in the morning, my Big Goal is to do my very best, to be my very best, and to grow as much as possible. Any money I've made is simply a by-product of my constant pursuit of personal growth. That's why I set Big Goals and work so hard.

So you have to be careful when you're trying to discover your Big Why. We hope that what motivates you isn't just money or a comfortable retirement. The truth is, you can achieve those things faster than you think; then, if you're not careful, you'll be left with a lot of life and little reason to live it. We hope you're getting in touch with what truly motivates you. Maybe you love to do the deal. Some of the best agents I know love nothing more than a difficult negotiation that gives them a chance to really shine, to acknowledge objections, to discover a solution with which both sides can be happy. This is the kind of Big Why that doesn't easily fade.

I've also known real estate agents who like nothing better than providing exceptional service to their clients and handing them a key to their dream home. This kind of Big Why has led them essentially to become invaluable financial advisers for their clients, guiding them on investments so they can eventually buy their dream home.

As you've probably guessed, my personal favorite is the Big Why that drives people to be the best they can be. You might try thinking of it this way: Being your best is actually a goalless pursuit. You can never ever really reach a point where you can truthfully say, "I just can't grow anymore." And what is so exciting is that this kind of Big Why can create a life that literally explodes with limitless possibilities and unlimited personal growth. It is where the unimaginable you dared not dream becomes the imaginable you dare to live. And as far as money goes, when you are always striving to do the best you can do, you will always be making the most money you can possibly make. Here is the best part of all: Once you have the money, what you can do with it (gifts, travel, charities, hobbies, etc.) can then become another why that supports your Big Why!

Now, stop for a second and take another look at your notes. What are the whys in your life? What is the biggest one for you? Whatever you place foremost will be your Big Why. If it is the right kind of Big Why, it will also tend to lend foundational support to all of your other whys. Like geese that fly in formation, the lead goose bears the brunt of the work and allows all the other geese to draft behind her. Your Big Why can and will do the same thing for all your other whys. It is the why that pulls all whys.

In the end, I am a strong advocate for placing personal growth ahead of any Big Why you have. It is simply that powerful. High achievers know this. They know that when they decide to be their best and place that at the forefront of all other whys, it will pull the rest in its wake.

Just as important, striving to be the best you can be will keep you from pulling up short and settling for "good" and letting "just good enough" be the theme of your life. In his bestselling book *Good to Great*, Jim Collins declares, "Good is the enemy of great. . . . Few people attain great lives, in large part because it is just so easy to settle for a good life. The vast majority of companies never become great, precisely because the vast majority become quite good—and that is their main problem." I have come to accept that one of the greatest challenges in life is pushing to be our best when we are already pretty good. The surest way to combat that natural tendency is to make "being your best" and "doing the best" the point of everything you do, to make it your Big Why.

Robert Browning is often quoted as having said, "Ah, but a man's reach should exceed his grasp—or what's a heaven for?" Significant whys led by the Big Why, "Be the Best You Can Be," will have you reaching for the sky every time.

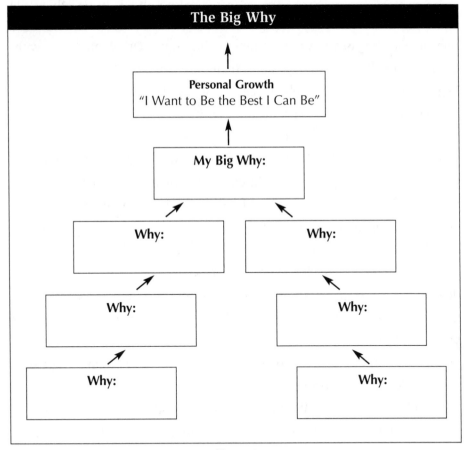

Figure 3

2. THINK BIG GOALS AND BIG MODELS

"I see no limit to the size of my business. My vision is to build a business that my children can take over and that will still pay an income to my husband and me."

Rachel DeHanas
Millionaire Real Estate Agent
Waldorf, MD
Sales volume—$52 million

The second foundational way the Millionaire Real Estate Agent thinks is to Think Big Goals and Big Models. In working with top real estate salespeople, we discovered that any time they tried to separate Big Goals and Big Models into two categories, it just didn't work. It turns out they are like the yin and yang of Chinese philosophy. One cannot exist without the other. If you have Big Goals, then to reach them you will inevitably begin a quest for Big Models. Likewise, Big Models will drive you toward the achievement of Big Goals, even if that was not your intention.

If anything, the power behind having Big Goals is really about the power of acquiring Big Habits by beginning with the end in mind. The professional habits you build will either empower or restrict you. What you must understand is that your habits will either serve as an empowering platform for the next level of your success or as a restricting box trapping you inside your current level. Big Goals are about reaching for your true potential. By focusing on Big Goals, you will be focusing on developing Big Habits that will always be appropriate to achieving your highest levels of success. And in taking this approach, you'll find as you grow that your Big Habits never hold you back. Small goals tend to facilitate small habits. Big Goals tend to facilitate Big Habits. Big Goals require Big Habits to drive Big Models.

Think of it this way. Why do we tell our children to sit up straight at the dinner table? Is it just about respect or manners? No. One reason we want them to sit straight is because we know that bad posture can inhibit the ability to be successful in sports and, later, can lead to serious back problems. When you look at your child slouching at the dinner table and think, "If he keeps that up, he won't be able to swing a golf club when he's fifty, much less pick up a bag of groceries without clutching his back" . . . you Think Big Goals for your child. You then show him a Big Model: You sit up straight, pull your shoulders back, and tuck your chin. That is the kind of Big posture Habit that will not limit your child's potential.

It really is that simple. Your task is to internalize this concept: that in order to become your very best, you will have to Think Big and have Big Models. The habits that you create will either help you reach your goals or hamper your attempts. Warren Buffett points out that most people discover too late that "the chains of habits are too light to be felt until they are too heavy to be broken." When you begin with a Big Goal in mind, you consciously build the kinds of Big Habits that will serve as key building blocks for your entire career.

> *"I watched other agents who were doing well. I began to do what they were doing. Every year I set higher goals—'double it' was my motto. It worked."*
>
> Elaine Northrop
> Millionaire Real Estate Agent
> Ellicott City, MD
> Sales volume—$71 million

What is amazing is that Big Goals and Big Models also have a powerful magnetic effect. They pull us through all the smaller goals along the way. First-time marathoners understand this principle well. A marathon is 26.2 miles, yet nonrunners, people who are often not even all that fit, regularly adopt proven training programs and manage to finish the full marathon. For a runner, 26.2 miles is a Big Goal. Now, after years of study and experimentation, Big Models are readily available to help anyone pursue a marathon. I love watching the evening news after one big marathon and listening to the interviews with some of the first-time marathoners. They say things like, "Before this race, I'd never run more than three miles! I can't believe I finished. I never would have thought it possible." It is a powerful thing to witness.

I've even talked to first-time marathoners about how they achieved their goal. On the path to 26.2 miles, each week they were hitting new personal bests. One weekend they ran five miles and the next seven and so on, until one weekend they discovered they'd run a half marathon. For most people a half marathon would be a daunting prospect. However, when you start with a bigger goal and a model to get you there, half marathons are reduced to small goals along the way. Isn't that awesome? They accomplished these small goals because their habits, their diet, all their training reflected a much larger goal. Big Goals and Big Models speed you to achieving your very best faster and more easily than you would have ever imagined possible.

The same principles can apply to your real estate career. Let's say it takes, on average, about $80 million in closed volume to Net a Million. For most of us, the $80 million in closed volume may as well be a 26.2-mile marathon! It appears possible only for the elite few.

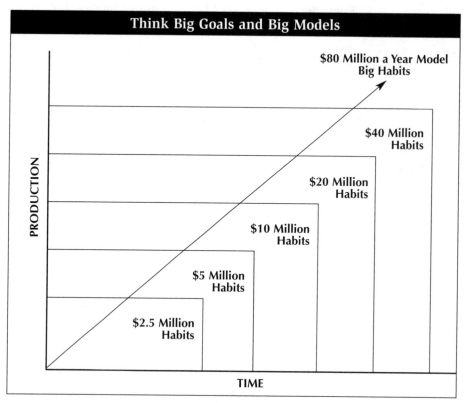

Figure 4

The Millionaire Real Estate Agent

Figure 4 tells the story. Inside the borders surrounding $2.5 million are the models and habits appropriate to that goal. But, when you look closer, you'll notice that these are just a subset of what is necessary to achieve the next level, $5 million. If all you have are the models and habits for $2.5 million, those borders will become a box that you will have to break through should you desire to achieve more. Before you can move forward, you'll have to unlearn your old models and old habits and reinvent yourself with appropriate models and habits to support your new larger goals. On the other hand, if you can begin with the models and habits of someone at the $80 million level, then the borders will simply serve as steps you climb on your way upward. Helen Keller observed, "One can never consent to creep when one feels the impulse to soar."

> *"If you don't have a dream, your life will be about your problems. Your future organizes you now—it is the power of the future pull."*
> Tim Wood
> Millionaire Real Estate Agent
> Big Bear Lake, CA
> Sales volume—$38 million

The trick to soaring to your best is to adopt Big Goals, Big Models, and then start building the Big Habits that will support them.

3. THINK POSSIBILITIES

If I've learned anything in life, it is that if you believe something is possible, you tend to focus on the constructive means necessary to make that possibility a reality. I've also learned to believe the opposite. If you don't think something is possible, then you will be blinded to the ways it could be done. It's like a self-imposed blind spot.

For anyone who wishes to achieve the very best, this becomes a defining moment. Now that you have a Big Why and you've decided to adopt Big Goals and Big Models to power it, the question is: "Do you really think it is possible to become a truly high-achieving real estate agent?" In my mind, it all comes down to your affirming or nonaffirming answer to this question: "Do you think it is possible?"

I believe there are three stages of possibility thinking that people can either get stuck in or go through: (1) Nothing is possible, (2) Something is possible, (3) Anything is possible. For many people, "nothing is possible" because they just don't think in terms of possibilities. Thus, they take no action and nothing happens—just like they thought. For most, "something is possible" because they believe in the power of possibility thinking. They believe that if you think something will happen, it probably will. The problem is that they have an erroneous mental map that says thinking possibilities is all they have to do. And since possibilities thinking, by itself, is so powerful, they do end up with something happening! But it stops there. Because they take no appropriate action, something is all they get. For a very few people, however, big things happen. Why? These people believe that anything is possible if you want it badly enough and are willing to do what is necessary to get it. When possibility thinking supports a Big Why with Big Goals and Big Models, watch out! Anything is possible.

> *"I've always thought big. The opportunities in real estate are limitless."*
>
> Gregg Neuman
> Millionaire Real Estate Agent
> San Diego, CA
> Sales volume—$113 million

When I was growing up, my mother always told me, "Where there's a will, there's a way." In essence, what she was saying was, "Son, if you want it badly enough, if you have a big enough reason for achieving what you want, then you'll figure out a way to get it." My father would be listening to these discussions, and he would invariably point out that history has shown that "necessity is the mother of invention." What my parents were trying to teach me was right. Anything is possible if you put your mind to it and take appropriate action. Millionaire Real Estate Agents understand this.

They have come to realize that while believing alone isn't enough believing is enough to constitute complete and total sabotage before ever get started.

We hope you've seen the Tom Hanks film *Cast Away*. In it, Hanks plays Chuck, a FedEx employee marooned for years on a desolate island. Much was made of Chuck's relationship with "Wilson," a volleyball salvaged from the packages in the wreck. The loneliness and depression evident in Chuck's relationship with his imaginary friend "Wilson" were poignant and, at times, humorous, and became emblematic of the film. But it was really the other package, the box painted with angel wings, that ultimately made the difference. Because Chuck refused to open the angel package until he was saved, it became an emblem of his eventual salvation. The screenwriter, William Broyles Jr., intentionally introduced the angel package to serve as a symbol of hope and possibilities. Broyles did extensive research, read numerous first-person accounts of shipwreck and wilderness survival, and picked up on what many experts know to be true—often the difference between those who survive and those who perish is the ability to believe in the possibility of rescue. In Chuck's case, the possibility of rescue was deeply tied to the package with angel wings.

Ask yourself this question: "When presented with a challenge, do you first think of the ways you could succeed or the ways you could fail?" This is a test. To get to your highest level possible, you will always have to be answering the question "If I want it, what must happen for me to get it?" And then believe that through your efforts, even trial and error if need be, your goals are possible.

Top real estate salespeople are deeply familiar with the saying "Act as though it were impossible to fail," and they build their careers on such an approach. Possibility thinking, when combined with appropriate action, pushes you not only into the realm of possibilities but beyond into the ultimate achievement realm of probabilities.

4. THINK ACTION

When you have Big Goals and Big Models with a Big Why powering them, you begin to Think Possibilities, and you begin to believe anything is possible. Now, when you begin to believe your Big Goal is possible, the natural result is that you start forming plans and get more focused on making things happen. It then follows that the next way to think is to Think Action.

> *"I love the action. It's what I love most about the real estate business."*
> Don Zeleznak
> Millionaire Real Estate Agent
> Scottsdale, AZ
> Sales volume—$77 million

Let's pause for a moment and revisit Tom Hank's character, Chuck, in *Cast Away*. While the package with angel wings was essential to his ability to think possibilities and survive through four trying years marooned on the island, what is more significant is that the package eventually instilled in him the willingness and faith necessary to take action. Fueled by the belief he would succeed, he built a raft and set himself adrift on the open sea, intent on rescuing himself or being rescued. Possibility thinking must be followed by action for those possibilities to have the chance of being fully realized.

The problem for most is that they assemble everything they need to pursue success and then, instead of actually pursuing it, they leave the raft of their salvation on the shore and decide to think about it some more. They hide behind continual inaction while calling it something else altogether—inaction in the form of additional research, planning, preparation, or, more plainly, procrastination. When you are ready, anything short of action is just plain inappropriate. Simply put, top agents know that no action leads to nowhere. And nowhere is not where they plan to be. When you know what to do, there comes a point when it is just time to "shut up, get up, and giddy up."

Millionaire Real Estate Agents clearly understand this. They know that to have results, they have to take action, so they make sure they take positive action toward their Big Goals every day. Truth be told, most high-achieving real estate salespeople have something of a natural advantage. They naturally tend to be decisive and have a high sense of urgency. But even they cannot rely on their natural behavioral style day in and day out. They, too, will need help to reach Big Goals.

Big Models assist the naturally action-oriented and the less naturally action-oriented get into action and stay there. Models represent a plan that was prepared in advance and, when properly systematized, should translate into a consistent set of actions you take every month, week, or day. Models help bring focus to your actions even when you yourself aren't feeling so focused. They help take the choice and decision making out of your actions, so each day your task is clear, your goals evident, and your actions powerful. Thus, total focus on implementing a Big Model takes "natural ability" largely out of the equation and can help anyone become and stay an action-oriented agent.

> *"If I do the right thing, the money will be there."*
> Barbara Wilson
> Millionaire Real Estate Agent
> Medina, OH
> Sales volume—$57.3 million

We've found that the Big Why that gives you an action-first, "damn the torpedoes" mind-set combined with a Big Model that gives you everyday focus provides a powerful one-two punch toward knocking out your Big Goals. It follows that those who concentrate on implementing Big Models get a huge boost in living the Think Action principle of the Millionaire Real Estate Agent.

5. THINK WITHOUT FEAR

Interestingly enough, one of the big obstacles for most people who want to Think Action is that as they set out actually to take action, they cannot Think Without Fear. They start to move forward, stumble into some obstacles, and find themselves paralyzed into inaction by the specter of failure. And then fear of failure itself becomes our primary fear. It can be arresting. It can stop anyone in her tracks. When you begin to focus on the fear of failure, you're cooked. When you can't see the possibilities for and the potential rewards of success because the fear of failure has blinded you, it is time to stop for a moment and reflect.

If you are a possibility thinker, that means you believe you can do this—it is possible. But to "do this," you will have to "do something." You'll have to take action. If you take action, you will most certainly make some mistakes or fall short of the initial progress you'd hoped for. To rephrase the popular bumper sticker: SETBACKS HAPPEN. The good news is that setbacks along the way do not represent total failure and should never get in your way unless you allow them. As we'll discuss in the next section, Think Progress, these momentary setbacks can even represent positives, such as learning opportunities. So never let fear of failure freeze you into inaction—very little good can happen when you're not acting at all.

Ironically, for some people fear of failure actually motivates them to take decisive action and that's a good thing. It can even be a part of their Big Why. Many high achievers have reached for their potential simply because they could not tolerate the thought of the alternative.

Look, we all have our share of failed attempts. It is really a matter of how we view them. Failed attempts are not failure, so never fear the attempt itself. And keep trying! Charles Kettering warns us of this when he writes, "The only time you can't afford to fail is the last time you try." It follows that if you never quit trying, you've never really failed.

The men's speed skating finals in the 2002 Winter Olympic Games demonstrates this point beautifully. The American skater, Apolo Anton Ohno, was widely predicted to win the gold medal, and, coming into the final turn of the race, he was in great position to take the top place on the medal podium. But then a skater lost his balance, tangled with the rest, and all the leaders were sent crashing to the ice. A cry went up from the crowd, and a stunned Steven Bradbury of Australia, the last-placed skater and the only one still standing, coasted across the finish line to take the gold. But while the other fallen skaters were paralyzed by the belief that all was now lost, Ohno had the presence of mind to rise and virtually throw himself across the finish line to take the silver medal. What would have been an utter failure for many athletes in his position was transformed into what was ultimately hailed as one of the defining moments of those Winter Games.

Having a Big Why will help you focus on what the Millionaire Real Estate Agent usually has going for him—the power and motivation that comes when your greatest fear is not reaching your goal. This allows him to slough off setbacks as they go without ever losing his faith or his momentum. He fears ultimate failure but is indomitable in the face of intermittent failure. Top agents persevere through the "failures along the way" so that they do not fail at the end of the day.

6. THINK PROGRESS

Think Progress is about the knowledge that breakthroughs more often than not come through effort and persistence. While clearly related to Think Without Fear, Think Progress takes your thinking a step further. Statistically speaking, the more you try, the better your odds at succeeding. If a scientist tells you the odds are a thousand to one against your achieving a particular result, they are also saying that if you attempt it a thousand times, you're guaranteed to achieve that result. Think

Progress is about quantity and repetition. Success is in the numbers.

David Bayles and Ted Orland in their enlightening book, *Art & Fear,* tell the story of the ceramics teacher who divided his class into two groups: One would be graded solely on the *quality* of their work and the other would be graded solely on the *quantity* of their work. He was very straightforward about his grading criteria. The group graded on quality would produce one pot, which needed to be perfect to get an A. The quantity group would have all their pots weighed. If they had produced fifty pounds of pots, they got an A. If they produced less, their grade would suffer. The results where quite revealing. The quality group spent much of their time planning the perfect pot, but when it came time to create it, they either made mistakes or their skills were too underdeveloped to fulfill their visions. On the other hand, the quantity group churned out pot after pot and, in the process, learned from their mistakes and perfected more advanced techniques. If you haven't guessed, the group that focused on quantity not only generated a greater quantity of work but also work of a superior quality.

The Millionaire Real Estate Agent does not see consequences in terms of positives or negatives. If something has an outcome, whether it has a positive or negative

result, they call it progress. Because they Think Progress, they know that failures are just stepping-stones, part of the learning process, and they don't let the negative outcomes derail their enthusiasm. These highly successful real estate agents also know that persistence and repetition will eventually yield tremendous results. They Think Progress all the time.

You will undoubtedly make some mistakes on the path to becoming a top real estate agent. Just remember that mistakes are progress. Business lore has it that legendary capitalist Andrew Carnegie once called a man into his office. The man, whose decision had just cost Carnegie's business $1,000,000, started the conversation by apologizing and saying he understood why he was being let go. Carnegie replied, "Why would I fire you when I've just invested a million dollars in your education?" Progress is important and is usually achieved by the person who makes the most attempts. The quality is in the quantity.

7. THINK COMPETITIVELY AND STRATEGICALLY

Most of us, when we sit down to play Spades, Monopoly, or Scrabble, expect to have fun. And because losing is more about your pride or who has to take out the garbage, you don't hold back. You try to outthink and outplay your friends. When I advise real estate agents to Think Competitively and Strategically, I'm really telling them to approach their career the way they do a game.

I've played the board game Risk with my son and witnessed an otherwise guileless, wonderful child morph into a little Napoleon plotting my demise. If everyone, even the sweetest child I know, is capable of this level of competitiveness, why don't we all apply the same level of strategic thinking and competitiveness to our careers? And, by the way, why shouldn't our work be just as entertaining?

> *"I want to win. I expect to get the deal. I didn't win a Cy Young Award as a Major League pitcher, but I have earned that level of award in real estate."*
>
> Mike Mendoza
> Millionaire Real Estate Agent
> Phoenix, AZ
> Sales volume—$60 million

Almost all of the Millionaire Real Estate Agents we've worked with or interviewed for this book were, by nature, very competitive people. They love what they do. They are competitive and tend to think strategically. As a result, their work has taken on the marvelous characteristics of a competitive and fun game. When they go on a listing appointment, they are analyzing it, working out the best approach for success. And when they get that listing—Yahtzee!

Once, I facilitated a panel discussion. On the panel were some of the top-producing agents in the city. One of the top agents was asked to talk about territory, and he related how his team had made it their goal to "own" a particular area. In fact, his personal sales team at the time had a 20 percent market share in that area. Another panelist then related a story of how this agent had reacted when she had gone after a listing in the heart of his targeted area. Well, he called her up and pretty much told her that he would do whatever it took to get that listing. And he meant it. Through intense competitiveness, he got that listing as well as the respect of his friend and competitor. Playing to win is not a bad thing.

Anson Dorrance, the legendary coach of the University of North Carolina (UNC) women's soccer team, struggled early on to get his players to play as competitively in practices as they did in games. They'd knock down a teammate on an aggressive play and, instead of pursuing the advantage, they'd stop to apologize. Dorrance knew that if the team practiced apologetically they'd likely play that way, too. He had to teach them that aggressive, competitive play among friends was something to be respected rather than avoided. He adopted a system where the coaches meticulously scored each athlete in drills and scrimmages. They were timed in sprints and were awarded points for winning 50/50 balls, etc. Each evening the coaches tabulated their scores, ranked every player, and then posted them on Dorrance's office door. Well, the atmosphere in practices changed dramatically. In the beginning, no one wanted to see their name at the bottom of the chart. Later, competitiveness became a mentality and a source of pride. They expected their teammates to bring their very best against them—anything less showed a lack of respect. Competition became a huge part of the team's culture, and they experienced tremendous success as a result. In the program's first twenty-two years, UNC won seventeen National Championships. Once when Dean Smith, UNC's Hall of Fame basketball coach, was asked what it was like to share the spotlight with the newly successful football program, he responded, "This is a women's soccer school. We're just trying to keep up with them."

Treating it like a game is also about learning to Think Strategically. The problem is that most real estate agents can't distinguish between rules (how you play) and strategies (how you win). In real estate, our rules have nothing to do with making money. They are about conduct, ethics, and protocol. You can be a master of conduct, ethics, and protocol and still be a pauper! Now, I'm not in any way insinuating that you need to break the rules to succeed. Rules are about proper requisites and restraints. I advocate playing by them; however, strategies are often found in the gray areas in between the rules. I can't relate to you how many times I've heard the following type of exchange:

LOW ACHIEVER: Can we do that?

HIGH ACHIEVER: Why? Did someone say we couldn't?

People who live by the rules live in a literal world. Strategic thinkers are exercising their creativity and living outside those limitations. When I think about great strategic thinkers, I think about guys like William "Candy" Cummings, who in 1863 introduced the curveball to baseball. Imagine the scene the first time he threw a ball that looked just like a fat, slow, perfectly hittable ball until "it drops off the table." Batters must have screwed themselves into the ground trying to hit it. And I bet they complained, saying things like, "That's not fair! He can't do that!" The rules of baseball precisely define the distance from the pitcher's mound to home plate, what constitutes a ball and a strike, and a half-dozen other elements, but they never said the ball had to fly straight. Cummings understood that, and, as a result, he is enshrined in the Baseball Hall of Fame in Cooperstown, New York. The game was forever changed by his strategic thinking. Any ballplayer will tell you that anybody can hit a fastball, but it takes a major leaguer to hit a "big league" curve. Every sport and profession has its own Candy Cummings. Strategic thinkers not only find tremendous success, but they also have the power to reshape their respective professions.

When you go to work, to get the most out of your career you should have the same attitude as when you sit down to play a game. Think Competitively and Strategically. Start where the rules stop and challenge your competition to "catch you, catch you if they can!"

8. THINK STANDARDS

If you plan to be successful in real estate, really successful, you'll have to embrace standards. Standards are about defining levels of performance and then holding yourself and others accountable to meeting or exceeding those levels. Think of it this way, we define our children's standards in school by creating consequences if they don't make good marks. We set a standard, and if they underperform and bring home a grade below that standard, we hold them accountable and enforce the consequences. When you're a one-person business, your challenge is to find, implement, and articulate those standards as your value proposition. When you have employees, your challenge is to define your standards clearly, to live them yourself, and to hold your staff accountable to them as well.

> *"We put all our people through the CC Boot Camp. We teach them how to sell real estate at our level. We tell them they are on a Super Bowl Team. We expect the best."*
> Chris Cormack
> Millionaire Real Estate Agent
> Ashburn, VA
> Sales volume—$70 million

Because you are doing the business and know your own standards, Think Standards is unlikely to be a serious issue until you hire your first assistant. The trouble most of us have is in communicating our standards and then enforcing them. When real estate agents make the leap into becoming employers and having a staff, they're often stretched to the limit and need help badly just to handle their current load. Because of that, they're often so grateful just to have help that they don't ever think to hold their new staff member accountable to their personal standards.

You just have to be disciplined and patient when you begin the hiring process. Experience shows that hiring an effective assistant should easily double your sales volume. (If you don't already have an assistant, read that last sentence again!) A bad assistant, well, that person can be difficult to recover from. So many of us make the mistake of hiring out of convenience rather than by standards. Your friend's daughter graduates from college and needs a job and because we need help or want to do our friend a favor, we hire her. We hire out of convenience and familiarity rather than looking for people who share our standards from the beginning. Here's a secret that high achievers have discovered but which most people usually miss: When you have the right staff, that same staff that can take you to $20 million can probably take you to $80 million. It's all about who you hire and the standards to which you hold them accountable.

So when it comes time to grow your business through people, you'll have to clearly articulate and enforce your standards from the beginning. "High intention" deserves "high attention!" And then you must regularly "inspect what you expect!" Highly successful real estate agents Think Standards for themselves and everyone around them.

9. THINK SERVICE

Virtually every top-producing agent we have ever worked with has a deep and almost inherent sense of service. They have a servant's heart and place their buyer's or seller's real estate experience above all else. They are always thinking service. In their quest for huge sales success, many top agents may not always show their competitors this service side—but trust me, it is there. It is the heart and soul of their business. And, as we have studied and probed this, we have discovered that their service approach exists at three levels. First, they know the underlying purpose of the real estate profession. They, in essence, know exactly why they should be hired. Second, they have a clear sense of how they deliver that purpose. Top agents can easily explain what services they will provide anyone who hires them. We have come to call these services the agent's value proposition. And third, they have a continual drive to always put their client's needs above all else. We call this their fiduciary commitment. Let's take a closer look at these three aspects of service.

Purpose

Top real estate agents always have a clear understanding of why they should be hired and they are able to articulate it to anyone at anytime. For sellers, their goal is to net them the most amount of money, in the shortest amount of time, with the least amount of problems. For buyers, their goal is to find them just the right home, at the best price, in the right time, with the least amount of problems. Great service begins with a clear purpose for why someone should work with you.

Value Proposition

Even beyond their sense of purpose, the very best real estate agents are able to translate this purpose and the reason people should hire them into a specific set of services that they will provide. We have come to call this the agent's value proposition. This value proposition lays out in detail what services the buyer or seller will receive. When we narrowed it down to what is really important, we discovered there are ten specific service areas for the buyer and ten for the seller. These are outlined and defined in the following graphics, Figure 5 and Figure 6.

Fiduciary

For the very best real estate agents there is a level of service they provide that goes beyond even their purpose and value proposition. It is

The Top Ten Service Areas of the Seller Value Proposition

1. Needs Analysis
a. Help clarify the motivating reasons to sell.
b. Determine the seller's timetable.

2. Pricing Strategy
a. Determine the best selling price strategy given current market conditions.
b. Show resulting net sheet.

3. Property Preparation
a. Advise on repairs and improvements.
b. Provide staging strategies.

4. Marketing Strategy
a. Develop marketing plan.
b. Establish marketing timetable.

5. Receive an Offer
a. Evaluate offers.

6. Negotiating to Sell
a. Negotiate counteroffers.
b. Advise on final terms and conditions.

7. Sell
a. Prepare postcontract work list.
b. Advise on repairs and vendor services.

8. Preclose Preparation
a. Coordinate and supervise document preparation.
b. Provide preclosing consulting.

9. Closing
a. Review closing documents.
b. Resolve last-minute items.
c. Complete transaction.

10. Post Closing
a. Coordinate move.
b. Assist with postclosing issues.

Figure 5

The Top Ten Service Areas of the Buyer Value Proposition

1. Needs Analysis
a. Analyze buyer's wants and needs.
b. Help buyer get clear picture of her ideal home.

2. Prequalification or Pre-approval
a. Guide buyer to loan officer.
b. Obtain prequalification or pre-approval.
c. Help choose best mortgage financing plan.

3. Neighborhood Information
a. Create broad neighborhood search profile.
b. Provide list of target neighborhoods and related information for each.

4. Home Search
a. Organize and schedule a home search process.
b. Ongoing updates, drive-bys, and showings of available homes.

5. Make an Offer
a. Compare homes and make decision.

b. Advise on terms and issues of offer.
c. Fill out purchase offer contract.

6. Negotiating to Buy
a. Present the offer.
b. Negotiate on buyer's behalf.

7. Vendor Coordination
a. Advise and supervise vendor selections.
b. Coordinate vendor services.

8. Preclose Preparation
a. Coordinate and supervise document preparation.
b. Provide preclosing consulting.

9. Closing
a. Preview closing documents.
b. Resolve last-minute issues.
c. Complete transaction.

10. Post Closing
a. Coordinate move-in.
b. Assist with postclosing issues.

Figure 6

the commitment they make to the buyer and seller to act as a true fiduci-ary—to place their client's interests ahead of the interests of all others. Even their own. This commitment to fiduciary service seems, in our observations, to go way beyond the technical issues of agency represen-tation. While the fiduciary agent abides by the legal requirements placed on them by their profession, they also treat all of their clients with great

The Difference Between a Functionary and a Fiduciary

FUNCTIONARY	FIDUCIARY
1. Low Level	1. High Level
2. Low Relationship	2. High Relationship
3. Assumes Little Responsibility	3. Accepts High Responsibility
4. Uses Low Skill	4. Masters High Skill
5. Records Information	5. Perceives Information
6. Responds to Needs	6. Anticipates Needs
7. Processes Data	7. Interprets Data
8. Narrow Picture Viewpoint	8. Big Picture Viewpoint
9. Delivers Information	9. Advises and Consults
10. Other-Directed	10. Self-Directed
11. Minimum Legal Responsibility	11. Maximum Legal Responsibility
12. Employee	12. Partner
13. Does the Task	13. Owns the Result
14. Tells and Sells	14. Educates and Guides
15. Stays out of Decision Making	15. Involved in Decision-Making
16. Follows Rules and Procedures	16. Uses Judgment and Intuition
17. Replaceable	17. Irreplaceable
18. Minimally Paid	18. Highly Paid

Figure 7

The Millionaire Real Estate Agent

fiduciary care. Actually, this may be an appropriate place for us to draw a distinction between the two types of service being provided in the real estate industry: Functionary vs fiduciary. A functionary is one who is in a specific task relationship with his clients—he does the job. While a fiduciary is one who not only does the tasks of the job, but is also in a high-trust relationship with his client and feels total responsibility for the outcome. Figure 7 gives a great illustration of the differences between a functionary and a fiduciary.

Interestingly enough, a fiduciary can easily do functionary work, but a functionary cannot easily do fiduciary work. Top agents understand this and, as a result, work really hard to provide fiduciary services to all their buyers and sellers. In many ways, this is the true difference between average service and exceptional service. Fiduciary service is the highest quality of service you can provide any buyer or seller with whom you work.

THE THREE L'S OF THE MILLIONAIRE REAL ESTATE AGENT

There is an amazing principle in life that when fully understood will probably change your life forever. It's called the Pareto Principle or the 80:20 Rule. This universal truth was originally discovered by the Italian economist Vilfredo Pareto in 1906 when he noted that 80 percent of the farmland in Italy was owned by 20 percent of the population. Pareto, also an avid gardener, subsequently noticed that 20 percent of the peapods in his garden yielded 80 percent of his harvest. This was all the validation he needed to launch an intensive study into this amazingly consistent theory that states that 80 percent of our results will come from 20 percent of our actions. I personally believe the 80:20 Rule is the best kept, most underutilized "achievement formula" in business. Richard Koch, in his groundbreaking book *The 80/20 Principle*, describes this rule as "the principle of greatest outcome for time and effort expended." Most people believe that time and effort alone deliver results, and, while this may be true, the 80:20 Rule teaches us that time and effort on the 20 percent that really matters will deliver 80 percent of the results we seek.

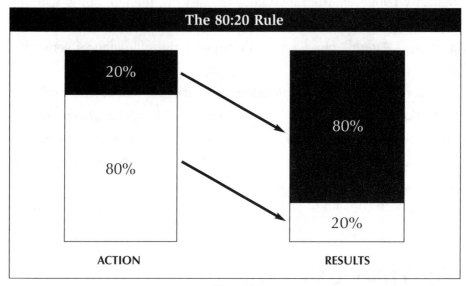

Figure 8

As Figure 8 above reveals, the opposite also appears to be true. When we are focused on the 80 percent that doesn't matter, we tend to get 20 percent of the results we want. The truth is that when our actions are not focused on the 20 percent that matters, the results we want usually don't show up. Doing a lot of things is never a substitute for doing the right things.

Like everything else, real estate sales has its 20 percent. The 20 percent the Millionaire Real Estate Agent focuses on are the Three L's—Leads, Listings, and Leverage. When you are concentrating on Leads, Listings, and Leverage, you are focusing on the key activities that will yield the greatest return for your business. Let's refresh our memory as to why these areas should always be foremost in your mind and go into a bit more detail.

LEADS—LEAD GENERATION VS LEAD RECEIVING

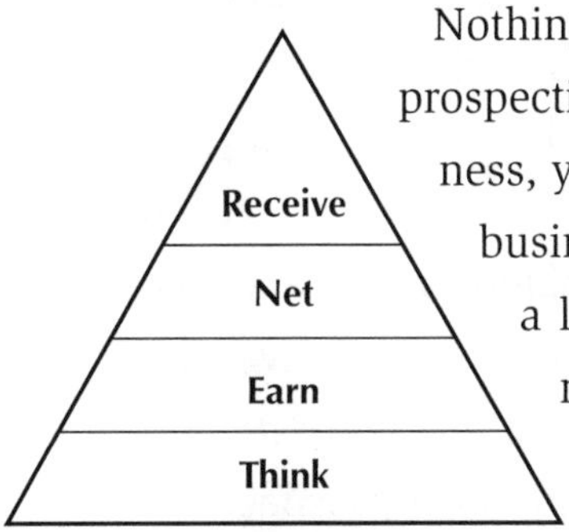

Receive

Net

Earn

Think

LEADS

Figure 9

Nothing is more important to your sales career than prospective buyers and sellers. To have a viable business, you simply must have the client leads. To have a business that pays you a lot of money, you will need a lot of leads. Funny, but some real estate agents miss this not-too-subtle point and end up spending their time on other less financially rewarding activities. I can't tell you why this is, but let's be perfectly clear about it in this book—no leads means no sales.

We must have leads, and, in fact, if it is helpful to you, you should think of yourself as being in the "lead-generation business." Many will say, "But I'm in the real estate business," to which I reply, "Fine, then try staying in the real estate business very long without leads." If it makes you feel any better, please realize that all businesses are, in addition to their particular business, in the lead-generation business. What you have to embrace is the fact that it is the number of qualified leads you have that will either grow your business, keep you in business, or put you out of business. Nothing else about your business will have

> *"Without leads, we wouldn't be in business."*
>
> Chris Cormack
> Millionaire Real Estate Agent
> Ashburn, VA
> Sales volume—$70 million

as big an impact on it as the number of leads you have. For this reason, Leads becomes the first of the Three L's. Without them, the other two are not nearly as important.

When I taught new agent sales training classes, I would sometimes start my class discussion on leads by asking the audience, "If I told you there was an out-of-town buyer who just got in this morning and who will be paying cash and needs to purchase a home by the end of the week, could any of you help him out?" Everyone would raise their hand.

"Well, I can guarantee you there is a buyer getting into town today who has cash and needs to buy a house now. The problem is we don't know where or who this buyer is. And that is the leads challenge of the real estate business." In a prosperous market, there are usually many agents relying on passive lead generators, casual referrals, and luck to create business. I call this Lead Receiving. Unfortunately, real estate agents who are in the business of Lead Receiving may find themselves selling very few houses when the market shifts. Conversely, if you actively and systematically focus on Lead Generating through direct prospecting and marketing activities, you will always be doing the best you can even in shifting markets. In the battle of Lead Generating vs Lead Receiving, Lead Generating always wins, no matter what the market. If you count on the market to deliver leads when times are good, you better count on it to take them away when times are bad. What is given can also be taken away. . . .

One of the first questions I ask when consulting one-on-one with someone who wants to earn more is: "Do you have enough leads that if you close them properly you'd be reaching your goals?" If they answer yes, then it would seem that they have a conversion problem. If they answer no, I tell them to put everything else on hold and go get more leads. The issue of leads should always be at the forefront of your business consciousness.

The catch is that lead generation is not something that can just be turned on and off. Some very good lead generators make the mistake of turning it off when they think they have more business than they can handle. They turn it off and six months later they suddenly realize that the market has made a slight shift and now they don't have enough leads. If their methods still work and work quickly, then they will be able to ride the roller coaster again. If they find that their methods aren't quite as effective as they once were, they may be in trouble. Lead generation stays on, even when the volume might appear overwhelming. This isn't a problem. Too many leads is a good thing. Now, you have choices you didn't have before. When your lead-generation methods are consistently bringing you more business than you think you can currently manage, that is when you know it is time to hire help. Or you can "cherry pick" the best and refer the rest.

Leads are foremost in the Three L's of the Millionaire Real Estate Agent. You need to make sure you are not in the business of Lead Receiving and make sure you are always in the business of Lead Generating (and stay in it). Until you have enough leads to exceed your goals, there is no other issue. And, if you're willing to be a Millionaire Real Estate Agent, you can never have too many.

LISTINGS—THE HIGH-LEVERAGE, MAXIMUM-EARNING OPPORTUNITY

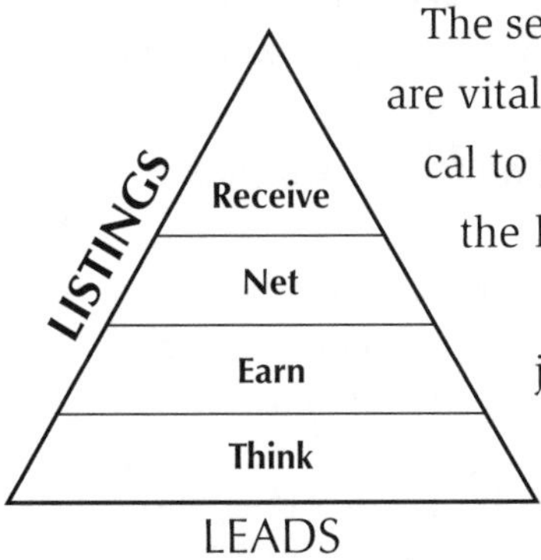

The second most important L is Listings. While leads are vital to your sales business, seller listings are critical to your ability to build it to its highest level with the lowest costs and highest net.

Let's explore a hypothetical situation. Pretend just for a moment that you are in a situation where you have to choose between working with someone who wants to list a $200,000 home and someone else who would like to buy it. Neither will be offended if you choose the other, so which do you choose? The listing opportunity or the buying opportunity? I would hope that 100 percent of you would choose the listing opportunity. Why? Let me count the reasons. . . .

Figure 10 (pyramid diagram): LISTINGS on left side, with levels from top to bottom: Receive, Net, Earn, Think. LEADS at the base.

Figure 10

> *"Listings make the business, and signs are our best source of leads."*
>
> David and Judie Crockett
> Millionaire Real Estate Agents
> Concord, OH
> Sales volume—$53 million

The Many Virtues of Seller Listings

1. Seller listings mean marketing opportunities:

   a) You get to put your sign in the front yard (and maybe directional signage, as well).

   b) You get to market the listing through direct mail and e-mail, etc.

   c) You get to advertise the listing through newspapers, magazines, the MLS, your website, etc.

2. You have more control of your time. There is usually not the sense of do-it-right-now urgency with sellers that buyers often have; therefore, you should be able to control your scheduling a little more.

3. Seller listings maximize your per-hour compensation. It usually takes a lot less time to obtain and market a listing prior to its selling than it takes to show for and sell to a buyer.

4. Volume, volume, volume. In our experience a highly focused, highly leveraged real estate agent can work fifteen to twenty-five seller listings per month. And keep it up. The same agent would be hard-pressed to work seven or eight buyers per month and continue to do so over a long period of time.

5. With seller listings you are on the frontend of pricing, which translates to an intimate knowledge of the market.

6. Properly marketed seller listings bring you more business. Because of the multiple marketing opportunities that are part of the listings process, we've found that on average, one well-marketed listing will generate one serious buyer who buys. So, if you focus on obtaining and marketing seller listings, you should be able to get all the buyers you need. It's the real estate industry's version of the "twofer."

Figure 11

Conversely, buyers present many fewer (if any) marketing opportunities. At best, buyer clients get us into the field, ensure that we are actively surveying our market firsthand, and can generate referrals. At worst, an indecisive buyer can demand weeks, if not months, of your attention before buying or, worse, deciding to wait until next year. There is simply too much upside to the listings business not to focus on listings first.

The Millionaire Real Estate Agent

So, if you would choose sellers over buyers in the hypothetical situation we described above, why aren't you placing seller clients at the core of your business? There are so many great reasons to devote all of your time and effort to taking and marketing listings. The Millionaire Real Estate Agent grasps the incredible advantages of making, obtaining, and marketing seller listings their primary lead-generation focus, and they do so almost exclusively. Over time, they will hire one or more buyer specialists to work the buyer side of the business and concentrate their energy on the high-return, high-leverage business of listings. (And once that is fine-tuned, they may then hire a listing agent to work the seller side as well.)

Listings are the second L in the Three L's of the Millionaire Real Estate Agent. All the Millionaire Real Estate Agents we worked with and interviewed devoted their time to listings first. The buyers they worked with were usually the result of their seller focus or their focus on referral and repeat business. Make listings your primary focus. Listings will help you gain more control over your time and money, and the rewards you reap from your efforts will be the highest they could possibly be.

LEVERAGE: THE WHO, HOW, AND WHAT OF REAL ESTATE

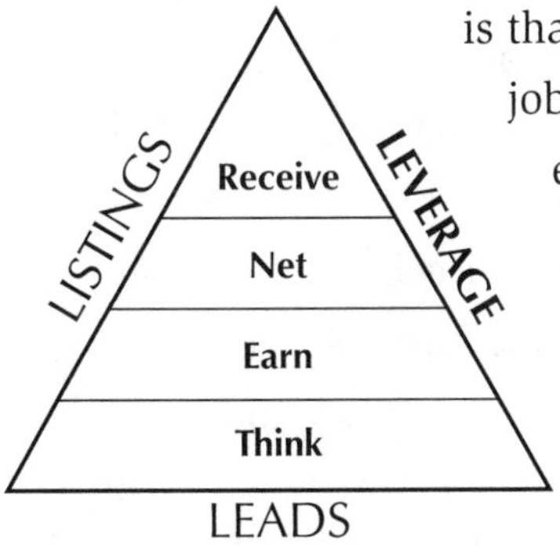

LISTINGS

Receive

Net

Earn

Think

LEVERAGE

LEADS

Figure 12

The interesting thing about the third L, Leverage, is that if you focus on the first two L's and do a great job, you will eventually have no choice but to either make less money or jump into becoming leveraged. An effective focus on leads and seller listings eventually brings you to a point where you have more business than you can possibly handle alone and will create the opportunity to start focusing on leverage. And that is how it should be. Until you have maxed out on what you can accomplish through focus on leads and listings, you should not be hiring another person. Why? Red Light, Green Light. You do it when you need it.

Let's revisit our mountain-climbing analogy. If following the path to becoming a Millionaire Real Estate Agent is like climbing Mount Everest, then leverage can be likened to the hiring of Sherpas, the native climbers who assist on almost every attempt at Everest's summit. Only a small handful of climbers have ever successfully climbed Mount Everest alone. None of the Millionaire Real Estate Agents we have worked with or interviewed claimed to have reached their current level of success alone. Look at it this way:

Leverage answers three key questions in your business:

1. Who is going to do it? People
2. How will they do it? Systems
3. What will they do it with? Tools

You might say Leverage is the "Who, How, and What" of your real estate business when you are not the only one doing it.

> *"Our staff is the key to our freedom. With our team, we no longer have to deal with every little problem."*
> Ronnie and Cathy Mathews
> Millionaire Real Estate Agents
> Houston, TX
> Sales volume—$99.5 million

Bringing people into your sales business to work with you has the potential to tremendously impact your business. Now, the challenge is to add the right people, because that impact could be positive or negative, depending on who they are and what they do. Great talent is irreplaceable. Great talent often meets and exceeds your standards and has the capacity to grow with you and the business. Poor hires, on the other hand, can do a lot of damage. Good talent should not be confused with great talent. Good is good and great is great. And, although good can really help, great can actually change your business forever. Therefore, it is crucial that you avoid settling for people who merely fill gaps and who do not have the capacity to grow. An agent and longtime friend of mine once jokingly explained why most agents were satisfied with good, rather than great, talent in their business; he said, "Gary, after you've hired bad, good is great!" That's true. But the greater truth is: "Once you've experienced great, good just isn't good enough."

In the very beginning you will seek people leverage to help with administrative duties, answer the phones, process transactions, and place the advertising and marketing you create. They are transaction coordinators, contract managers, marketing specialists, and bookkeepers, and sometimes they are all those things rolled into one. Eventually, if they are talented enough,

> *"Take the leap of faith—hire someone. It will open you up and free you up."*
> Valerie Fitzgerald
> Millionaire Real Estate Agent
> Los Angeles, CA
> Sales volume—$160 million

they will help you create and implement systems to run your business more efficiently and consistently.

When you look for people leverage to help with the administrative side of your business, do not underestimate the importance of this first hire. We've found that great administrators have the ability to run a real estate business and may eventually become the person who takes your place when you move on to Receive a Million. Why? Because they are not real estate agents themselves, their ambitions should not run counter to your own. The opportunity to manage a million-dollar business as its CEO is a great career path, and, as the owner, you have less reason to fear they will eventually walk away with your business. Finding a replacement for yourself is the final step on the path to becoming the Millionaire Real Estate Agent, and we'll discuss that tricky maneuver in detail in the final stage, Receive a Million. In the interest of getting the big picture first, to help you Think a Million, you should bear in mind that Receive a Million may well begin when you hire your first great administrative person.

I'm convinced that one of the greatest Realtors of our time is Ebby Halliday in Dallas, Texas. Ebby's first assistant was Mary Francis Burleson. Today, some thirty years later, Mary Francis is president of Ebby Halliday Realtors, a thriving real estate business with more than twenty-five offices around Dallas. Never underestimate the importance of your first hire! Sharon Gibbons was my first hire in 1983, and, like most first hires, she was in charge of "doing it all," from typing to answering the phone to you name it! By the late 1990s, Sharon had taken over the entire financial department. And who knows what responsibilities she'll have next year or the year after that. If you do it right, your first hire could be a lifetime hire.

So your first step to leverage will be administrative help who will eventually help create and implement systems. Systems are simply the repeatable processes that allow us to duplicate magnificent results easily. You may create a listing-appointment checklist or a ten-point marketing plan for your listings. Whatever the case, it will be defined by your standards and repeatable by others. Your administrative people leverage should also bring tools. Tools are what they do their work with, from phone systems to computer networks to websites and marketing packages. As you progress, you'll want to spend less and less time selecting and implementing tools. Your people leverage can take these tasks away from you and allow you to concentrate on the dollar-productive activities like lead generation, going on listing appointments, or hiring and training additional talent.

"You must have a vision and build a talent pool to deliver it."
Chris Cormack
Millionaire Real Estate Agent
Ashburn, VA
Sales volume—$70 million

Only after you have great administrative help (who in turn bring systems and tools), and they have helped grow your business to a point where there are more clients than you can handle, do you begin the process of hiring real estate salespeople leverage. Buyer assistants come first (probably in the form of a showing assistant who matures into a full-fledged buyer assistant), and much, much later a listings specialist. In Earn a Million, we'll diagram a suggested organizational growth chart to take you from Earn a Million to Receive a Million. For now, we'll simply say that people are the most powerful form of leverage. Hire carefully. Seek those who can exceed your standards, and don't settle for less. And, remembering our Red Light, Green Light discussion, add leverage incrementally! Leverage often represents salary, which will be the biggest costs on your profit and loss sheet. Whenever you add an additional person, you must hold that individual accountable for bringing corresponding positive growth. Only after each new piece of leverage—be it people, systems, or tools—is magnificent can you add the next.

Leverage becomes the "Who, How, and What" of your business when you really want to grow. So when you find you have maximized your personal productivity and have hit a ceiling of achievement, it is time to think about adding appropriate leverage to break through to the next level.

THE EIGHT GOAL CATEGORIES OF THE MILLIONAIRE REAL ESTATE AGENT

It's the fourth quarter—quick, what's the score, who has the ball, and how much time is left? Don't you expect everyone on your favorite football or basketball team to know these simple facts? Of course you do. People expect the players on their team to know the key information about the game at any point during the game and after. You're in business, you're treating it like a game, and you're no different. You and everyone on your team need to know your key numbers at all times!

> *"You have to track your numbers!"*
> Bill Ryan
> Millionaire Real Estate Agent
> Chandler, AZ
> Sales volume—$54 million

The Eight Goal Categories of the Millionaire Real Estate Agent is about knowing your numbers. You simply cannot run a business properly without tracking expenses and the results you net from your efforts. It is also about guiding you through and focusing you during the goal-setting process. CEOs (worthy of the title) should be able to tell you exact performance numbers for their company (expenses, profit, market share, etc.) for the previous year and year-to-date. You could then pick any single set of numbers and ask them what their goal is for the year. This is what you expect from people who responsibly run businesses. And as a real estate businessperson, you'll need to start expecting it of yourself. So you'll need to track numbers and set goals in key categories, and, as CEO of your business, you'll have to know those numbers backward and forward.

There are two sets of numbers the Millionaire Real Estate Agent is always aware of:

1. goal numbers

2. actual numbers

The first set defines your annual goals for your business. The second set, if monitored on a weekly (or at least monthly) basis, acts like a compass. Each time you assess your actual numbers, you'll get a pretty clear picture of how you are doing in regard to your annual goal numbers. If you are falling short in one area, you can throw your resources at the shortfall and get it back in line before your next assessment. When you find yourself on track to exceed all your goal numbers, you know it is time to consider raising the bar. Even with all the billion-dollar prognostic equipment available to NASA, their average shuttle mission is not a simple matter of charting the course and then logging the milestones of the journey. Because the stakes are so high, they monitor progress in nanoseconds and make literally thousands of course corrections during an average mission. NASA takes the "know your numbers" and Red Light, Green Light concepts to the ultimate extreme.

Millionaire Real Estate Agents know their goal numbers and track them to make sure they know how they're doing at all times. They set big "someday" goals, three-year, annual, monthly, and even weekly goals. And they set them using a consistent set of goal categories. In our experience, these categories can be effectively narrowed down to the eight most important areas of a real estate sales business.

> *"I've been looking at my real estate practice as a business. . . . Now, I track all the numbers and watch my P&L."*
>
> Rachel DeHanas
> Millionaire Real Estate Agent
> Waldorf, MD
> Sales volume—$52 million

The Eight Goal Categories of the Millionaire Real Estate Agent

1. Leads Generated
2. Listings
3. Contracts Written
4. Contracts Closed
5. Money
6. People
7. Systems/Tools
8. Personal Education

For each of these eight categories, you should set "someday," three-year, one-year, one-month, and one-week goals.

Figure 13

By creating key goal categories, goal setting becomes simpler and highly focused. You simply have to run down the list and fill in the blanks:

1. How many leads must I generate this year? this month? this week? to be on track for my three-year and "someday" goals?
2. How many listings must I take this year? this month? this week? to be on track for my three-year and "someday" goals?

3. How many contracts must I write this year? this month? this week? to be on track for my three-year and "someday" goals?

4. How many contracts must I close this year? this month? this week? to be on track for my three-year and "someday" goals? And so forth.

This is by far the most efficient and effective way to set goals and to focus your attention and efforts on those areas that will impact your business. If you don't have a system that can be reused each year with little change, you really have to work at setting goals. For most people it is too tiring and, as a result, they focus on a couple of New Year's resolutions and spend the next twelve months reacting to all the other areas in their life. Categories act as placeholders. When you have them in place before you begin the goal setting or evaluative process, it is harder to forget or ignore areas that need your attention.

> *"I run it like a business. I track all my numbers on a big board in my office. . . . "*
>
> Cristina Martinez
> Millionaire Real Estate Agent
> San Jose, CA
> Sales volume—$136.3 million

THE FIRST GOAL CATEGORY OF THE MILLIONAIRE REAL ESTATE AGENT: LEADS GENERATED

Leads are the most important number you need to know. You must know how many leads you must generate to meet your other goals (e.g., seller listings taken, contracts written, contracts closed, etc.). Every time you receive an e-mail, or your phone rings and it's business, you should be keeping a record of how many leads you're receiving. We hope you'll be finding out where the leads are coming from as well. Tracking these two things will help you make better decisions about how to invest your lead-generation dollars. Eventually, you'll be able to work backward and work out which forms of lead generation are the most dollar productive.

One of the most important things you can learn from tracking your leads is the conversion rates for you and your staff. You'll be working to get at two key conversion rates:

1. Conversion rate for converting calls into buyer appointments
2. Conversion rate for converting calls into seller appointments

Over time, you'll also get a sense of how many buyer appointments and seller appointments you'll need to net a certain number of buyer listings (agency agreements) and seller listings. From there you'll be able to track how many buyer and seller listings you'll need to net a certain number of closed sales. Once you have a good understanding of these numbers, you'll be able more accurately to predict the relationship between the leads coming to your business and how they translate to closed sales and gross income. You can break it down and go into even more detail if you choose, but the ultimate goal is for you to be able reliably to predict the number of leads you will need to generate in order to meet any production goal.

THE SECOND GOAL CATEGORY OF THE MILLIONAIRE REAL ESTATE AGENT: LISTINGS

This is the second most important number a Millionaire Real Estate Agent needs to know. Your entire business model should be built around obtaining a certain number of seller listings each month and year. Seller listings, as we have mentioned, are the high-leverage, maximum-earning opportunity in this industry. Seller listings properly marketed will generate more leads and buyer contracts. If you don't get them, your model can quickly begin to break down.

In Earn a Million, we will prescribe a certain number of seller listings you should strive to get each month and year. Your conversion rates will then dictate how much lead generation is necessary to get you the right number of seller agreements to net your listing goals. If you choose to track only two areas of your business, track your leads and your listings.

THE THIRD GOAL CATEGORY OF THE MILLIONAIRE REAL ESTATE AGENT: CONTRACTS WRITTEN

Here is what you need to know about your sales contracts written:

1. Number of units written
2. Total volume written
3. Gross income written

The best practice is also to track how many of your contracts written were listings and how many were buyers.

THE FOURTH GOAL CATEGORY OF THE MILLIONAIRE REAL ESTATE AGENT: CONTRACTS CLOSED

To properly set goals for and track sales contracts closed, you need to know:

1. Number of units closed
2. Total volume closed
3. Gross income closed

As with contracts written, you'll also want to keep track of how many of your contracts closed were listings and how many were buyers.

THE FIFTH GOAL CATEGORY OF THE MILLIONAIRE REAL ESTATE AGENT: MONEY

This is approached as a business and as such money and the issues of money must always be accounted for and respected. The big money issues to track are:

1. Gross closed income—How much money did we make?
2. Budget—How much money did we spend?
3. Net income—How much money did we earn as profit?
4. Agent compensation—How much do I (the agent) personally get to take home?

The Sixth Goal Category of the Millionaire Real Estate Agent: People

People are the first and most important type of leverage you bring to your sales business. When there is more work than you can handle, you must hire additional help. Individuals never maximize their potential by themselves—so you will need help. The three key goal areas you will always have to address regarding your people are:

1. Recruiting—What people needs do I have?
   a. Who do I need and what do I need them to do?
   b. Where will I find them?
2. Training—What training needs do I have?
   a. Now that I have someone, how and when will I teach them what to do and how to do it well?
3. Consulting—What performance or accountability issues do I have?
   a. Now that my people are in the job and trained, what/how/when will they be supported and held accountable so they can excel?

Even if you do not currently have any people needs, it is important that you keep this placeholder in your goals. Begin with the end in mind, right? If you're tracking the other aspects of your business properly, you'll probably begin setting goals in this category long before you actually need to make a hire. You will see that your leads are increasing, and, with them, you'll be seeing a corresponding increase in listings taken and contracts written and closed. Eventually, you'll be looking to the future and saying, "If this continues for much longer, I'll need to have help."

Having the placeholder on your goal sheet at all times helps prompt you to ask this question early instead of late. The advantage to you is that you'll have the opportunity to take your time and look for an outstanding candidate. Because you're tracking your growth in specific areas, you'll also have a head start on creating a job description that fits your current and future needs.

THE SEVENTH GOAL CATEGORY OF THE MILLIONAIRE REAL ESTATE AGENT: SYSTEMS/TOOLS

After people, systems and tools make up the remainder of leverage. Before you hire your first staff member, you should think about what systems and tools you will need in place. Systems are about documenting your methods. You want your people to document your methods and then be able to duplicate your excellent results. Creating systems can be challenging. Your first hire, your administrative help, will help you to create initial systems for them and any future hires in your sales staff. Tools are everything from computers, equipment, and phone systems to something as simple and as vital as a job description.

Actually, the job description is an extremely important tool for establishing your standards for performance and behavior on the front end. They should be detailed and thorough. If it is helpful to do so, try thinking of them as the syllabus college professors hand out on the first day of class. A typical syllabus will not only provide a description of the material to be explored, but it also sets standards for passing and failing. Your staff needs to understand how they can succeed with you and how they might fail with you. The management of almost all your other tools can be delegated to your staff.

The systems/tools goal category manifests itself as the following questions:

- What new systems or tools do we need to add?
- What current systems or tools do we need to improve or upgrade?

Because system/tool leverage can take time to research, create, and deploy, they should always be present in your goals and tracking. You'll want to predict these needs well in advance so you can give them the attention over time they may require.

The Eighth Goal Category of the Millionaire Real Estate Agent: Personal Education

If there is one thing that our experience has shown over the years, it is that Millionaire Real Estate Agents are always focused on personal development. For themselves, they attend seminars, seek out consulting relationships, and require their staff to do the same. They are always looking for ways to improve how they and their staff operate professionally and personally.

Your personal education goal category will show up in your thinking as:

1. What knowledge do I need to learn? What skills do I need to acquire?
2. What knowledge do the individuals on my staff need to learn? What skills do they need to acquire?

There is always an ongoing need to improve your understanding of the key areas of your business. On the road to becoming your best, school is never out.

Keeping goal categories is one of the areas that changed my life as a businessperson. Back in 1979, I attended a Lewis R. Timberlake seminar on goal setting. Timberlake advocated using goal categories, and before long I was scratching out notes on what should be the core goal categories for a highly successful real estate agent. These categories were originally tried and tested by none other than myself. Now, over the course of my career, they have withstood my personal scrutiny as well as the original doubts and skepticism of thousands of real estate agents who have consulted with me. While goal categories are magical and can bring amazing focus to your business life, they shouldn't be compartmentalized to just your business life. I encourage you to explore taking advantage of the power of goal categories in your personal life as well.

CONCLUSION

Think a Million is designed to be a crash course in the mental and planning aspects of becoming a Millionaire Real Estate Agent. Hopefully, this chapter has provided valuable insight into the way high achievers think and the principles that dictate their actions. Start with an awareness of the mind-set, the Nine Ways the Millionaire Real Estate Agent Thinks; absolutely focus on the Three L's of the Millionaire Real Estate Agent; and methodically use the goal-setting placeholders we described in the Eight Goal Categories of the Millionaire Real Estate Agent. If you can do those things, you'll be very well positioned to apply the models we will describe in the next chapter, Earn a Million, and start taking your real estate career to a higher place.

If you now feel you can Think a Million, then congratulations! You're well on your way! It's time to move on and explore how to Earn a Million.

POINTS TO REMEMBER: Think a Million

- How you think matters. Thinking Big at the beginning is like building a twenty-lane highway for your vision of the future.

- Work to learn before you work to earn. That learning will more than make up for any lost time and will, in fact, earn you more money in the end.

- The Nine Ways a Millionaire Real Estate Agent Thinks:
  - Think Powered by a Big Why—Having a clear purpose, mission, or need gives you focus and powers your actions.
  - Think Big Goals and Big Models—Big Goals and Big Models foster Big Habits early and pull you through smaller goals on the way to greater things.
  - Think Possibilities—Believe that anything is possible and then act as though it were impossible to fail.

- Think Action—When you are ready, anything short of action is just plain inappropriate. Shut up, get up, and giddy up!

- Think Without Fear—Failed attempts are not the same thing as failure, so never fear the attempt itself. The only time you can ever truly fail is if you give up or refuse to try at all.

- Think Progress—Success is in the numbers. The quality is in the quantity and achievement often comes to the person who makes the most attempts.

- Think Competitively and Strategically—Treat it like a game and learn to think strategically! Winners dare to compete.

- Think Standards—You have standards. Your challenge is to learn to communicate them clearly and to instill them in your team.

- Think Service—Know the purpose of your profession. Articulate the details of your value proposition and deliver on it with fiduciary commitment.

■ The 80:20 Rule is always at work and Leads, Listings, and Leverage are the 20 percent of your focus that ultimately gives you 80 percent of your results.

- Lead generation is never a passive activity!

- Listings are the high-leverage, maximum-earning opportunity in real estate.

- Leverage is the Who, How, and What of a powerful real estate sales team.

■ Bring the power of goal categories into your business life. Goal setting becomes easier and more effective when you have a consistent set of goal categories.

■ Businesspeople know their numbers. They know their goal numbers and their actual numbers and so should you. The Eight Goal Categories of the Millionaire Real Estate Agent are: Leads Generated, Listings, Contracts Written, Contracts Closed, Money, People, Systems/Tools, and Personal Education.

EARN A
MILLION

*"If a man knows not what harbor he seeks,
any wind is the right wind."*

Seneca

Figure 1

THE SCIENCE OF SUCCESS

There is both an art and a science to achieving your highest potential in your real estate sales career. The art is the motivation and inspiration that comes from reexamining your MythUnderstandings and the way a Millionaire Real Estate Agent thinks. However, motivation to go down a path with no map to follow—no clear way to turn your dreams into reality—is like a mystery door with nothing behind it. It can feel like a false promise.

Our focus in this book up to now has been mostly on insight and perspective, facing your fears, and thinking big. We've been studying the art of real estate sales success. It is now time to turn our attention to another focus. It is time to be instructional. We've seen the art, now it is time to discover the science.

MODELS MATTER

As we've discussed, models are very important tools to help us achieve our goals. To put it plainly—models matter, and the right models matter most. If you don't know where you're going, I guess any model will do. But if you're trying to become your very best and achieve the most you possibly can, you'll need Big Models to match your Big Goals. Now that you've set aside your myths and learned how to think like a high achiever, it is time to get down to the work of becoming one. In the sales business, everyone, whether they realize it or not, is following a model. The difference between everyone else and top achievers is that top achievers purposefully choose Big Models in the key areas that matter so they can achieve their highest potential. They understand that you must be a "20 percenter" and find models that help focus your efforts on the 20 percent of activities that lead to 80 percent of the results. One of our discoveries in working with and interviewing Millionaire Real Estate Agents is that they all seem to follow four key models: an Economic Model, a Lead-Generation Model, a Budget Model, and an Organizational Model.

The Four Fundamental Business Models of the Millionaire Real Estate Agent	
1. The Economic Model	3. The Budget Model
2. The Lead-Generation Model	4. The Organizational Model

Figure 2

It turns out these four models are foundational. They represent the four areas everyone must ultimately tackle on the way to high real estate sales achievement. In a nutshell, here is what they teach:

1. The Economic Model—A formula that shows you how to plug in specific numbers you'll have to achieve in specific areas to receive a specific net income.

2. The Lead-Generation Model—The specific approach you must take to systematically generate a specific number of leads.

3. The Budget Model—An outline of the specific budget categories you should track and the percentage of your gross revenue you should spend in each of them.

4. The Organizational Model—The specific staff positions you will need to fill and the job responsibilities they will be given as your business grows.

Simply think of the four models as adding up to a formula that says: To achieve the amount of net income you desire, you will need to generate X number of leads, spend X amount of money in specific areas to support those efforts, and hire X number of people to service it all.

On the following two pages are two key diagrams. They provide an overview of the four models, but show two distinct perspectives. The first perspective is a high-level look at the key areas in each model and the second drills down to the specific issues and numbers you'll need to focus on to pursue the path of the Millionaire Real Estate Agent.

Please take a few moments to review Figure 3 and Figure 4 on the following pages and get your bearings before we dive into the science of success at the Millionaire Real Estate Agent level. Try not to get too caught up in the numbers shown in Figure 4. They will be explained in detail in the second half of this chapter. For now, we just want you to get a sense of where we are headed.

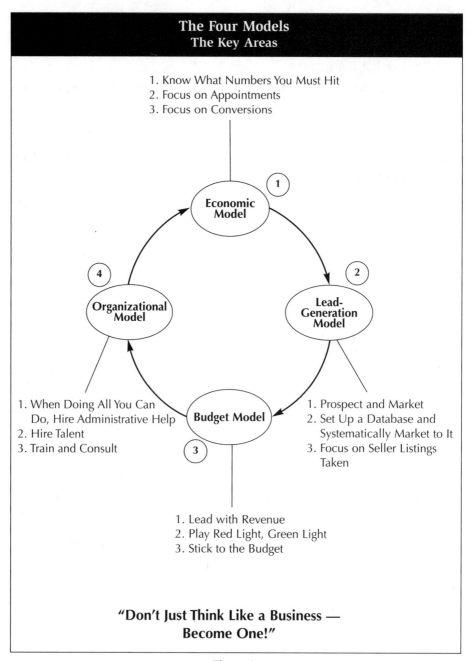

The Four Models
The Key Areas

1. Know What Numbers You Must Hit
2. Focus on Appointments
3. Focus on Conversions

Economic Model (1)

Lead-Generation Model (2)

Organizational Model (4)

Budget Model (3)

1. When Doing All You Can Do, Hire Administrative Help
2. Hire Talent
3. Train and Consult

1. Prospect and Market
2. Set Up a Database and Systematically Market to It
3. Focus on Seller Listings Taken

1. Lead with Revenue
2. Play Red Light, Green Light
3. Stick to the Budget

**"Don't Just Think Like a Business —
Become One!"**

Figure 3

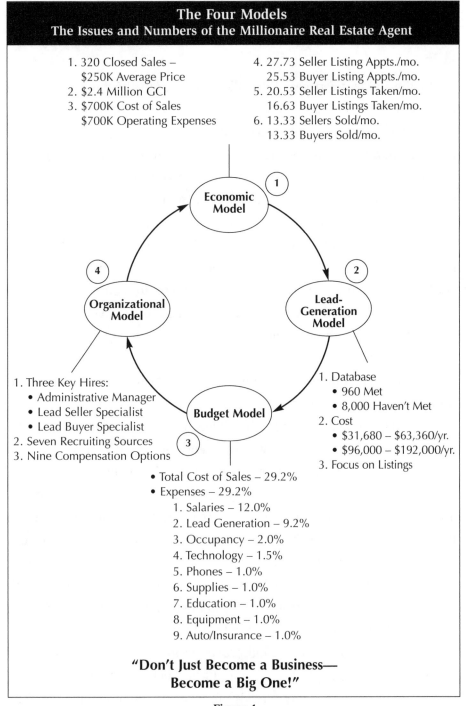

The Four Models
The Issues and Numbers of the Millionaire Real Estate Agent

1. 320 Closed Sales –
   $250K Average Price
2. $2.4 Million GCI
3. $700K Cost of Sales
   $700K Operating Expenses

4. 27.73 Seller Listing Appts./mo.
   25.53 Buyer Listing Appts./mo.
5. 20.53 Seller Listings Taken/mo.
   16.63 Buyer Listings Taken/mo.
6. 13.33 Sellers Sold/mo.
   13.33 Buyers Sold/mo.

Economic Model

Lead-Generation Model

Organizational Model

Budget Model

1. Three Key Hires:
   • Administrative Manager
   • Lead Seller Specialist
   • Lead Buyer Specialist
2. Seven Recruiting Sources
3. Nine Compensation Options

1. Database
   • 960 Met
   • 8,000 Haven't Met
2. Cost
   • $31,680 – $63,360/yr.
   • $96,000 – $192,000/yr.
3. Focus on Listings

• Total Cost of Sales – 29.2%
• Expenses – 29.2%
   1. Salaries – 12.0%
   2. Lead Generation – 9.2%
   3. Occupancy – 2.0%
   4. Technology – 1.5%
   5. Phones – 1.0%
   6. Supplies – 1.0%
   7. Education – 1.0%
   8. Equipment – 1.0%
   9. Auto/Insurance – 1.0%

"Don't Just Become a Business— Become a Big One!"

Figure 4

HOBO SHACKS OR HOUSES

In the following pages, I'll walk you through the fundamentals of these four sound and proven models. Then, once we have the basic concepts down, I'll show you how Millionaire Real Estate Agents apply them in their efforts to earn and net a million in annual income. However, before you start absorbing them and are tempted to personalize them, it is a good and appropriate time to remind you of our earlier discussion on modeling and creativity. I believe that until you have implemented and worked with a model, you have little business trying to change or improve it. Remember, trust those who have lived before you. And if you've done your research properly, then there are compelling reasons for selecting the models you've chosen. You need to have faith in your research. The time to question was then, now it is time to give the models your full faith and effort. Personal hands-on experience is the only true route to obtaining a clear understanding of if, when, or how you should ever deviate from a foundational model.

Strangely enough, against all advice to the contrary, most agents begin by implementing their own ideas and models. It seems they have always wanted to do things their own way and be creative, so they start off their business lives with creativity. Then, as a result of success or failure, they start adding more and more creativity to the mix. Before long, they have no solid foundation upon which to build and no framework upon which to hang their thinking and actions. The structure of their business begins to look like a "hobo shack" of ideas and creativity, with no plan or vision driving it. Creativity is the theme of their business. We believe that the best houses and the best businesses get built from clear blueprints, solid foundations, and proven frameworks.

If you've ever tried to find a shortcut in a neighborhood you weren't familiar with, you probably already understand this phenomenon. The

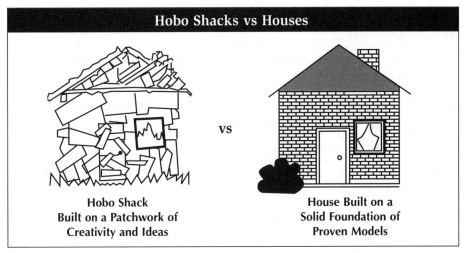

Figure 5

all-too-common story goes something like this. You're driving your clients down a busy thoroughfare and figure you could save five or ten minutes if you cut over a couple of blocks to a street that might have less traffic. So you take a quick right, drive down a few blocks, and pick a side street that appears to run parallel to the main street you were on. Everything looks great until, a few blocks from where you started being creative, the unexpected happens and the new street angles off in the wrong direction, away from your intended destination. So you compensate by being creative again and start angling through the neighborhood trying to get back on track. Well, you probably know how this story ends. At some point you apologize to your clients, pull over, and break out the map (which you had with you all along). Instead of gaining five minutes, you've lost fifteen, and you have to retrace your steps back to the beginning and start over. Not to mention the embarrassment you feel and the loss of confidence your bewildered clients likely feel.

There are multiple avenues to the highest levels of success in the real estate sales business; however, these paths are not laid out on a physical grid like some city streets, so they may not be quite as obvious as you wish them to be. Intuition and a good sense of direction are probably not enough to get you there if you venture off to explore new, unpaved avenues to success.

Look at it visually this way. In the diagram below (Figure 6), the straight line represents models and the dotted line represents creativity. When you start with models, you always have a sound, proven basis from which to work. The model serves as a reference point that allows you always to know why you made the creative decision you made and where to return if your creativity proves unsuccessful. When you don't have a model to provide direction and focus, your last creative effort becomes your reference point, and you can easily become lost.

The good news is that the models presented in the coming pages represent one proven and well-traveled path to your ultimate destination. They can be your map, your primary route, if you're faithful to them and consult them often. Even in Venice, Italy—the most labyrinthine of cities—first-time visitors regularly find their way from the famous opera house to obscure, off-the-beaten-path cafés because they faithfully take the time to consult their map at each fork in the road.

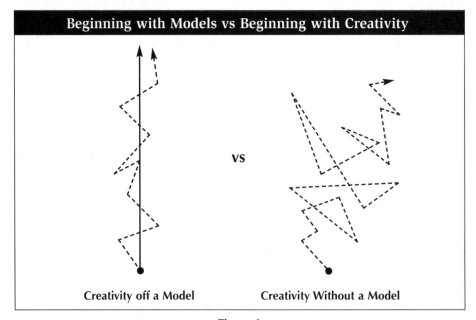

Beginning with Models vs Beginning with Creativity

VS

Creativity off a Model   Creativity Without a Model

Figure 6

Start with the proven model and—only when you're confident you have your bearings and know your reference points—dare to strike down a new path of creativity.

When agents don't follow models, they tend to say things like, "I'm reinventing my business this year." That's often just another way of saying, "I'm lost and starting over." When you are models-based, you occasionally need to tweak or readjust, and when you're creativity-based, you get to start over. There's a big difference between the two.

A LESSON FROM WARREN BUFFETT

Warren Buffett, arguably the greatest investor of all time, understood how to be faithful to models. In graduate school, Buffett studied the teaching and models of economist Benjamin Graham, the author of *Security Analysis*, a classic guide to investing. The book is a thorough examination of investment strategies and models, and Graham published four editions from 1934 to 1962. In *Buffettology*, the authors write that Buffett believed that "one learns through experience, and if not from experience, from those with experience." In other words, the greatest investor of our time, possibly of all time, understood the power of learning from others and following models. Later, after getting some professional investing experience, Buffett vowed not to make another investment until he had read *Security Analysis* twelve more times. You see, he was not content simply to be familiar with the leading models in his field, Buffett wanted to be a true student of them. Purportedly, he still keeps all four editions of the book on his desk and regularly consults them, picking up on subtle nuances each year based on his continued working experience applying the models. For Warren Buffett, the right models really do matter. And, his tremendous success proves that following the right models can have really *big* rewards.

It is our hope that the Four Fundamental Business Models of the Millionaire Real Estate Agent might serve you as the theories in *Security Analysis* have served Buffett. Start with them as they are. As you implement them and understand them more profoundly, you'll find the occasional need to experiment to see what works best for you in your market. Ultimately, everyone will end up with their own personalized versions of the models, which, while faithful to the underlying principles, will reflect your style and your market. Just remember to base your efforts on a solid proven model rather than on unproven, ungrounded creativity.

THE FOUR FUNDAMENTAL MODELS OF REAL ESTATE SALES SUCCESS

From all our experience and research, four key models stand out as foundations for a highly successful real estate sales business. Following these models should put you on the surest and quickest path to great real estate sales achievement. Our discussion of these four models will be divided into the two sides illustrated in the figures we saw earlier. First, as an overview, we will briefly explore the key areas of each model. Then we will analyze in much greater detail the key issues and numbers of each model as they specifically relate to the goals of the Millionaire Real Estate Agent. We'll walk the surface of the models to get familiar with them and then dive deep to reach the understanding you'll need to apply these models at a high level.

To be highly successful in your real estate sales career it is important that you understand that you need not only to think like a businessperson—you need to become one as well. You must take on the actions of a successful business in order to have one. Models are about action. These four models represent the four major arenas in which you must take effective action to build your real estate sales career to its highest level of success.

MODEL ONE:
YOUR ECONOMIC MODEL

Think of your Economic Model as a formula that describes the way your business works. It is your equation for success. Essentially, the Economic Model describes the relationship between a series of activities and the specific outcomes they produce. Actually, you can work the formula in reverse just as easily. If you start with an outcome, it will dictate the specific actions you must take to produce it.

Now, whether you realize it or not, you have an Economic Model. Every business does—every real estate agent does. The issue is not about having an Economic Model; rather, the issue is whether you understand the one you have and whether it can get you the net income you want. A sound Economic Model should do three basic things for you:

1. Show you where your money comes from (gross revenue)
2. Show you where your money goes (expenses)
3. Show you how much is left for you (net income)

This is basic economics and sounds very simple, but, in actuality, most people follow very unsound Economic Models.

1. They are not sure where their money will come from.
2. They are not sure which costs are critical and which ones are not.
3. They can't be sure how much will be left at the end of the year.

The problem is their Economic Model is based on activities with no projected outcomes attached. They have bought into the common fallacy that if they just work hard and spend money on their business, then somehow they deserve to make all the money they want. Sorry—it simply doesn't work that way. Fortunately, highly successful real estate agents have lived before us, and we now have lots of examples to guide us. We can now put together a basic and proven real estate agent Economic Model that you can trust to help you achieve your maximum potential.

The Economic Model we propose is about approaching your economics and this business in a manner that works for any real estate sales business, from a one-person sales operation to a large, dynamic team. Big Models work for everyone and lead to Big Goals. In fact, the model advocated here has no known limits.

THE THREE KEY AREAS OF YOUR ECONOMIC MODEL

There are three critical areas of focus in your Economic Model. First, you need to focus on knowing the key numbers you must hit. Understanding how the different aspects of your business interact to produce financial results is essential to making sound decisions. Then you'll have to focus on the number of appointments you must make, the driving numbers in your Economic Model, and the conversion rates you must achieve, the key variable in the equation. Let's quickly touch on all three.

1. Focus on the Numbers You Must Hit

The greatest thing your Economic Model will tell you is what numbers you must hit in order to net the income you want to receive. The formula shown in Figure 7 is simpler than you might have thought.

"We begin with the end in mind. We know the numbers we must hit and we never lose sight of them."

Chris Cormack
Millionaire Real Estate Agent
Ashburn, VA
Sales volume—$70 million

With a model like this, you can fill in performance numbers and see in a very clear way how high or low averages in one area affect the rest. Once you get a feel for the way the numbers interact, you can take the guesswork out of your planning and set specific goals in specific areas to achieve specific results.

The Basic Formula for the Economic Model of the Millionaire Real Estate Agent	
For Sellers	**For Buyers**
_____ Seller Listing Appointments	_____ Buyer Listing Appointments
x _____ % Conversion Rate	x _____ % Conversion Rate
= _____ Seller Listings Taken	= _____ Buyer Listings Taken
x _____ % Conversion Rate	x _____ % Conversion Rate
= _____ Sellers Sold	= _____ Buyers Sold
x _____ Average Sales Price	x _____ Average Sales Price
= _____ Seller Sold Volume	= _____ Buyer Sold Volume
x _____ % Commission	x _____ % Commission
= _____ Gross Revenue from Sellers	= _____ Gross Revenue from Buyers

= _____ Total Gross Revenue

− _____ Expenses

= _____ Net Income

Figure 7

2. Focus on Appointments

When you look at your Economic Model, you can clearly see that it has a beginning and an end. The end is the net income you will receive. What causes that net income starts with the beginning activity—appointments. These are appointments to make listing presentations to sellers and buyers. (Please note, we refer throughout this book to listing both sellers and buyers. Seller listings are multiple listing service agreements, and buyer listings are buyer agency representation agreements. We "list" both sellers and buyers.)

> *"Every day, I try to work fifteen files and have three seller listing appointments."*
>
> Mike Mendoza
> Millionaire Real Estate Agent
> Phoenix, AZ
> Sales volume—$60 million

Pure and simple, if you don't have the appointments, nothing else happens; therefore, they become a critical point of focus for your Economic Model. Appointments drive income. So target appointments first, get as many as you need, and go on from there.

3. Focus on Conversion Rates

Your Economic Model hammers home that you must focus on getting appointments to have any chance at all of earning income. It also makes clear that how many of these appointments you can convert to seller and buyer listing agreements and then convert to sales will determine just how much income you can actually earn. Given that you must turn appointments into tangible business, you could distill the Economic Model down to the following statement: Appointments converted to seller and buyer listings converted to sales equals gross income. Conversion rates are the key variables in your income equation.

If you step back and look at your Economic Model, something should stand out big and bold to you. Converting leads to appointments and converting appointments to listings are huge drivers of your economic success. They are both accomplished by a skilled presentation with a firm grasp of scripts and dialogues. If you can't make a convincing presentation, deliver purposeful scripts, or engage in effective dialogues, you won't be very successful, no matter how many leads you may have.

"We've discovered that the more we master our scripts and dialogues, the better our conversion rates are."

Gary and Nikki Ubaldini
Millionaire Real Estate Agents
Palm Harbor, FL
Sales volume—$28 million

So now your Economic Model has given you another gift. It has highlighted the key skills you must learn to be successful in real estate sales—the skills to convert leads to appointments and the skills to convert those appointments to listings. Make no mistake, mastering your presentations, scripts, and dialogues is what will drive your conversion ratios.

MODEL TWO:
YOUR LEAD-GENERATION MODEL

As important as your Economic Model is, your Lead-Generation Model is just as important. Why? One relies upon the other—the two go hand-in-hand. Once you know how many appointments you must have, you now have to generate the leads necessary to generate those appointments. That's where your Lead-Generation Model comes in. Leads are fuel to your economic engine. And here is a truth that you must never lose sight of: You can never have enough good leads. Never.

THE POSITIONING BATTLE

One of the great "ahas" I took away from reading the marketing classic *Positioning: The Battle for Your Mind*, by Al Ries and Jack Trout, was the idea that the human mind is an "inadequate container." The basic idea they share is that under the constant bombardment of advertising and marketing, the human mind becomes saturated by brands and can hold only a finite number at any one time. Ries and Trout cite the work of Harvard psychologist George A. Miller when they assert that the maximum number of product brands we can remember for a given category—the brand "saturation point" for the mind—is seven. That's when I had a huge "aha." Their book is about major brand advertising, the multimillion-dollar campaigns behind soft drinks, airlines, cars, and fast-food chains. It made me wonder what the implications were for the local real estate agent marketing to their target audience. Chances are, if the average person can't name more than seven brands of potato chips, they can't possibly name more than two or three real estate agents in their market.

Data gleaned from the 2002 National Association of Realtors (NAR) Profile of Buyers and Sellers tends to back this up. According to NAR research, 76 percent of all sellers contacted only one agent and 16 percent contacted just two. On the buyer side, the statistics are just as revealing. According to the same NAR research, 59 percent of all buyers interviewed only one agent and 22 percent met with just two!

From this we can clearly see what Ries and Trout are talking about—"mind share" for real estate agents is slim to none. Considering all the information people are assaulted with, they tend to block out all but the bare minimum, if for no other reason than self-defense. Clearly, with so many choices, people will tend to limit what they remember. Average out the NAR statistics, and you'll see that roughly 86.5 percent of all buyers and sellers seem to have room in their minds for only one or two real estate agents. In the battle for real estate consumer mind share, you're either first or second or you're out of contention. You're either at the head of the class or with the rest and lost in the mass!

> *"Invest in yourself. Market your name and presence."*
>
> Elaine Northrop
> Millionaire Real Estate Agent
> Ellicott City, MD
> Sales volume—$71 million

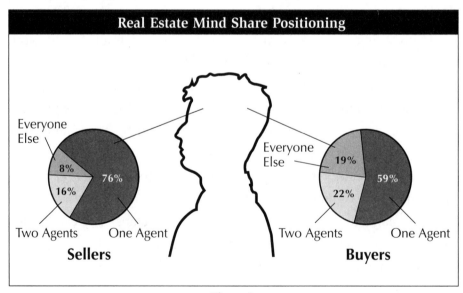

Figure 8

So the big question and challenge is how to win those first two positions of real estate mind share with enough people. The answer is through a systematic lead-generation effort.

PLAYING THE NUMBERS GAME

It is undeniably true that the higher the quality of your leads, the better your conversion rates. This truth is so self-evident that many real estate agents focus most of their lead-generation efforts on getting "quality leads." But this truth can be misleading. The real issue is even bigger than conversion rates. It is your net results—the number of converted leads you achieve and the sales volume into which they translate. High conversion rates will allow you to generate the same income from fewer leads than if you had lower conversion rates. But lower conversion rates can be just as effective if you can amass a great number of leads. So while your conversion rates are very important, the number of leads you must generate is even more critical. The octane of your fuel is irrelevant if you don't have enough to get you to your destination. Big real estate sales destinations need a big number of leads.

Highly successful real estate agents will tell you that as far as lead generation is concerned, "the quality is in the quantity." Whereas most real estate agents do modest lead generation and get modest results, a few do massive lead generation and reap massive rewards. They are the Millionaire Real Estate Agents.

Interestingly, many agents are seduced by the search for the perfect marketing image and invest large amounts of time and money in this pursuit. Now, there is no question about it, your marketing look and message are very, very, very important. However, we must keep them in perspective. Our experience working with top agents has taught us that even as important as your look and message are, there is a much stronger correlation between sales leads generated and the consistency and frequency of your message than between sales and the creativity of the message. No matter how you slice it, lead generation will almost always come down to a game of numbers. For effective lead generation, you need to be systematic (frequency and consistency) and go for sheer volume.

Your lead-generation plan must always be more ambitious than your income goals. Emerson was right when he wrote, "We aim above the mark to hit the mark." And that was never more true than when applied to lead generation; markets shift, conversion rates slide, and things just happen over time that could cause you to need more leads than you originally thought you would need. Your best defense against these unforeseen possibilities is to go on the offensive and build a lead-generation plan that will generate more than you think you'll need. If you then end up with more than you originally planned, is that a bad thing? No. But the opposite would be. It's a numbers game—always has been, always will be.

THE THREE KEY AREAS OF YOUR LEAD-GENERATION MODEL

There are three key areas in your Lead-Generation Model. First, there is the prospecting and marketing aspect, where you generate leads and move them into your inner circles. Second, there is the work to set up your database and feed it constantly. And, lastly, there is the systematic marketing to that database to generate new, repeat, and referral business. Let's take a closer look at all three.

1. Prospect and Market

The goal of your "achieve big" lead-generation program is twofold: to generate leads and to build stronger relationships for future business. Before we get into the details, let's take a look at the Strategic Model for Generating Leads and Building Relationships (Figure 9).

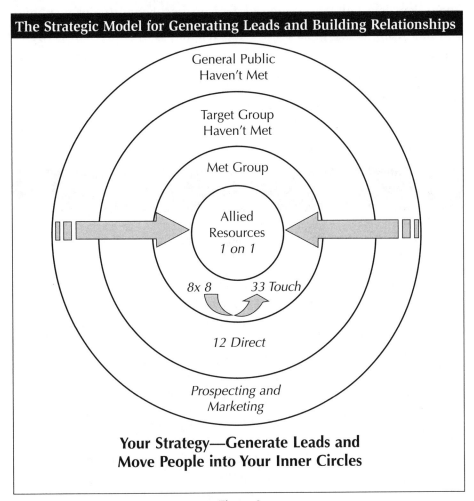

The Strategic Model for Generating Leads and Building Relationships

General Public
Haven't Met

Target Group
Haven't Met

Met Group

Allied
Resources
1 on 1

8x 8   *33 Touch*

12 Direct

*Prospecting and
Marketing*

**Your Strategy—Generate Leads and
Move People into Your Inner Circles**

Figure 9

"*Our business comes from referrals and reputation, but we still do a lot of marketing. We mail to our client base quarterly and to our farm area monthly.*"

Jill Rudler
Millionaire Real Estate Agent
Westerville, OH
Sales volume—$58 million

Let's briefly walk through this strategic model. The General Public is just that—the people out there whom you haven't met and who don't know you. You will use a large variety of prospecting (you find them) and marketing (you attract them and they find you) sources to generate leads in this category. In our experience, there are two broad prospecting categories and eleven broad marketing categories from which to choose (see Figure 10). The market, your preferences, your budget, and your goals will usually dictate the types and total numbers of sources inside those categories you employ.

Prospecting (Proactive and Direct)	Marketing (Proactive and Indirect)
1. Telemarketing ❑ FSBO (For Sale By Owner) ❑ Expireds ❑ Just Solds ❑ Just Listeds ❑ Past Clients ❑ Allied Resources ❑ Geographic Farm Area ❑ Apartments ❑ Corporations ❑ Builders ❑ Banks ❑ Third-Party Companies **2. Face-to-Face** ❑ Allied Resources (Meals) ❑ Door-to-Door Canvassing ❑ Open Houses ❑ Client Parties ❑ Networking Events ❑ Social Functions and Community Events ❑ Seminars ❑ Booths at Events ❑ Teaching and Speaking Opportunities	**1. Advertising** ❑ Newspapers ❑ Billboards ❑ Personal Vehicles ❑ Yellow Pages ❑ Radio ❑ Television ❑ Magazines ❑ Grocery Carts ❑ Bus Stop Benches ❑ Moving Vans **2. Promotional Items** (Magnets, Calendars, etc.) **3. Internet Websites** **4. Direct Mail** ❑ Postcard Campaigns ❑ Newsletter Campaigns ❑ Just Sold/Just Listed Cards ❑ Special Events Cards ❑ Quarterly Market Updates **5. IVR and Computer Retrieval programs** **6. Broadcast** ❑ Voice ❑ E-mail ❑ Fax **7. Signs/Directional Signs/Brochure Boxes** **8. Name Badges/Logo Shirts/Car Signs** **9. News Releases/Advice Columns** **10. Farming** ❑ Geographic ❑ Demographic **11. Sponsorship** ❑ Little League ❑ Charities ❑ Community Events

Figure 10

The Millionaire Real Estate Agent

Chances are, if you are already in the real estate business, you have a large number of lead-generation opportunities left to exp Exploring all these options could leave you spread too thin. We recommend making a list of the prospecting and marketing options you currently pursue and then adding a number of those listed above. You may already be attending social and community events, but not focusing on lead generation while you are there. Ads used for one form of marketing can often be cheaply and quickly adapted for other formats. Look for ways to "kill two birds with one stone."

When you have your final list, systematize it. Create a written plan on how you propose to attack each of the areas over the course of the next twelve months. Set time aside for that task and chip away at it every week. Our interviews with top-producing agents clearly reveal that they purposefully employ a wide variety of techniques to a greater-than-average number of sources. Think of it as diversifying your lead-generation portfolio. The multiple methods and sources will not only bring you more business in prosperous times but will also diversify and help protect you during uncertain times.

The Target Group consists of people you haven't met and don't know, but it differs from the General Public in that you have targeted them as people with whom you'd specifically like to do business. As a result, you will implement a very specific marketing campaign to the Target Group in order to generate business leads from them over time.

The Met Group are those individuals who know you because you have met them either in person or by phone. Your goal is to launch a tighter, more directed marketing campaign to this group, in hopes of building a really strong relationship and generating more business per person than from the Target Group.

Lastly, Allied Resources comprise a very select subset of your Met Group. These are individuals you expect either to do business with or to receive business leads from every year. This is your core group in your database, so in addition to marketing to them in the same manner as the Met Group, you will be meeting with each of them one-on-one for a meal, a visit, or a party several times a year. Some (the most influential) you would see as often as once a month.

> "If you don't have a network, you won't be successful."
>
> William Barnes
> Millionaire Real Estate Agent
> Taylors, SC
> Sales volume—$59 million

If there is a basic formula for working with your Allied Resources, it can be summed up this way: Educate, Ask for Help, and Reward. Each time you make contact with someone in your database, you should be "educating" them; in other words, you should reinforce the notion that you are in the business of real estate sales, that you are very good at what you do, that you have knowledge to share, and that you really prefer to do business on a referral basis. You are "asking for help" by asking them to contact you if they or someone they know is thinking about buying or selling a home. These two steps are the areas in which your proficiency with scripts and dialogues will pay the biggest dividends. The last area, "reward," is much more about being systematic in your approach to rewarding a referral. You need to have a system in place that will immediately reward the act of referring a client to you. Your rule of thumb should be to "treat the referral source even better than the referral." Show your appreciation at every point: when you take the referral call, when you meet with the referral, when you do business with the referral, and when the transaction is complete. Too many real estate agents make the mistake of rewarding only those referrals that turn into closed transactions. Reward the right behavior! Your sphere of influence isn't in the business of screening clients before they refer them to you—the act of referral is what should be meaningfully rewarded. That is what you want them to do again and again.

These four groups—the General Public, your Target Group, your Met Group, and your Allied Resources—represent the total population from which you will be trying to generate leads. The goal is to prospect

The Millionaire Real Estate Agent

and market yourself to these groups in such a way that as many as possible will, over time, place you in their number one or number two real estate agent "mind share" positions. This can lead to conducting immediate business or future business with you, and to referring immediate or future business to you. For a full overview of how to generate referrals from your Allied Resources, please consult Allied Resource Referral Generating Program (Figure 11).

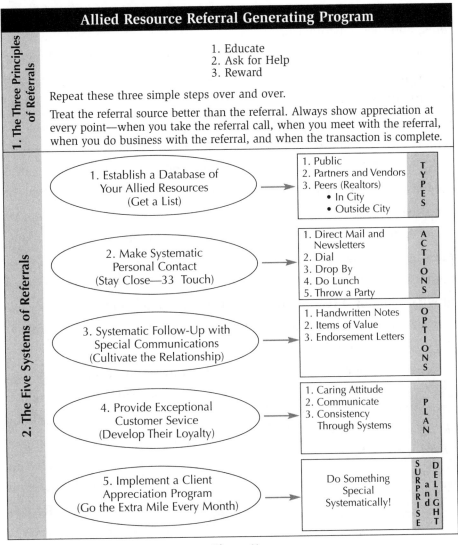

Figure 11

2. Set Up a Database and Feed It

At the heart of your lead-generation program will be a large, powerful contact management database. Think of the names of the people in your database and the relationship you have with them as "your business." When you hear of anyone in the personal services industry selling their business, what do you think they mean? What is it that a doctor or an attorney really sells? Since they don't have a product per se, what they're selling usually boils down to a few things: their staff, their systems, and their customer base.

Many years ago, I went in for my annual allergy checkup. Imagine my surprise when a doctor I had never heard of or seen before stepped into the room and introduced himself as my new allergist. Turns out he had bought my former allergist's "business" when my former allergist retired. Now, of all the things he might have bought from my former doctor, what did he buy that was the most important? Me! My name in a database and my relationship with the former doctor is why he bought the business! If you grasp the simplicity of this concept, then you've understood one of the most important concepts in this book, albeit a simple one. Your database is your business. Building up the number of names in it and a relationship with those names is really at the very core of what building a real estate business is all about. Think of it this way: The size of your real estate sales business will be in direct proportion to the size and quality of your database.

The best approach to lead generation is to set up a model that you systematically execute. Once you've got the model, your entire focus becomes implementing the model. A series of systems you can follow will make this quite simple for you to do. You just need to do it!

> "I came from the insurance business, so I know how to build a client base that brings repeat business."
>
> Russell Shaw
> Millionaire Real Estate Agent
> Phoenix, AZ
> Sales volume—$50.6 million

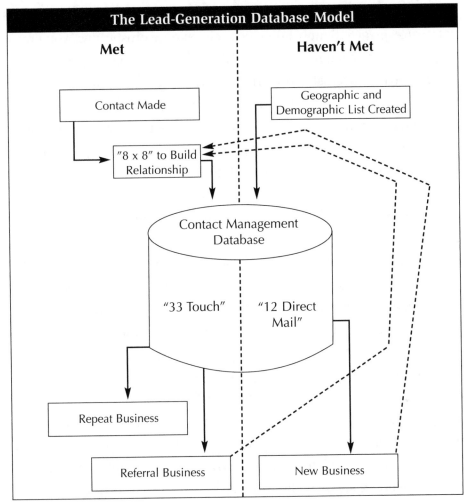

Figure 12

To operate your database model, you first need to realize that you'll be trying to generate leads from two groups: (1) people you have met and (2) a targeted group of people whom you haven't met. We refer to these groups in our lead-generation database strategy as Met and Haven't Met.

Marketing and prospecting to your Met and Haven't Met databases will yield three types of business: new (from Haven't Met), repeat (from Met), and referral (most likely from Met). While prospecting and making direct contact with these two groups is a very powerful approach, it is not very leveraged. Simply put, if you rely on pure prospecting, you probably will never generate enough leads to reach your highest potential. To become highly successful you will need to make sure your lead generation is marketing-based, which is highly leveraged. Now, a pure marketing approach to the Haven't Met might work, but our research suggests that you probably still need a prospecting program to drive leads to your business and protect against market shifts. Peak performance in sales requires you to have a systematic marketing-based Lead-Generation Model, which is then enhanced by personal prospecting. That way you can enjoy the benefits created by both activities.

So even if you have intellectually accepted the idea that you have two professions—lead generation and real estate sales—it can still be hard to maintain your focus on a complete lead-generation program. This is especially true when the business cycle in your market is up and there just seems to be an endless stream of leads. The danger of slacking off and not following a systematic marketing-based, prospecting-enhanced lead-generation system at all times is that each time the market shifts (and it always does) you'll have to reinvent your lead-generation approach. The best in the industry never allow their lead-generation systems to fall prey to the ebb and flow of enthusiasm or the market. They systematize such that little energy or enthusiasm is required to keep the machine running at all times. Their plan is ongoing, with monthly and even weekly installments. Their lead-generation planning and review meetings go on their calendars and are faithfully kept. To be extremely successful in the long term, your approach to lead generation needs to be purposeful and consistent. Enthusiastic entrepreneurial "get go" just isn't enough for the long haul. There is simply too much chance in that approach. Remember, success in the lead-generation game is in the numbers, so you simply can't overdo it. Again, let me reiterate that you can never have too many leads.

The Millionaire Real Estate Agent

As you prospect and market to the General Public, your Target Group, and your Met Group, you will constantly be evaluating the size of your database and the names in it. Think of it as a living thing that will need constant feeding to be kept alive. People will need to be added regularly as you make new relationships and lose old ones. Feed it, fatten it, but, whatever you do, don't put your database on a diet!

3. Systematically Market to Your Database

Real estate sales is a contact sport. Actually, it is a close contact sport, and the best players believe it is a frequent and systematic close contact sport. To succeed at a high level in real estate sales, you must commit to frequent contact with a database with the intent of building close rela-tionships. And you will need to approach it systematically to make absolutely sure that this gets done.

We advocate three general approaches when marketing and prospecting to your two main audiences, Met and Haven't Met. All three have a common theme—overkill! Why? Because no matter

> *"The key is to get people to call you. I do all kinds of marketing—the Internet, newsletters, real estate magazines, newspapers, and investment groups."*
>
> William Barnes
> Millionaire Real Estate Agent
> Taylors, SC
> Sales volume—$58.8 million

how much frequent and systematic lead generation is emphasized, most real estate agents still tend to underdo it. If you take one thing away from this discussion, please remember that when you market yourself to your audience, it needs to be systematized such that your audience is "touched" numerous times in a consistent fashion. The three methods we recommend to achieve this are: 8 x 8, 33 Touch, and 12 Direct.

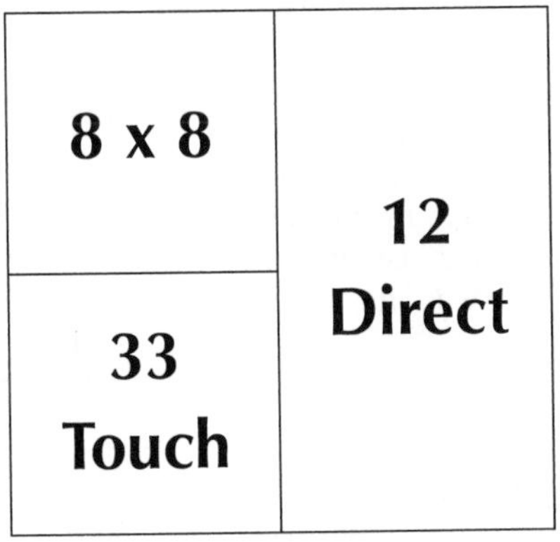

8 x 8

12 Direct

33 Touch

Figure 13

1. 8 x 8

Everyone you know or meet (your Met Group) first goes into your 8 x 8 program. Your 8 x 8 program is a systematic way of establishing relationships and cementing in their mind who you are and the opportunities your business represents for them. Simply put, once a week for eight weeks you will make meaningful contact with these individuals via letters, cards, and phone calls, with an aim toward establishing yourself as the number one real estate agent in their mind. Remember, if you aren't first or second in their mind, you probably won't get the business. This program begins this "mind share" positioning process in

---

8 x 8

- **Week One**—Drop off a letter of introduction, your personal brochure, a market report, and your business card.
- **Week Two**—Send a recipe card, inspirational card, community calendar, or market statistics.
- **Week Three**—Send a recipe card, inspirational card, community calendar, or market statistics.
- **Week Four**—Make a telephone call:
  "Hello, this is _____ from _____ Realty. Did I catch you at a bad time? How are you? Did you happen to receive the _____? Have you had a chance to look at it? The reason I'm calling is to find out if you happen to know of anyone who might be buying or selling their home. . . ."
- **Week Five**—Send one of your free reports.
- **Week Six**—Send a real estate investment or house maintenance tip.
- **Week Seven**—Send a refrigerator magnet, notepad, or other usable giveaway (not throwaway!) with your name, logo, and contact information on it.
- **Week Eight**—Make another telephone call:
  "Hello, this is _____ from _____ Realty. Did I catch you at a bad time? How are you? Did you happen to receive the _____ that I sent you? That's great. Did you have any questions? As you can tell, I really hope you will allow me to be your Realtor for life. And also, let me just give you a quick reminder that if you happen to know of anyone who might be buying or selling their home, could you please share their name with me or my name with them. . . ."

**8 x 8 is About Building Relationships and
Winning the Real Estate Agent "Mind Share" Battle**

Figure 14

a very powerful way. Figure 14 depicts what a typical 8 x 8 program might include.

For you, four mailings and four telephone calls may work just as well. Or maybe you'll choose to run the program for twelve weeks instead of eight. You can adapt the program to your personal strengths, but you should hold true to the foundational idea of no less than eight touches over eight weeks. This has proven to be the minimum number of touches required to establish a bond between you and the individual. And always remember that every touch should include a reminder and instructions on how to send you referral business.

Make sure time is set aside every week to follow through on your 8 x 8 program. Once you've completed the 8 x 8 program, these new contacts go into the Met portion of your contact database, where they will be included in your ongoing 33 Touch program.

2. 33 Touch

Your 33 Touch program will be a systematic marketing and prospecting technique, which will ensure year-round contact with the Mets. As with any core task, I recommend time be blocked off each week to make sure these important contacts occur. You must accept this as a basic but crucial job in your business—your ultimate success depends on it. The following graphic (Figure 15) shows all the elements a typical 33 Touch program might include.

---

33 Touch

- **18 Touches** A combination of eighteen e-mails, mailings, letters, cards, or drop-offs (which might include your business card) and may be one of the following: A letter of introduction, your personal brochure, market reports, Just Sold or Just Listed cards, holiday cards, your personal newsletter, recipe cards, property alerts, real estate news or articles, investing news or articles, community calendars, invitations, service directories, promotional items, etc.

- **8 Touches** Thank you or "thinking of you" cards

- **3 Touches** Telephone calls

- **2 Touches** Birthday cards (husband and wife)

- **1 Touch** Mother's Day Card

- **1 Touch** Father's Day Card

33 Touches Each Year

Figure 15

While e-mailing is inexpensive and convenient, we recommend preceding your telephone calls with real mailings. This simply makes it much easier to say, "Did you receive the _____ I sent you?" and break the ice. Each touch should include a reminder to send you referral business and instructions on the best way to do so. Any promotional items you send should be items of value that they can use. If it has a really long shelf life, like a refrigerator magnet or a notepad, then so much the better.

As with the 8 x 8 program, the foundational idea here is that you will make 33 systematic contacts, or brief touches, over the course of the full year. Please be aware that 24 might do it, but, then again, it might not. Twelve touches a year certainly isn't enough to guarantee you are in the number one or two spot in their mind when they think of real estate. Research has backed up our experience where frequency is concerned.

Our research shows that what all this activity will do for your business is this: For every twelve people in your Met contact database to which you market yourself thirty-three times (33 Touch) you can reasonably expect to net two sales. One of those sales will likely be repeat business, and the other will likely be referral business. Marketing to your Met contact database is generally the most cost-effective form of lead generation. In terms of reaching annual production goals and using a conversion ratio of 12:2, if you wanted to make fifty sales a year, you'd need to have three hundred people in your Met database whom you had sent through your 8 x 8 program and who were in your 33 Touch program. That represents a lot of time and effort, no question about it. However, this database and your relationship to it is the heart of your business. My question to you is, if you aren't doing this, then what researched and historically proven lead-generation strategy are you following?

3. 12 Direct

The 12 Direct program is how you work the Haven't Met portion of your database. It stands for twelve direct mail pieces mailed out annually.

Now, your Haven't Met database includes your mailing lists for farm areas and/or any other demographic groups. Considering the time involved and the work that can be delegated, there is no question that this is a highly leveraged form of lead generation to the masses. Personal telephone calls and drop bys are not required, so in the same amount of time you would work a handful of names in your Met contact database, you can shape a message that can be sent to thousands in your Haven't Met database.

Our research and experience have taught us that for every fifty people you market yourself to twelve times a year, you can reasonably expect to generate one sale. At a 50:1 ratio, you'll have to have 2,500 people in your database to consistently hit an annual goal of fifty closed sales. Amassing a database of 2,500 people in your market might seem difficult and expensive, but it isn't. However, it will take some focused effort and time devoted to getting the names, moving them into the database, and planning out your 12 Direct marketing campaigns each year. To save time and money, we suggest you plan and set up each twelve-month campaign all at once at the beginning of the year; then it can go on automatic pilot for the year.

The key word used over and over again is *systematic*. The reason I'm hammering that one home is that it is the crucial concept behind your lead-generation program. When you get this down to a systematic level, then you've probably gotten it down to an automatic level. That's when you're really in business! And in more ways than one!

FOCUS ON SELLER LISTINGS

If there is a creative angle to your lead-generation program you'll want to pursue, it is to create your message, image, and methods such that they are conducive to generating seller listing leads. Why? Research shows that if your lead-generation program consistently delivers seller

The Natural Balance of Seller and Buyer Listings		
GCI	Seller Listings Sold	Buyer Listings Sold
$ 40K	4	6
$ 80K	8	11
$ 150K	15	16
$ 250K	25	25
$ 750K	64	56

Figure 16

listings, you can count on the marketing of those seller listings to deliver buyer leads. The above graphic, the Natural Balance of Seller and Buyer Listings (Figure 16), is the product of a study we conducted using data collected from more than ten thousand agents.

This graphic illustrates that, as an agent's business grows, that individual's percentage of listings grows as well. While natural balance is achieved at about a quarter million in GCI, beyond that point the number of buyer listings sold largely depends on the goals and priorities of the agents. Our interviews with the best agents in the business have led us to believe that a seller listing properly marketed will consistently yield one or more buyer sales. So, if you wanted to have fifty sales in one year, you'd really need a lead-generation plan that delivered twenty-five salable and marketable seller listings and then effectively market them. If you're not sure exactly how to do that, please consult the Basic Fourteen-Step Marketing Plan for Listings (Figure 17).

"When we successfully list, everything else seems to fall into place."
Gary and Nikki Ubaldini
Millionaire Real Estate Agents
Palm Harbor, FL
Sales volume—$28 million

Try to remember this simple truth: If you focus on marketing your seller listings—the buyers will come!

I've intentionally kept our discussion of the Lead-Generation Model to the foundational issues, which we believe will have the greatest

Basic Fourteen-Step Marketing Plan for Listings

1. Staging and Pricing Strategies

2. For Sale Sign, Ryder Signs, and Directional Signs

3. Tube or Box with Flyers and Distribution of Flyers in Neighborhood

4. Flyers in House/Home Book/Comment Cards

5. MLS

6. Web Listings with Virtual Tour (Strategic Placement)

7. House Featured in "Marketing Vehicle" (Calendar, etc.)

8. Open House Program

9. E-mail/Fax/Voice Broadcast

10. Track Showings/Collect Feedback

11. Target Marketing

12. Weekly Seller Updates

13. Property Caravans

14. Creative Marketing Ideas (10K, Cable, etc.)

Truth: The only real difference between agents is that some "list" houses and some "market" them. Are you a listing agent or a marketing agent?

Figure 17

impact on the success of your lead-generation program. But make no mistake, there are other issues at play, as well as a number of skills you will need to develop through experience and training to make your lead-generation effort truly effective.

Foremost of these are the disciplines of sales scripts and dialogues. If you haven't internalized your scripts and dialogues for buyer and seller presentations such that you can face almost any situation with confidence, your lead-generation activities will not likely yield the kinds of results we describe here. Confidence is the key. If you know (and I mean *really* know) your scripts and dialogues, you will feel confident and empowered when you go about the otherwise intimidating business of making or receiving calls, approaching FSBOs, and working your Allied Resources. The bottom line is that script and dialogue proficiency builds confidence and that confidence leads to decisive action.

A strong marketing-based, prospecting-enhanced lead-generation plan backed by script and dialogue mastery is the best formula for creating the greatest number of leads for your business.

MODEL THREE:
YOUR BUDGET MODEL

In our discussion of the Economic Model, we began with the premise that you need to understand where your money comes from in order to effectively build your sales business. Your Budget Model is about understanding what happens to your money between the time you receive it (as gross revenue) and keep it (as net income). In short, it is about expenses or, more to the point, minimizing your expenses to maximize your net income.

> *"In the past four years, I have gotten very focused on profitability. I now review my P&L almost every day."*
>
> Gregg Neuman
> Millionaire Real Estate Agent
> San Diego, CA
> Sales volume—$113 million

COST VS INVESTMENT

In reality, you probably would equate a budgeting seminar with a yawning festival. Right? Admit it. And you wouldn't be alone. Most agents just can't get their heads around the fact that a budget is a powerful financial-planning tool. They tend to see budgets as a necessary evil, more a record for income tax purposes and audits than anything else. I'm here to tell you this is wrongful thinking and, I hope, to change your paradigm, your way of thinking about budgets.

When people sit down to discuss refinancing a mortgage or maybe costing out the potential return on renovating their kitchen—despite all the math and calculations—don't they tend to get energized? Of course they do. They get energized because they understand that implicit in these calculations is the opportunity to save thousands on their mortgage or markedly increase the value of their home through renovations. It can be the same with your budget. When you view the money you spend (expenses) as simply the cost of doing business, budgeting remains a chore. However, when you see every dollar spent as an "investment in your future," you'll approach budgeting with more excitement and a high level of interest. Budgets can be interesting, and it is time to change your perspective.

Your philosophy should be that for every dollar invested in a business expense, you should receive some multiple of that dollar back. Dollar for dollar isn't enough. Why? If you were to invest a dollar and get only a dollar back, why would you go to the trouble of spending it in the first place? Just keep the dollar and save the time. However, if you can get multiple dollars in return for a dollar investment, then you know you are not spinning your wheels. Every dollar in your business can be accounted for in this way. And when you view budgeting in this manner, where expenses are investments, you'll get excited and see your budget for the powerful financial-planning tool it is.

THE THREE KEY AREAS OF YOUR BUDGET MODEL

When it comes to your Budget Model, you'll want to concentrate on three areas in particular. First, you'll want to adopt "Lead with Revenue" as your financial motto. Next, you'll need to get into the habit of playing the mental

> *"We analyze our P&L monthly and we have gotten better at controlling our expenses."*
> David and Judie Crockett
> Millionaire Real Estate Agents
> Concord, OH
> Sales volume—$53 million

game of Red Light, Green Light with your expenses. This is about getting incremental results from incremental increases in expenses through accountability. And lastly, you'll have to develop the self-discipline actually to stick to the Budget Model you've adopted. Let's quickly take a look at these important budgetary issues.

1. Lead with Revenue

The key to budgeting and spending is to subscribe to one critical discipline: Lead with Revenue (not expenses)! The basic idea is to try to spend only money that your business has generated. Or, to put it simply, make money before you spend it. The beauty of the real estate sales business is that the actual cost associated with getting a single buyer or seller listing is really quite low. With a proportionally small investment, you can generate revenue in your real estate sales business that will, in turn, fund the growth of your business. The key is to start with this approach as early as possible and keep it as a discipline throughout your career.

Often, the difference between a successful start-up business and an unsuccessful one is usually decided before the business ever opens its doors. Companies that successfully minimize their start-up cost and debt before they open for business and start generating revenue quickly have a much better chance of survival. As we saw in the dot.com boom-and-bust era, some companies perceived as having smaller "upsides" ended up outliving many of the high-profile companies by following better business practices. A good example is a now-defunct software company in my hometown, which was a poster child for what we call "leading with expenses." Here was a company that spent millions on Super Bowl ads before they had positive cash flow in their business! Unfortunately, many real estate agents take this same Field of Dreams ("if I spend it, they will come") approach. They think that if they spend a lot of money up front or build the infrastructure of a big sales organization up front, the business will come. If you hold to the Lead with Revenue approach, it will force you to lead with lead generation and sales—not expenses. As the dot.com bust helped remind us all, when you continually lead with expenses instead of forcing the business to generate its own income, what often comes is a total loss.

2. Play Red Light, Green Light

You should never be as concerned with how much money you're actually spending as you are with the results you get by spending it. At some point in your career, it will take the careful spending of money to make money, so over time be prepared to invest money back into your business to build it. It is not the spending of money that is the problem. The problem is holding the money you're spending accountable for results. And the solution is the same old game: Red Light, Green Light. So, if you begin the process by Leading with Revenue, and you are always investing money your sales business has already generated, then your job is to hold that investment accountable.

> "*I do all my own budgets, I track my P&Ls and I have a great accountant who understands business.*"
>
> Don Zeleznak
> Millionaire Real Estate Agent
> Scottsdale, AZ
> Sales Volume—$77 million

Now at some point the dreaded "cost creep" will probably occur. However, you can greatly minimize your risks by following sound business practices like Leading with Revenue and Red Light, Green Light. When your costs just creep up with no corresponding increase in results, that is when you really have risk. We call that "good money chasing bad business practices." You correct it by pulling out your stop sign and reevaluating that expense. In terms of insulating your company against unexpected income shifts, you want to concentrate on keeping your fixed costs (like rent, salaries, leases, etc.) as low as possible. If you have higher fixed costs and face a shortfall in revenue, you might be tempted to cut back on variable or unfixed expenses (like lead generation), which drive your business. This can create a wicked catch-22 situation in which, because of falling revenue, you cut back on investing in the very activities that are likely to increase your revenue. Keep your fixed expenses as low as is practical and hold your discretionary expenses accountable to appropriate results.

3. Stick to the Budget

Obviously, as your business grows from one stage to the next, your actual costs will be very different; however, your percentages may not be. What we have discovered is that no matter where you are on the continuum, the percentages remain remarkably stable. Figures 18 and 19 illustrate some general examples of what budgets at various production levels might look like.

> *"Over my twenty plus years I've learned that you must budget and control your expenses. That is how I can take 75 percent to the bottom line."*
>
> John Toye
> Millionaire Real Estate Agent
> Westland, MI
> Sales Volume—$39.2 million

Budgets are to be respected. They are there for a reason—to guide you as you invest in your business. Doing the research to determine how the money in your business should be spent and then not following it can be summed up in two words: *Sheer folly.*

NATURAL RHYTHM

Lastly, I want to point out to you that there is a natural monthly rhythm to business, which demands that you examine your books at least once each month. I'll go so far as to recommend you keep a monthly budget but address it on a weekly basis. Why? Because Leading with Revenue and Red

GCI	(6M) $180,000	(10M) $300,000	(16.7M) $500,000	(26.7M) $800,000	(40M) $1,200,000
Cost of Sales*	21,000	21,000	100,000	250,000	350,000
Gross Profit	159,000	279,000	400,000	550,000	850,000
	88%	93%	80%	69%	71%
Expenses	59,300	93,000	152,500	238,000	344,000
	33%	31%	31%	30%	29%
Net Income	99,700	186,000	247,500	312,000	506,000
	55%	62%	50%	39%	42%

* Assumes Cost of Sales includes company desk fees or splits, commissions or salaries paid to buyer or seller agents helping you in the business, royalties and referral fees.
** All percentages have been rounded up to the nearest percent.

Figure 18

EXPENSE DETAIL					
1. Salaries	20,000	36,000	65,000	100,000	144,000
	11.1%	12%	13%	12.5%	12%
2. Lead Generation	18,000	30,000	50,000	80,000	120,000
	10%	10%	10%	10%	10%
3. Occupancy	1,500	2,500	3,000	4,000	5,000
	0.8%	0.8%	0.6%	0.5%	0.4%
4. Technology	4,000	4,500	7,500	12,000	18,000
	2.2%	1.5%	1.5%	1.5%	1.5%
5. Phone	2,600	3,000	5,000	10,000	12,000
	1.4%	1%	1%	1.3%	1%
6. Supplies	1,800	3,000	5,000	8,000	12,000
	1%	1%	1%	1%	1%
7. Education/Dues	1,800	2,000	5,000	7,000	12,000
	1%	0.7%	1%	0.9%	1%
8. Equipment	3,600	6,000	6,000	8,000	12,000
	2%	2%	1.2%	1%	1%
9. Auto/Insurance	6,000	6,000	6,000	9,000	9,000
	3.3%	2%	1%	1.1%	0.8%

All percentages figured as a % of Gross Income. These are a rough approximation and have been rounded up to the nearest tenth of a percent.

Figure 19

Light, Green Light require you to stay in touch with your spending. Some agents choose to review their financials much more frequently.

For Millionaire Real Estate Agents, budgeting is not only a core part of their business practice, it has also taken on the aspects of a game. And that is what we mean when we say once you understand it, budgeting can be fun and engaging.

MODEL FOUR:
YOUR ORGANIZATIONAL MODEL

You do all you can do. You go as far as you can go. You get all the results you can get, and when you can't go any further, you look for help. This help should come in the form of a talented person.

People are always asking me when or how they'll know when it is time to hire their first person. I tell them that it is like knowing when to hire a contractor or a maid. We could easily do most of the work that needs to be done around the house, but at a certain point in our lives we realize that our time could be better spent on other things. We start to look for help at home in a very natural way. When you don't have anyone to do that work for you, it is like a second job. On Thursday nights, you are a housekeeper. On Saturdays, you're the lawn man. And so on . . . In other words, if you don't have a maid, you are one. If you don't have a lawn man, you are one. And in business, if you don't have an assistant, you are one!

At the beginning of your real estate career, you are a lead generator, a showing agent, a seller listing agent, a bookkeeper, a runner, a call coordinator, and many other things all in one. When you aren't having fun or when you are feeling overwhelmed is the time to find someone to help with your "other" jobs. You don't have enough arms and legs to do everything all the time. In fact, at some point, everyone should aspire to have assistance just to avoid burning out. And the leverage that hiring some-one can bring to your business is the fastest, surest way to continue up the path to becoming a Millionaire Real Estate Agent.

THE THREE KEY AREAS OF YOUR ORGANIZATIONAL MODEL

We've identified three key aspects of your Organizational Model that can make a big difference in your chances for success. The first area is about acknowledging when you need help and then seeking the right kind of help. No matter what you might think, the first person you hire should always be an administrative assistant. Second, you need to hire T-A-L-E-N-T. Hiring talent is the key to gaining leverage in your business life. Lastly, you'll have to learn to train and consult with your staff. There is no point in hiring talent if you don't plan to teach them how to do their jobs well and challenge them to grow and learn. Let's take a quick tour of the key areas of focus in your Organizational Model.

1. When Doing All You Can Do, Hire Administrative Help

Adding staff members is just one of the three ways you can add leverage to your sales business. Besides people leverage, you could also turn to systems or tools. While traditional thinking would have you put systems in place to push you further along, we've discovered a problem with that thinking. Designing and implementing systems takes more time than you think and very specific skills. For most real estate agents, trying to put multiple systems in place by yourself will actually reduce productivity. Creating effective systems can be as complicated as it is time-consuming, and many

> *"As my business increased, I put people in place so I could do what I enjoyed. I was not afraid to add staff. I got more time for the dollar."*
> Mike Mendoza
> Millionaire Real Estate Agent
> Phoenix, AZ
> Sales volume—$60 million

agents quickly become frustrated. Frustration then leads to poor systems or no systems at all.

What we've learned is that the best way to put systems in place is to hire a person with the skills to document and later implement your systems. I realize this may sound crazy. I mean, why hire someone to document something you know and do so well? Actually, on this point I may know you better than you know yourself. Despite my best efforts working with hundreds and hundreds of real estate agents over the years, only a handful managed successfully to document their systems without outside help. At first, I thought the agents who didn't document their systems were the odd-balls. Now I know the truth—the agents who did document their systems were! So I've learned my lesson: hiring a person, specifically administrative help, comes before the full development of systems and tools.

One major point you'll have to address right up front is this: Should you hire a licensed assistant or a nonlicensed assistant? We have discovered that there are almost as many agents with assistants who have real estate licenses as there are those who don't. The graphic below provided by the Jeff Hooper team of Ottawa, Canada (Figure 20), lays out the pros and cons to consider.

The Pros and Cons of Hiring a Licensed Assistant	
THE PROS	**THE CONS**
1. Assistant allows agent to focus on lead generation by having the business knowledge, experience, and the ability to do other tasks. 2. Assistant has already made a career decision to be in real estate. 3. Assistant understands the commission business. 4. Assistant is already trained in the business.	1. Assistant may cost more. 2. Assistant tends to bring his own clients and wants to work with them. It can get messy.

Figure 20

The Millionaire Real Estate Agent

2. Hire Talent

The fundamental principle guiding any hiring decision you ever make is this: Always strive to hire talent. We say people are talent when they are a superb match for the criteria you have established for a particular position. By this we mean their natural abilities, skills, experience, and aspirations all line up around the job description and give them every reason to succeed at a very high level. This allows you to judge people against clear criteria instead of judging them as people. A candidate is therefore either a "great fit" or "not a fit" for the job, rather than being a good or bad person. It may sound like splitting hairs, but it probably represents a significant shift in your paradigm. When you surround yourself with talent, your life will never be the same. Hiring a truly talented person can take your business further than an entire busload of less talented ones. Here's how you'll know when you've hired talent:

- Talent pushes to get answers.
- Nontalent will have to be pushed to want answers.

- Talent shares your goals and fulfills your needs as a natural by-product of fulfilling their own.
- Nontalent doesn't fulfill your needs and ends up giving you back pieces of its job.

- Talent knows what it wants or is actively searching to know.
- Nontalent doesn't know what it wants and isn't searching.

- Talent pushes you constantly.
- Nontalent requires you to push it.

- Talent is continually raising the bar and wants to be associated with talent.
- Nontalent may not know where the existing bar is set or even what bar you're talking about.

Lastly, you can recognize talent by the way they talk. Their language is the language of challenge and achievement. When you work with them, talent is about as inconspicuous as a mighty redwood in a field of Christmas trees. Talent stands out.

One challenge with hiring talent is the level of compensation they may require. Many agents approach compensation with the worst possible point of view. Many of the discussions I've heard at real estate seminars and classes on the subject can be boiled down to this philosophy: "How little can I pay someone and not have them leave?" I'd like to advocate the exact opposite approach: When you make it your business to hire talent, I want you to ask yourself, "How much can I afford to pay them, so I can keep them as long as possible?"

> *"You must surround yourself with talent—loyal, strong people who want to work, like to work, and are productive."*
>
> Allan Domb
> Millionaire Real Estate Agent
> Philadelphia, PA
> Sales Volume—$135 million

If you remember our Red Light, Green Light discussion of incremental expenses being held accountable to direct incremental gains, you understand that when you hire talent, they should pay for themselves (and usually in spades). Therefore, you should reward your staff members based on how you expect them to perform and then hold them accountable to perform at that level. When you have talent, any compensation you are paying is really an investment on which you should expect substantial returns. It is totally true in life that you get what you pay for. So what is it you want, talent or nontalent? Get the most or pay the least?

Most real estate agents who consider becoming employers believe that hiring someone will cost them money. The truth is that a bad hire will not only cost you money, it will also cost you opportunities. A good hire will actually save you money and probably won't cost you any opportunities. A great hire—talent—will not only make you a lot of money, but will also create opportunities for you and your business. Please take a long look at the following two diagrams.

As Figure 21 and Figure 22 illustrate, the actual compensation you must pay someone won't burn you nearly so badly as a bad hire will. Get the idea out of your head that you'll hire talent when you have more

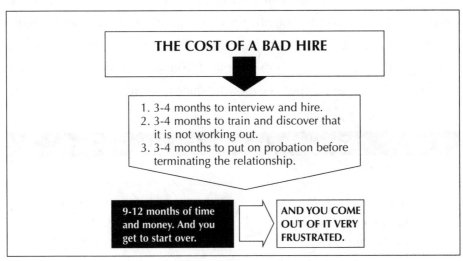

Figure 21

Figure 22

money. Talent may cost more than the average person, but the return on your investment is obvious.

3. Train and Consult

The last key area of your Organizational Model is training and consulting. What you pay talent to help you makes up a huge percentage of your annual costs, so you will always want to make sure you get the most out of your people investment. (And this is for their benefit and yours!) You'll get the best results from people if you do two things: train and consult them. To get perspective on how this will work, take a look at the model below.

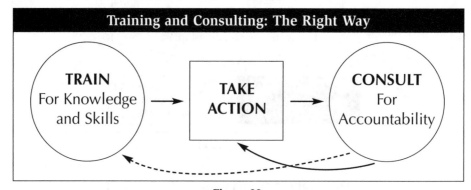

Figure 23

This is the way training and consulting should work. You train people initially to understand the job, learn the skills, and develop the systems required to do the job at a high level. They then start taking action. Every week, you meet with them to review their goals, priorities, and weekly tasks, and to hold them accountable. As necessary, you'll also be making sure they get the additional training needed to continue their growth and improve their ability to excel at their job. Just like you, your employees should set annual goals and break them down into monthly and weekly ones. Their goals should contribute to your goals. And your weekly meetings are designed to keep them on track toward meeting and exceeding those goals.

Now that is the supercondensed version of how training and consulting should be done. As you probably noticed, it is not a one-time thing. You begin with training and consulting, and it continues for as long as your employees work with you. Most agents either conduct training for only a short period following a new employee beginning or simply skip it altogether.

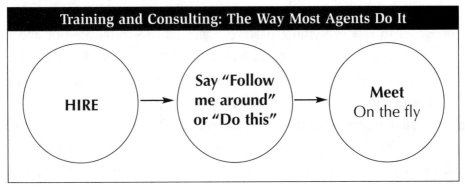

Figure 24

These agents are practicing "sea gull" management. They do very little training (or none at all) and then they just swoop in, make a lot of noise, dump on people, and fly off. Is it any wonder they can't find or keep talent to work with them?

We've discovered that over time talent will not need to be micromanaged. Trained, yes. Consulted, yes. Micromanaged, no. Reviewing goals weekly and then consulting on ways to help them achieve them is usually enough to get great results. If you find yourself still micromanaging a staff member three to six months into his employment, he may not be talented and may not be motivated to reach his goals (your goals) on his own. That may be the case. Or you may learn that you haven't quite learned to let leverage work for you and

> *"We now only want people who have a work ethic and share our value system. They need to crave learning."*
> Mary Harker
> Millionaire Real Estate Agent
> Dallas, TX
> Sales volume—$52 million

are overmanaging your staff. Be warned that nothing will scare away talent faster than micromanagement. They don't need it, don't enjoy it, and won't tolerate it. Talent expects that if they exceed your goals and expectations, you will train, consult, and hold them accountable, but no more.

Generally speaking, micromanagement is usually something to be avoided. Sometimes, inexperienced managers pay too much attention and get trapped in "hover mode." This is when your employees feel obligated to run everything past you, and you feel obligated to check on everything they do. That is a bad place to be, and, at the end of the day, no one feels empowered to take decisive action. Let's take a quick look at the Ten Principles for Empowering People (Figure 25). They are great guiding principles for managing your staff.

From clearly communicating and getting agreement on their responsibilities to treating them with respect, these ten principles will help you have the highest possible success with the people you employ.

Ten Principles for Empowering People
1. Tell people what their responsibilities are. Get agreement.
2. Give them authority equal to their assigned responsibilities.
3. Set standards of excellence and guidelines.
4. Provide initial and ongoing training that will enable them to meet standards (skills, knowledge, etc.).
5. Hold them accountable. Define consequences.
6. Provide them with weekly feedback on their performance.
7. Recognize them for their achievements (praise in public; correct in private).
8. Trust them. Allow them to grow into self-leadership.
9. Give them permission to fail.
10. Treat them with dignity and respect.

Figure 25

The Millionaire Real Estate Agent

Consulting your employees is at the very heart of the empowerment process. Although many agents think of accountability as tough confrontation, I want you to think of it as "carefrontation." You're doing it because you care. When done right, it holds people accountable to their job and goals in a timely, agreeable manner. Consulting begins by setting and agreeing to specific annual, monthly, and weekly goals. Your weekly consulting meetings to cover whether your employees are on target with their goals should be fairly straightforward. Figure 26 illustrates the formula we use when consulting from a common platform of shared goals.

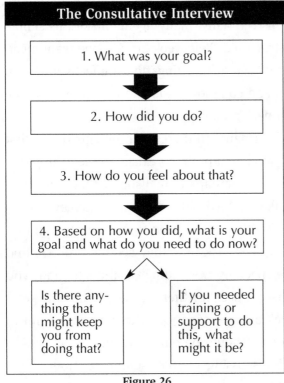

Figure 26

It is a simple but highly effective formula. This simple process of asking questions really brings out accountability. You don't have to do anything but follow this interview process each week. When people are meeting their goals, they require little corrective management. If anything, you'll mostly be reviewing their goals and priorities, and consulting with them on improving techniques or solving problems. The main trouble you will have is when people are not regularly meeting their goals. This requires an additional approach and much more involvement from you.

The first step to take when people are underperforming over time is to shift gears from the normal consultative interview and get their agreement that a problem exists. This should be done in private. (Remember, it's always: Reward in public; correct in private.) A staff meeting or when other employees are present is a poor forum for working with people on performance issues. When confronted publicly, even in the nicest way possible, the people you are seeking an honest dialogue with may withdraw or, worse, become defensive. Many, many agents make this simple mistake because they have structured their week around one team meeting. The truth is you need two sets of meetings to be effective: a team meeting to share information and common goals and private one-on-one meetings to address personal performance.

In addressing personal performance, if there is a problem you are first seeking their agreement that an actual problem exists. In fact, the possibility remains that the goals were perhaps unrealistic or that work conditions have conspired to make talented individuals underachieve. So, if you can eliminate those possibilities, you'll need to get their buy in that a productivity problem exists. Next, ask how they see the problem and then honestly share your perspective. Depending on the situation, you may need to discuss the consequences for them if there is no change in the situation. You should seek an agreement on what you both want to see happen. This short-term goal should be put in writing.

A big part of the process is discussing alternate solutions. "How are we going to solve this problem?" Let them know that you're willing to participate in the process and get their ideas on how to fix it. What emerges from this conversation can be very revealing. It may be that the people do not believe in your models and aren't following them. They may think they have better ideas. Keep an open mind, but the point of the discussion is to arrive at a mutually agreeable course of action. This needs to be specific and should spell out expectations, responsibilities, and time lines. Again, write it down. What you will have then is a kind of short-term contract for personal performance course correction. You have a copy, and they have a copy. They have agreed to the terms and understands the consequences. Next, you begin the process of following up and measuring progress.

Stick to your proven models and approaches during this process. Underachieving employees will many times try to convince you that it is the models or systems that are wrong and not their behavior. You have to remember that you are judging results and not people. If people aren't right for your system, you can still "love them to death" while parting ways. Conversely, you'll need to positively reinforce achievement and progress as it occurs.

As an ongoing reminder, think of your Organizational Model this way:

> Talent to shine,
>
> Systems to define,
>
> Train and consult to refine.

THE TWO D'S IN YOUR ORGANIZATION

Time out. Before we leave our discussion of your Organizational Model, we need to address systems and tools. We've put forth the idea that when you hire the right people, they will develop and implement your systems and tools. That is exactly right, and it's why we've dedicated the bulk of our analysis of leverage to the people aspect. But we need to realize that while the third L—Leverage—begins with people, it also includes these other two important aspects. Systems and tools bring leverage to your staff, and they bring more D to your business. Let's take a moment and explore the concept of bringing D to your organization.

All truly successful businesses are successful because they get things done. The best businesses get things done by bringing two D's into the business. The concept of D comes from the popular DISC behavioral profiling tool used by many organizations during the hiring process. In that system, D loosely stands for the "drive" we associate with doers. In other words, "D gets things done." It is sometimes referred to as Leadership D. On the opposite end of the spectrum is another kind of D that I've identified over the years. It's the D of the business itself, which is about the "drive" created by infrastructure—powerful systems and tools. This is called Business D. In a business organization, unless you address it, the two tend to exist in inverse proportion to each other. The more Leadership D there is, the less emphasis is put on developing Business D and visa versa. Leadership D and Business D. Having them both in your business is the key to building a truly great business.

Most real estate agents power their sales business by their Leadership D and heavily favor leveraging their growth on their personal drive. This is the classic model we see every day in the real estate industry, where the agent provides the lion's share of the D. On the other side of the spectrum are mature businesses, which base their success on the quality and effectiveness of their infrastructure, systems, and tools. This brings to mind massive systems-based companies like FedEx, which have exceptional leaders like Fred Smith but which also have amazing Business D. The Business D derived from systems and tools that are so effective that the company could essentially fly on autopilot for a long while without the leader's everyday influence. Their business model demands that their systems be that powerful and self-sufficient. Such a balance of Business D

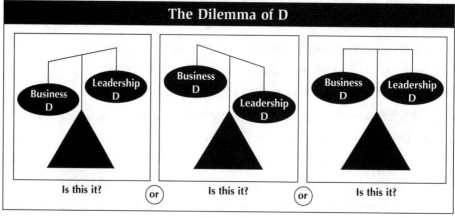

Figure 27

The Millionaire Real Estate Agent

and Leadership D is hard to find, but when present, the agent has the best of both worlds: Strong momentum from their Business D, powerful drive from their Leadership D.

In our industry, the main challenge for real estate agents is bringing Business D to the organization. Many high-achieving agents have difficulty making this happen and aren't comfortable depending on systems and tools to move their business forward. The truth of the matter is, to reach your highest level of success, you will have to incorporate a certain amount of Business D in your organization or it will always be 100 percent dependent on you.

Your Organizational Model is the key to adding Business D to your company. The right people will discover and implement the right systems and tools, while bringing some Leadership D of their own.

POINTS TO REMEMBER: The Four Fundamental Business Models of Real Estate

- Models are the science of business.
- Build your house with a blueprint or risk ending up with a hobo shack.
- Warren Buffett teaches us to master the proven models before we add creativity.
- The Economic Model shows you where your money comes from, where it goes, and how much is left for you.
  - Focus on the numbers you must hit.
  - Focus on appointments.
  - Focus on your conversion rates.

- The Lead-Generation Model shows you how to win the positioning battle for customer mind share.
  - Understand that lead generation is a numbers game.
  - Prospect and market to move people into your inner circle—your Allied Resources.
  - Set up a contact database and feed it daily.
  - Use 8 x 8, 33 Touch, and 12 Direct to contact your database systematically.
  - Focus on seller listings and market them for more leads.
- The Budget Model shows you what happens to your money from the time you receive it until the moment you get to keep it.
  - View your budget as a powerful financial-planning tool.
  - Lead with revenue, not expenses!
  - Play Red Light, Green Light to hold your investments accountable for appropriate results.
  - Stick to the Budget Model percentages and review them monthly.
- The Organizational Model shows you who will do what as you add people to your growing business.
  - Hire administrative help first. They will systematize and document your business.
  - Always hire talent. It will pay you back big when you take the time to find and keep talent.
  - Train and consult your people for maximum productivity and hold them accountable to standards.
- Add Business D (systems and tools) to your Leadership D (influence and accountability). It makes things happen even when you're not there.

THE MILLIONAIRE REAL ESTATE AGENT MODELS

Now that we've introduced and covered the four models high real estate sales achievement is built upon, let's take a close look at them from the Millionaire Real Estate Agent's point of view. Let's now study the issues and numbers of becoming a millionaire in real estate sales.

One of our discoveries while working with and interviewing Millionaire Real Estate Agents was that the transition between Earn a

Million and Net a Million was quite seamless. The same models are effective throughout. Netting a million in annual income is more a reflection of mastering your models than of pursuing a different path. In this section, we'll present to you the details that will take you all the way to netting a million and possibly beyond. In the subsequent chapter, Net a Million, we'll outline the primary issues you are most likely to encounter on the way from earning to netting a million.

As we cover these models, you must still remember to maintain your focus on the core issues that will drive your real estate sales business—the Three L's. The point is to put these models in place quickly and efficiently. If you follow them systematically and leverage their implementation through a few key hires, you should be able to maintain them with minimal distraction from your primary areas of focus—Leads, Listings, and Leverage.

Above all you'll be focused on generating leads. I like to say lead generation comes "first, last, and always." The difference between the Millionaire Real Estate Agent and an average real estate agent is that the millionaire never drops the ball on lead generation. It doesn't matter whether his computer crashed or his assistant quit, he systematically pursues leads and, when finished, then turns his attention to the problems of the day. He knows that if he allows himself to be distracted from his core job, he'll always be lagging behind and exposing himself to the vagaries of shifting markets. If lead generation doesn't get done, everything else could become unnecessary. The truth is that the opportunities you have to build your business begin or end with the number of leads you have. After lead generation, you'll focus on listings. From listings come inventory, market presence, and opportunity. And if you work them properly, they will also become a reliable source for buyer leads, usually on a one-to-one basis. Lastly, you'll be focused on gaining leverage through hiring, training, and consulting with the talented people you'll need to keep your leads and listings focus going strong. The right people will document and refine systems and add the proper tools as needed. So while these four models will provide clarity about the numbers behind how a Millionaire Real Estate Agent runs his business, don't forget that the Three L's are at the core of all these models and will be responsible for the vast majority of your millionaire results.

A QUICK WORD ABOUT QUALITY SERVICE

When I've consulted with agents, I've told them that the key to growing their business is to follow four models to focus on Leads, Listings, and Leverage. Sometimes they object. They want to know how significant a role quality service plays in becoming a highly successful real estate agent. Well, here is the answer: Just as we discussed in Think a Million, quality service will be a critical component of your success. And oddly enough, quality service will be the natural by-product of a business built on documented systems, accountability to standards, and hiring talented people. In fact, our experience is that agents who build a team of carefully selected, highly trained specialists provide a level of fiduciary service that is consistently and predictably higher than the service provided by a single person.

Top-producing agents are inherently committed to their clients and have a passion for helping them meet their home-ownership needs. While the commitment to delivering high-quality real estate service is fundamental to becoming a top-producing agent, it is not the primary determining factor in creating a million-dollar business. It is necessary, but not sufficient in itself. To build that business, you'll have to focus primarily on four models that become the main drivers for the Three L's: Leads, Listings, and Leverage.

> *"The cleverest thing I've ever done is to learn to delegate. My people actually do things better than I do."*
> Russell Shaw
> Millionaire Real Estate Agent
> Phoenix, AZ
> Sales volume—$50.6 million

THE FOUR MODELS

The Four Models of the Millionaire Real Estate Agent are the same four models we've been discussing. At the millionaire level, the difference is not in the models, but in the issues and the numbers you will need to fully execute them.

MODEL ONE: THE MILLIONAIRE REAL ESTATE AGENT ECONOMIC MODEL

THE FUNDAMENTALS

The Economic Model of the Millionaire Real Estate Agent begins with a basic snapshot of the cash flow of the business. At its simplest, the Economic Model looks like this:

All we've really done is just break the expenses category we presented earlier for the average agent into the

Gross Commission Income (GCI)

— Cost of Sales (COS)

— Operating Expenses

= Net Income

Figure 28

two expenses of the Millionaire Real Estate Agent: cost of sales and operating expenses. Now, to help make sure there are no misunderstandings going forward, the four elements of our model are defined as follows:

- **Gross Commission Income (GCI)** is based on an assumed 6 percent total commission with 3 percent for each side of the sale. (Although this will vary by agent and by city and is always negotiable, we had to pick a basic commission standard. For simplicity's sake, we have included all additional transaction fees charged buyers and sellers in the commission rate. It was the inclusion of these fees that brought the commission up to approximately 6 percent.)

- **Cost of Sales (COS)** is related to the amount of money paid to a listing specialist and the commission split paid to a buyer specialist. From our experience, a talented listing specialist will cost you between $65,000 and $100,000 (and the conservative, high end is assumed for all calculations). For the buyer side we assumed a 50/50 split for buyer specialists. Again this is a conservative figure. If your value proposition to your staff is such that you can compensate at a lower rate and still recruit and retain talent, you're in a much better position to net a higher income. Cost of sales can also vary widely based upon such variables as local market conditions, average price, support provided, source of leads, local employment conditions, etc. What must be understood is the implications for your net income when you raise or lower these costs.

- **Operating Expenses** are all the other costs of doing business, including marketing, rent, salaries, equipment and supplies, advertising, etc. Our research shows that as your business grows, this can reasonably be held at or below 30 percent of gross revenue (GCI). The impact operating expenses have on your income goes straight to the bottom line. When they rise, your net income will fall, and when they fall, your net income will rise.

- **Net Income** is the amount of profit your sales business earns. Because you are following the Millionaire Real Estate Agent model to pull you through smaller goals, your net income goal will always be set at $1,000,000. Bear in mind that net income is always your primary goal. It is natural to have goals in other areas, but always work backward from your net income. Always ask yourself, "If I lower/raise the percentage of any specific element, how will it affect my net income." This perspective will assure that you never lose your grasp on the interplay between these four economic categories.

Before we address the Economic Model, let's quickly examine one more assumption reflected in the model. We're assuming an average sales price of $250,000. This is well above the national median price but is backed up by our experience working with and interviewing top-producing agents. You can, and we hope you will, substitute numbers that reflect your business and your market. Once you've digested the proposed model, feel free to consult Figure 31 and Figure 32, which highlight the key changes in the model for average sales prices ranging from $150,000 to $300,000. Now, I think we're ready to start building the Economic Model of the Millionaire Real Estate Agent.

DOING THE MATH

Working backward, after adding back in COS and operating expenses, you will need approximately $2.4 million in GCI to net a million dollars in personal income. Here is a snapshot of the simplified version of the Economic Model:

There are two primary sources of income driving your GCI: seller listing sales and buyer sales. Of these two, seller listing income is

	$2.4 Million	GCI
—	$700,000	COS
—	$700,000	Operating Expenses
=	$1 Million	Net Income

Figure 29

the most important. Seller listings provide the greatest opportunity for net income; they are a marketing platform and a key source of leads. As detailed earlier, each seller listing properly marketed should generate one buyer sold if the leads are properly captured, followed up, and converted. The top agents we've worked with also confirm this. A seller listing-based agent who captures and converts buyer leads properly can reasonably expect her revenue to be divided equally between listings sold and buyer sales. In truth, this should be your strategy.

So, if your revenue is evenly divided between buyers and sellers, your $2.4 million in GCI will be divided equally between buyers and sellers, with $1.2 million coming from each side. To do that kind of business, you'll more than likely need leverage, which is where your cost of sales (COS) comes in. On the buyer side, due to the 50/50 split as compensation for buyer specialists, $1.2 million in GCI has a COS of $600,000. Seller listings are the better leverage opportunity for your business in the long run because you can expect your COS to be substantially lower. Your seller listing specialist will more than likely need to be ultimately compensated at a rate of around $100,000 per year.

With all those numbers in place, we can begin fleshing out the Economic Model in greater detail. Below is a quick overview of the basic cash flow of our model.

Now, we must determine the number of sales it will take to reach $2.4 million in GCI. Given our assumptions that the average sales price for the Millionaire Real Estate Agent will be $250,000 and that she will earn an average of 3 percent commission on each sale, we can conclude that it will

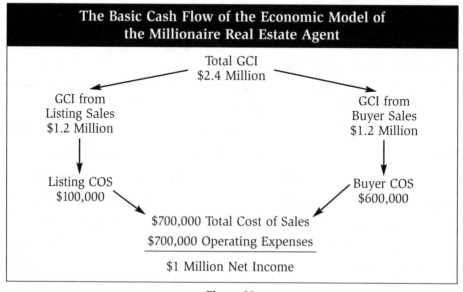

Figure 30

take 320 closed sales each year to reach $2.4 million in GCI. Since we are also advocating a seller listing-based perspective, where each properly marketed and worked seller listing generates one buyer sold, this divides clearly into 160 listing sales and 160 buyer sales each year. The charts below (Figure 31 and Figure 32) show the relationship between average sales price and the number of closed units necessary to reach $2.4 million in GCI.

As you can see, there is a direct relationship between average sales price and the number of units you

The Effect of Average Sales Price on Unit Sales	
Goal = 2.4 Million in GCI	
Average Sales Price	Closed Units
$150,000	534
$200,000	400
$250,000	320
$300,000	267

Figure 31

Percentage Decrease in Closed Units Per 10% Price Increase to Reach $2.4 Million in GCI Goal

% Increase in Price	Average Sales Price	Commission	Closed Units/Yr.	Difference	% Decrease Closed Units
10%	150,000	4,500	534		
				50	9.4%
	165,000	4,950	484		
				44	9.1%
	181,500	5,445	440		
				39	8.9%
	199,650	5,990	401		
				37	9.2%
	219,615	6,588	364		
				32	8.8%
	240,990	7,227	332		
				30	9%
	264,990	7,950	302		
				28	9.3%
	291,489	8,745	274		

Figure 32

will need to close each year to meet your GCI goal. Obviously, the higher your average sales price, the lower the number of units needed.

Closed units and average sales price are important drivers to Earn a Million and Net a Million, but they are not the only areas of focus for Millionaire Real Estate Agents. We need to concentrate on key activities that lead to closed sales. For starters, buyers and sellers must first agree to do business with us. And for this we need their written, contractual agreement to do business in the form of buyer representation agreements and seller listing agreements. To get these agreements, we'll need appointments with buyers and sellers to present our value proposition and secure the business. While our Economic Model ends with net income, it begins with lead generation and buyer and seller appointments. If we need 320 closed units to reach our GCI goal, we'll still need to work backward a bit further. We'll need to know:

1. the number of buyer listings and seller listings we'll need to take to net 320 closed sides per year
2. the number of buyer and seller appointments we will need to go on to take the appropriate number of buyer listings and seller listings
3. most importantly, the amount of lead-generation activity needed to generate the appropriate number of buyer and seller appointments.

> "We focus now on lead tracking. As a result, we have increased our speed of response and our percent of conversion."
>
> David and Judie Crockett
> Millionaire Real Estate Agents
> Concord, OH
> Sales volume—$53 million

The only way to get at these numbers is to track your lead-generation efforts carefully and get a firm grasp of your conversion rates.

Conversion rates may vary depending on a number of factors, including current market conditions, the effectiveness of your presentation, the quality of the leads, and the consistency of your follow-up. Our extensive research and experience can guide you to some solid benchmarks:

- For seller listings, approximately 80 percent of prequalified appointments should lead to listing agreements and approximately 65 percent of those listings should sell.

- For buyers, the ratios are reversed. Approximately 65 percent of prequalified appointments conclude with the buyer agreeing to be represented (hopefully with a buyer representation agreement in place), and approximately 80 percent of these buyers should go on to close.

Figure 33 illustrates how to work backward from your monthly target of 26.7 closed sales (320 sales/12 months) to get your monthly goals for buyer and seller appointments.

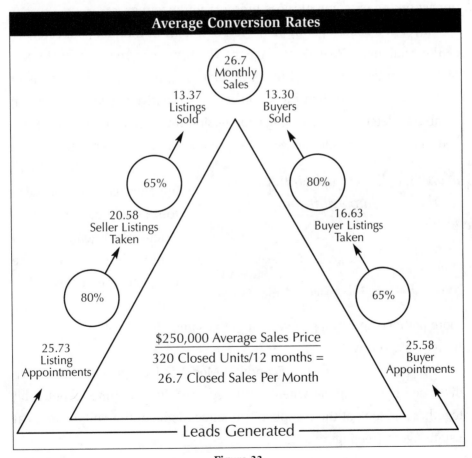

Figure 33

Using the 80/65—65/80 benchmarks, to reach the annual goal of 320 closed sales, you'll need to have a minimum of 25.73 listing appointments and 25.58 buyer appointments each month. Those 51.31 monthly appointments are some of the most important for you and your team. If you can turn up your focus for those appointments, the results can be amazing. Interestingly enough, some of the top agents we have interviewed reported conversion rates as high as 95 percent on seller listing appointments. Credit for this can be divided equally between the quality of their client leads, the excellence of their presentations (scripts and dialogues), their years of experience, and their value proposition. These factors almost always outweigh the market conditions in terms of having an impact on the outcome of these presentation meetings.

Buyer and seller appointments are both part of the first goal category of the Millionaire Real Estate Agent, which we covered in the Think a Million chapter. You'll need to set annual, monthly, and weekly goals in these categories and then track your results attentively. Over time, you'll be able to determine the average conversion rates for you and your team and update your Economic Model appropriately. The better your conversion rates, the fewer appointments you'll need to schedule each month to reach your goal. Or you could view it from the perspective that the higher your conversion rates, the more net income you'll generate from the same number of appointments. Either way, you win.

> *"Converting calls into appointments is one of the most important things for me to do."*
>
> Sherry Wilson
> Millionaire Real Estate Agent
> Purceville, VA
> Sales volume—$102.6 million

The last element of the Economic Model is lead generation. As we discussed before, this is where it all begins. Now it is time to put it all together and look at the complete Economic Model of the Millionaire Real Estate Agent (see Figure 34).

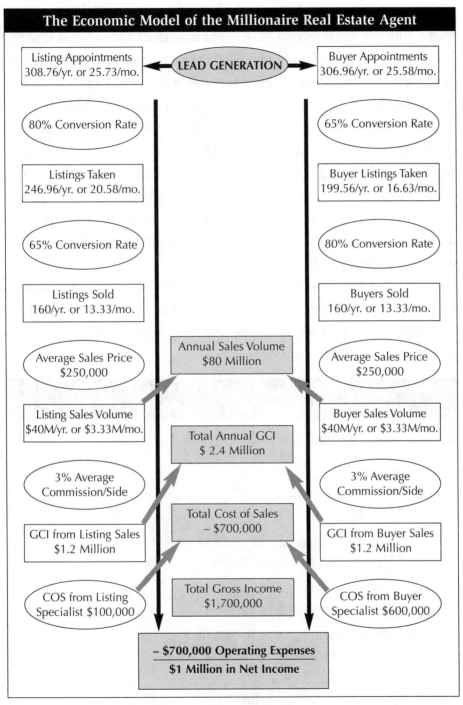

Figure 34

The Economic Model of the Millionaire Real Estate Agent accounts for all the principle variables that lie between your leads and your net income. If you already know your key numbers, then it becomes a simple exercise to convert these numbers to represent your current production numbers. If your conversion rates, average sales price, or average commission per side are better than our benchmarks, their inclusion will have a positive net effect on the model. You'll either net more or be able to lower your buyer and seller listing appointment goals to make the same amount. You and everyone on your team must own these essential numbers and know precisely how a change in one affects the others. If you or your team doesn't yet know your numbers, then your immediate mission should be to start tracking them in detail. In the end, knowing your numbers and how they interact in your Economic Model builds confidence and stability into your business. This is when it really starts feeling like a business!

Below is a recap of the key issues and numbers of the Millionaire Real Estate Agent's Economic Model:

The Big Issues of the Economic Model of the Millionaire Real Estate Agent
1. 320 Closed Sales with an Average Sales Price of $250K
2. $2.4 Million in GCI
3. $700,000 Cost of Sales $700,000 Operating Expenses
4. 27.72 Seller Listing Appointments per Month 25.58 Buyer Listing Appointments per Month
5. 20.58 Seller Listings Taken per Month 16.63 Buyer Listings Taken per Month
6. 13.33 Seller Listings Sold per Month 13.33 Buyer Listings Sold per Month

Figure 35

You now have six goals that you and your team can put on your goal sheet and post around your workspace so they are in clear sight at all times. If this is your business focus, then let it be your visual focus as well.

The Economic Model of the Millionaire Real Estate Agent is a Big Model for Big Goals. It should serve you well from start to finish. If you do not yet have a listing or buyer specialist, leave those areas in your personal model as placeholders for the future. Eventually, you will need talented people to help grow your business, and before you hire them, you need to understand the impact they will have on your cash flow and net income.

Model Two: The Millionaire Real Estate Agent Lead-Generation Model

Let's face facts. To achieve big in real estate sales, you will need a lot of leads. To be a Millionaire Real Estate Agent, you will need enough leads to drive your millionaire Economic Model. It's that simple. If you follow the Economic Model of the Millionaire Real Estate Agent, your annual lead-generation goal is quite clear—lead generate in order to net 160 listings sales, which will in turn lead to 160 buyer sales. It is anticipated that you will have to go on about 308 seller listing appointments (25.7/month) and about 306 buyer listing appointments (25.58/month) in order to achieve your 160 seller listings sold and 160 buyers sold goals.

Marketing Based—Prospecting Enhanced

To generate this level of numbers, you will need to follow a highly leveraged lead-generation plan that is marketing based and prospecting enhanced. The reason we keep saying marketing based is because marketing is a leveraged activity. To be able to generate the number of leads you will need, prospecting just won't be enough. Only marketing

> *"I mail to my database of 7,000 every month, and I try to make 100 past-client calls a day. I also do my own PR— I give the newspapers stories and then they call me."*
>
> Allan Domb
> Millionaire Real Estate Agent
> Philadelphia, PA
> Sales volume—$135 million

actively can give you the leverage you'll need to generate a large number of leads. Then, you might ask, why do prospecting at all? You will continue to do a certain amount of prospecting because this is your way of keeping your business in an active vs reactive state. By regularly prospecting, you will continue to keep your hand in proactive customer-creation activities that will be critical to your ability to hit your numbers when the market shifts and you're in a period when attracting through marketing doesn't generate enough leads. If you wait until the market shifts to get back to some prospecting activities, the lag time between when you start and when the leads come in could be longer than you want. If it would be helpful, refer back now to Figure 12 on page 143 and refamiliarize yourself with this model.

Basically, here is how the Lead-Generation Model works to become a Millionaire Real Estate Agent. You will run an aggressive marketing and prospecting campaign built off of the list in Figure 10 on page 138. These activities generate leads. All of these leads go into your 8 x 8 program to establish your relationship with these individuals. Their names are then added to your Met database and they get the 33 Touch treatment each year. The 33 Touch program should then result in repeat and referral business at a rate of one referral and one repeat for every twelve people in the program (or a 12:2 ratio*).

---

*Note: The reason we say 12:2 instead of 6:1 is because we're differentiating between a repeat sale and a referral sale. Studies show that when you follow the 8 x 8 and 33 Touch programs, you can expect to get two transactions for every twelve people in this program: One repeat sale and one referral sale.

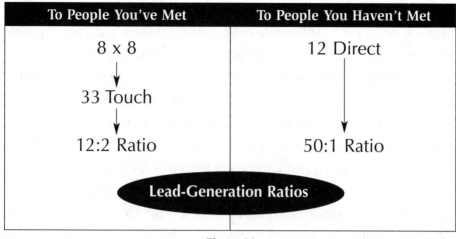

To People You've Met	To People You Haven't Met
8 x 8 ↓ 33 Touch ↓ 12:2 Ratio	12 Direct ↓ 50:1 Ratio

Lead-Generation Ratios

Figure 36

On the other side, you are marketing to geographic and demographic lists you have dropped into the Haven't Met portion of your contact database. These go through your 12 Direct program. Through twelve contacts over twelve months, your 12 Direct program can then be expected to generate one piece of new business for every fifty people in the program (a 50:1 ratio).

At those conversion rates, the Millionaire Real Estate Agent will need either 1,920 people in his Met database (Option 1) or 16,000 in his Haven't Met database (Option 2), or some combination thereof (Option 3), to reach the annual goal of 320 sales.

The Lead-Generation Numbers Game		
	MET	HAVEN'T MET
Option 1	1,920 in database +	0 in database
Option 2	0 in database +	16,000 in database
Option 3	960 in database +	8,000 in database
Net 320 Sales Per Year		

Figure 37

If you want to go the overkill route, which we encourage, you could also set out to put 1,920 people in your Met database and 16,000 people in your Haven't Met database! Now that is really aiming high!

While those numbers may look intimidating, it really isn't all that complicated. If you account for vacations, weekends, and sick days, the average person works roughly 240 days a year. (I realize the average real estate agent probably works more, but I'm sticking to the broad averages because I really, really, really want you to have a life!) If you were to add one person to your Met database each of those 240 working days, eight years later you would have enough people in your Met database to create 320 annual sales. Adding two people a day would get you there in four years. Three a day would get you to your goal in less than three years! And that's assuming you have to start from zero. So filling your Met database could take forever, or it could reasonably be done in as little as three years. The alternative is to go out and just accumulate mailing lists over time until you have 16,000 people in your Haven't Met database. The most powerful and proactive approach would be to do both in some combination of "overkill" that ensures you the right minimum number of sales leads to reach your goals.

Below are the Millionaire Real Estate Agent's Four Laws of Lead Generation, which we have found to be a helpful tool in getting real estate agents to maintain their focus on daily lead generation:

The Four Laws of Lead Generation
1. Build a database.
2. Feed it every day.
3. Communicate with it in a systematic way.
4. Service all the leads that come your way!

Figure 38

THE COSTS OF MASSIVE LEAD-GENERATION SUCCESS

When I throw out these kinds of numbers to agents who are striving to become Millionaire Real Estate Agents, one of the first assumptions they make is that it will cost a fortune. While it will cost more money than most agents spend, it is actually not nearly so costly as you might think. Let's break it down to a per-sale cost for sales generated through marketing and prospecting to your Met and Haven't Met databases.

The Cost of a Millionaire Lead-Generation Program	
Met (Big Goal = 1,920 People = 320 Sales)	**Haven't Met** (Big Goal = 16,000 People = 320 Sales)
1. Every 12 people in your Met database marketed to 33 times each year (33 Touch) = 2 sales. (One sale is a referral and one is repeat business.)	1. Every 50 people in your Haven't Met database marketed to 12 times a year (12 Direct Mail) = 1 sale.
2. Restated: 396 touches (12 x 33) = 2 sales.	2. Restated: 600 touches (50 x 12) = 1 sale.
3. So, 396 touches x $0.50 (average cost of a touch) = $198 for 2 sales OR **$99 per sale**. (If you double your costs for a worst-case scenario, count on $198/sale.)	3. So, 600 touches x $0.50 (average cost of a touch) = **$300 per sale**.
4. To reach your goal of 320 sales, how many people would you need in your Met database? Answer: 320 x 12/2 = 1,920 people	4. To reach your goal of 320 sales, how many people would you need in your Haven't Met database? Answer: 320 x 50 = 16,000 people
5. **Cost = 320 x $99/sale = $31,680/yr.** (OR a worst case scenario of Cost = 320 x $198/sale = $63,360)*	5. **Cost = 320 x $300/sale = $96,000/yr.** (OR a worst case scenario of Cost = 320 x $600/sale = $192,000)

* Note: The cost of the 8 x 8 program is not included.

Figure 39

So, unless you have 1,920 people in your Met database or 16,000 people in your Haven't Met database, you'll need to pursue a combination of the two approaches. Also, bear in mind that in the forthcoming analysis of the Budget Model of the Millionaire Real Estate Agent, we will make the recommendation that lead-generation costs should be about 10 percent of your gross income. So if your 396 Touches to a database of 1,920 costs you only $63,360, that will add up to only 2.6 percent ($63,360/$2.4 million). The 12 Direct program marketed to 16,000 people will cost $192,000, which is the other 8 percent ($192,000/$2.4 million). The conclusion, as you can probably see, is that you could generate "double" the leads you need to generate 320 closed sales for just a little over the recommended budget. I guess if you did that, you'd actually become a Multimillionaire Real Estate Agent. It's our hope that if you can do both the Met and the Haven't Met at full capacity, your gross income will more than account for this variance!

The numbers in the Cost of the Millionaire Lead-Generation Plan (Figure 39) are, nevertheless, rough, round figures. We're averaging the cost of a touch (considering that in addition to mailings, you will also be using the phone and cost-effective e-mails) at $0.50 per touch. Some agents whom we interviewed marketed to their farms for less than $0.20 per touch. Others chose the four-color, first-class mail route and averaged a dollar or more. The idea is that you need to be tracking your costs such that you can plug in the appropriate numbers.

The numbers presented in the Cost of the Millionaire Lead-Generation Plan allow us to make some interesting deductions. Repeat and referral business (lead generation from your Met database) require less money per sale than new business. We also understand that while these cost less, they take more time and effort (thirty-three touches as compared to twelve direct mails). Unless you can get more referral and repeat business per person (i.e., establish a clientele of real estate investors), your time will limit the amount of referral and repeat business you can do. Furthermore, the kind of personal attention required to successfully lead generate from your Met database may also prevent you from eventually stepping out of the business and achieving the final stage, Receive a Million. This is one reason most of the Millionaire Real Estate Agents aggressively pursue Haven't Met lead generation in addition to their formidable Met marketing and prospecting programs.

FOCUS ON LISTINGS

The Millionaire Real Estate Agent understands the importance of listing sellers' houses. They realize the huge benefits and advantages of seller listings covered earlier on page 102, and therefore build their entire Lead-Generation Model around generating seller listings. By focusing on seller listings, they put the two biggest advantages in the business to work for them:

> *"I have a broad marketing plan, but our yard signs alone generate over 7,000 leads a year."*
>
> Joe Rothchild
> Millionaire Real Estate Agent
> Katy, TX
> Sales volume—$106.9 million

1. Economic Advantage: Seller listings, as cost of sale, are less expensive to obtain than buyer listings and sales. At a cost of sale of around $100,000 vs $600,000 for the same volume of buyer sales, the Millionaire Real Estate Agent realizes a $500,000 cost savings.

2. Lead-Generation Advantage: Properly marketing seller listings not only begets a 2 for 1 (1 seller = 1 buyer) but also begets

more seller listings. Until a way is invented to effectively market buyers so sellers will contact us, marketing the seller has a huge leverage advantage for the real estate agent.

Millionaire Real Estate Agents are seller-listing lead generators first, marketers of those seller listings second, and buyer-listing lead generators third. Any other order and the odds of achieving millionaire sales numbers drop dramatically.

MODEL THREE: THE MILLIONAIRE REAL ESTATE AGENT BUDGET MODEL

While your monthly budget is your power tool for tracking and evaluating the investments you make in your company, the Budget Model of the Millionaire Real Estate Agent (Figure 40) is a more high-level look at your spending. What it does is highlight those areas where your focus and attention will pay the highest dividends.

The Millionaire Real Estate Agent's Budget Model is divided into two broad categories: cost of sales and operating expenses. Now, to be the most effective you can be and get the most out of these investments, you should be able to explain why every budget item is there, why it is a certain amount, and exactly what you expect to receive from it. With that in mind, let's break these two categories into their relevant parts and get a better understanding of them.

Your cost of sales reflects the actual costs of capturing and converting your leads to sales, which would be handled by your seller specialist(s) and your buyer specialist(s). Seller specialist(s) are responsible for five key activities:

- Converting seller leads into appointments
- Making listing presentations
- Securing seller listings

The Budget Model of the Millionaire Real Estate Agent

There are two key areas of expenses:

1. Cost of Sale*

This is the cost of acquiring the income and includes the salary and commission of a listing specialist and the commission of buyer specialists.

Seller Specialists	4.4%	$100,000
Buyer Specialists	24.8%	$600,000
Total Cost of Sales**	29.2%	$700,000

2. Operating Expenses*

This is the cost to generate leads and run the business. Key categories here are:

1) Salaries	**12%**	**$288,000**
2) Lead Generation	**9.2%**	**$220,000**
3) Occupancy	2.0%	$48,000
4) Technology	1.5%	$36,000
5) Phone	1.0%	$24,000
6) Supplies	1.0%	$24,000
7) Education	1.0%	$24,000
8) Equipment	1.0%	$24,000
9) Auto/Insurance	0.5%	$12,000
Total Expenses	29.2%*	$700,000

The Big Two (Salaries and Lead Generation) make up 72.6% of Operating Expenses!

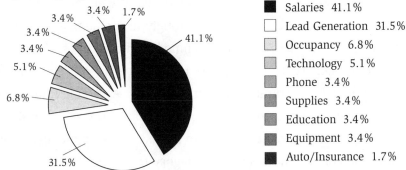

* Reflects percentage of annual $2.4 million GCI goal from the Economic Model of the Millionare Real Estate Agent
** Referral fees would also be included in Cost of Sales

Figure 40

- Handling communications during the marketing period
- Negotiating purchase offers

Based on our experience, we recommend this individual be paid a salary plus bonuses based on specific criteria such as the number of listings taken, number of listings sold, or the net profit of the business. Depending on the market, talent for this position will demand between $65,000 and $100,000 a year. Our model reflects the conservative end of the spectrum. Your buyer specialist is responsible for six key activities:

- Convert buyer leads to in-office presentation appointments
- Make the presentations
- Secure the buyer listings
- Show houses
- Negotiate purchase offers
- Handle communications from contract to closing

> *"I study my P&L all the time. Currently we take 35 percent to the bottom line. I want to get that up to 50 percent."*
>
> Glen Calderon
> Millionaire Real Estate Agent
> Ozone Park, NY
> Sales volume—$73 million

Typical commission splits range from a low of 35/65 to a high of 60/40 (or possibly beyond depending on any unique circumstances). However, you should know that going higher than 50/50 can have extremely adverse effects on your Economic Model, and we strongly recommend against it.

Operating expenses are divided into nine broad categories. There is no miscellaneous category. I repeat: There is no miscellaneous category. All expenses should be accounted for. In Appendix A, you'll find a very specific Chart of Accounts with more than 135 categories of expenses we have identified over the years. If you use it (and we recommend you do), you should be able to find a specific category for every check you write. Why? So when you are comparing expenses with other real estate agents, both of you will be talking the same language.

When you look closely at the Budget Model you will notice that of the nine categories, two account for the lion's share of your operating expenses:

We call these the "big two." Chances are if you can be successful in holding these two operating expenses accountable to results,

The "Big Two" as a Percentage of Operating Expenses	
Salaries	41.1%
Lead Generation	31.5%
Total	72.6%

Figure 41

your budget will be a healthy one. Those two budget items translate to two important areas of focus for you: staffing productivity (leverage) and cost-effective lead generation (leads) with an emphasis on seller listings (listings)—the Three L's.

Staffing productivity becomes an even larger issue if you now include your cost of sales as part of your staffing compensation costs. The compensation you pay your seller listing specialist and buyer specialist above the line (in cost of sales) accounts for another 29.2 percent of your gross income. Combine that with the "big two" and you'll see that lead generation and compensation as a whole add up to over half your gross income. Compensation is a full 40 percent! So what's your aha? Now you can see why we place so much emphasis on lead generation (that leads to listings) and leverage (as it pertains to your staff). These issues have a remarkable impact on the overall welfare of your business. In fact, they are your business.

Obviously, as your business grows from one stage to the next, your actual costs will be very different from the numbers on either of your Big Models, which represent the end picture. What we have discovered through research and experience, however, is that no matter where you are in the continuum, the percentages remain remarkably stable.

MODEL FOUR: THE MILLIONAIRE REAL ESTATE AGENT ORGANIZATION MODEL

From your first hire to your last, the key to knowing which people to bring onboard and what skills they should have on their résumés is to have a detailed Organizational Model. The Organizational Model of the Millionaire Real Estate Agent identifies a division of labor and the assignment of responsibility among your current and future staff.

> *"Every time I added people, my business grew."*
> Rachel DeHanas
> Millionaire Real Estate Agent
> Waldorf, MD
> Sales volume—$52 million

For a real estate sales business, there are three distinct areas of staffing:

1. **Administrative**—Marketing and administrative manager, transaction coordinator, listing manager, telemarketer, lead coordinator, assistant, and runner
2. **Buyer**—Lead buyer specialist, buyer specialists, and showing agents
3. **Seller**—Lead listing specialist and listing specialists

These staffing categories also represent a prioritization of the order in which you should seek help in each area. Administrative help is at the heart of the Organizational Model of the Millionaire Real Estate Agent. Only after a solid administrative staff is in place do we begin to even think about hiring buyer and seller help.

In the end each area should have a highly talented person in place—your marketing and administrative manager, your lead buyer specialist, and, finally, your lead listing specialist. Your primary focus under leverage from the start of your career until the end is to find and keep magnificent talent for these three essential positions. If you have

> *"I got an assistant early. I love sales, not paperwork."*
> Elaine Northrop
> Millionaire Real Estate Agent
> Ellicott City, MD
> Sales volume—$71 million

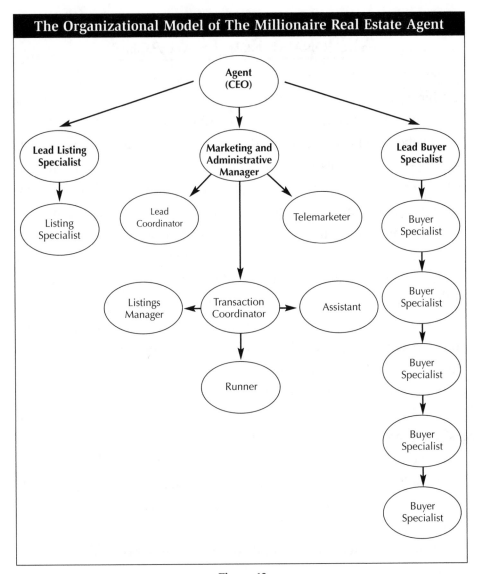

The Organizational Model of The Millionaire Real Estate Agent

Agent (CEO)

Lead Listing Specialist

Marketing and Administrative Manager

Lead Buyer Specialist

Listing Specialist

Lead Coordinator

Telemarketer

Buyer Specialist

Listings Manager

Transaction Coordinator

Assistant

Buyer Specialist

Runner

Buyer Specialist

Buyer Specialist

Buyer Specialist

Figure 42

extraordinary talent in all three, your chances of becoming a Millionaire Real Estate Agent are greatly enhanced. Magnificent talent is not easy to find. It takes time, patience, and dedication. But the encouraging revelation many agents come to is that you could be just three exceptional hires away from having the business of a Millionaire Real Estate Agent!

The Hiring Path of the Millionaire Real Estate Agent

So many agents make the mistake of seeking sales support first, usually buyer agents. As we've asserted before, salespeople are not by and large particularly talented at creating and implementing systems, nor are they the best people to identify and employ the proper tools for your business. In essence, agents who hire a buyer agent first have hired someone who is poorly suited for at least half of their job. In our experience, an agent should first hire administrative help. This allows the agent to focus on more dollar-productive sales activities such as lead generation, buyer appointments, and listing appointments. Depending on your personal production limits, your first, second, and possibly even your third hires will be talented administrative help. The idea is eventually to reach a point where you are wholly focused on lead generation, listing, and selling while your administrative team handles everything else in your business. Only after reaching that point, when you find you have more sales-oriented work than you can handle alone, do you add staff for sales, specifically a buyer specialist to handle many of the time-consuming tasks and processes of working with buyers.

Some Millionaire Real Estate Agents may opt to make the buyer specialist a "graduated hire" and begin with a licensed showing assistant. This allows them the option of being directly involved in initial consultations, negotiations, and preparing offers and contracts, while avoiding potentially long afternoons escorting buyers around town. By getting help in the selling side, you can increasingly devote your attention to the two most important sales activities in your model, leads and listings. As we have discussed, the more listings you have and market properly, the more buyers you will have. As you increasingly devote your energies to listings, you may need more than one person on the buyer side to handle the selling side of your business. In the end, you will need a talented lead buyer specialist who will eventually manage your other buyer specialists and showing assistants and hold them accountable to the goals of the business.

The next step in your organizational growth will probably be to add more administrative infrastructure if it is not already in place. Your marketing and administrative manager—who may have been your very first hire—is now managing your entire administrative team. That person will help you fill your other future administrative needs: transaction coordinator, telemarketer, listings manager, lead coordinator, assistant, and runner. These hires are added incrementally and in proportion to your sales growth. All the while they have been helping you document and implement systems and identify and implement tools in your business.

The lead coordinator is an interesting piece of the administrative puzzle. This is the person charged with receiving, sourcing, assigning, and tracking your leads through a database. In the beginning, your assistant will probably handle much of the call sourcing (i.e., where did the call come from) and database entry for you while you are working alone. When you have sales help, you, the Millionaire Real Estate Agent, will be personally assigning the leads and tracking conversion rates. Only later, when you have a fully developed sales team, will this become a large enough job for a full- or part-time employee.

The last piece of the puzzle is on the seller side of the business. At some point your lead buyer specialist and any additional buyer specialists will handle almost all the buyer business and your marketing and administrative manager will handle all aspects of your systems and tools. They will be two of your three key points of leverage that you will need to manage actively or, if they are magnificent, with whom you'll consult. All your attention will be on shaping the message behind your lead-generation efforts and handling the seller side of the business. When you find that you still have more seller listings than you can handle alone, you'll hire a listing specialist. Eventually, you could have a team of them and a lead listing specialist who oversees and reports directly to you. This

Basic Job Descriptions for the Organizational Model of the Millionaire Real Estate Agent

AGENT
- Lead-Generation Strategy
- Hire/Fire/Manage
- Train/Coach/Consult
- Meet with Executive Staff (Weekly for Accountability and Strategy)

LEAD LISTING SPECIALIST
- Secure Appointments
- Get Listings
- Weekly Seller Calls
- Negotiate Offers

LEAD BUYER SPECIALIST
- Secure Appointments
- Get Buyer Agreements
- Show and Sell
- Weekly Buyer Calls
- Negotiate Offers

LEAD COORDINATOR
- Receiving
- Sourcing
- Assigning
- Database Entry
- Tracking

MARKETING AND ADMIN. MANAGER
- Lead Generation and Systems Execution
- Communication Systems
- Financial Systems
- Oversee Staff

TELEMARKETER
- Get Lists
- Make Calls
- Get Leads

LISTING MANAGER
- CMA's
- Listing Marketing
- Seller Comm./Admin.

TRANSACTION COORDINATOR
- Contract to Close
- Select and Manage Vendors
- Client Communication

ASSISTANT
- Answer Phone
- Administrative Overflow

RUNNER
- Physical Tasks/Outside Office

Figure 43

is your third key point of leverage. These three people—the marketing and bookkeeping manager, the lead buyer specialist, and the lead listing specialist—will play a large role in helping you become a Millionaire Real Estate Agent.

To get a little more clarity on the roles each of these people will play in your Millionaire Real Estate Agent business, let's take a look at their abbreviated job descriptions. Years ago, we created a detailed list of the 170 tasks related to doing business as a Millionaire Real Estate Agent and to whom in this Organizational Model those tasks fall. While this was great exploration for a high-level understanding of the business, we believe the diagram opposite (Figure 43) is more effective in that it simply lays out the four or five most important job responsibilities of each staff member. True talent, when given responsibilities, will drill down to the details on his own and deliver.

We divide the diagram into three areas to show how the responsibilities are divided between front and back office staff. Your sales team is at the forefront of your business. In the middle is your lead-generation team. Your back office is where the principle administrative and support tasks are handled. When you are ready to step out of your business and let someone else take over, your future CEO will come from the front or middle office personnel—this individual must be an active part of your lead-generation machine because this is where the power of the company comes from.

So you will first add administrative help, then staff for selling, and lastly bring in someone to help you with the seller side of the business. With the exception of the order, the different specific pieces will fall in place rather naturally as your business grows. Figure 44 shows how your organization might grow following the Organizational Model of the Millionaire Real Estate Agent.

The 7th Level (in Figure 44) is a kind of Nirvana for the business person. It represents the place where you can actually step out of the business and start earning passive business income. Later, in the Receive

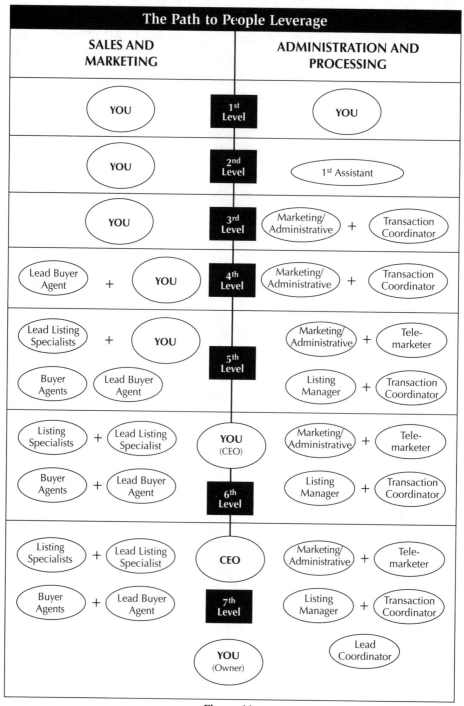

Figure 44

a Million section of this book, we'll discuss in greater detail the process of transitioning your business to the 7th Level.

In my experience, the average person thinks the goal of a business leader is to run a successful business. Well, I'm here to tell you it isn't. That is just the first goal of a businessperson. The ultimate business goal is to have a successful business run by other people! That's what we call having a "7th Level business." Getting there requires you to have loaded your organization with exceptional talent, particularly at the three key positions: marketing and administrative manager, lead buyer specialist, and lead listing specialist.

To sum it up, you are building a three-headed sales production machine. You'll have an administrative team with up to five members. (Your accounting, tax preparation, and filing may be outsourced both to simplify your life and to protect you in case of error.) You'll have a buyer team with three to five members including your lead buyer specialist. And you'll have a seller team with up to two staff members: a lead listing specialist (you in the beginning) and possibly another listing specialist. Every position will have a written job description identifying the core responsibilities of the job and the performance standards you expect.

SEVEN RECRUITING SOURCES

Because Millionaire Real Estate Agents have made a commitment to succeed through others, they will continually need to look for talent. There are seven main sources they use:

1. Ads
2. Allied Resources
3. Job Websites
4. Temporary Employment Agencies
5. Permanent Employment Agencies
6. Other Agents in Your Market Place
7. Real Estate Schools.

The Seven Recruiting Sources: 1–4

1 — ADS

"Immediate opening for assistant to assist real estate executive. You should be an organizer, a fast learner, a positive person, and a great communicator. Good word-processing and computer skills are a must. You'll work in a fast-paced real estate office in ____(City/State). We offer an exciting atmosphere in a people-oriented business. This is not an entry-level position. Your first step is to send your résumé to _____(e-mail) or fax to _____(fax number)."

PLACEMENT SOURCES: Small local newspaper preferred.

2 — ALLIED RESOURCES

"Hi, _____, this is _____ with _____ Realty. The reason I'm calling is to ask for your help. My business is expanding and I am looking to hire an outstanding person to help me take my business to the next level. The kind of person I'm looking for is:_____
_____.

Do you know of anyone who might fit this description? (Wait for answer and then ask for the appropriate means to contact them: Phone number, e-mail, etc.) Thank you for this lead. I really appreciate it. May I also ask you, if you were in my shoes, whom you might call to see if they knew of a good person for this opportunity?"

3 — JOB WEBSITES

Go to your favorite Internet portal (Yahoo.com or Google.com) and search for job sites with the following key words: job site, employment listings, employment connection, job postings, career search, etc.

Local sites, which are typically sponsored by your local newspaper, are best.

4 — TEMPORARY EMPLOYMENT AGENCIES

Hire a temporary employment agency. Go interview three to four temporary agents and choose one or more. These agencies will screen candidates in advance for you. The upside with a temp is you get to try out an individual with no commitment. The downside is the candidates get to work for you with no commitment either, and you may have to try out many to find a good fit (all the while paying more on an hourly basis than you otherwise would). Should you hire someone permanently, be sure to read the fine print as to your costs. You may have to pay their agency one to two months in salary as compensation.

Figure 45

The Millionaire Real Estate Agent

5	**PERMANENT EMPLOYMENT AGENCIES**	Hire a permanent employment agency. Go interview three to four temporary agents and choose one or more. These agencies will screen candidates in advance for you. The upside is that they screen better candidates in general. The downside could be the cost. Should you hire the candidate, you may pay one to two months of their permanent salary to the employment agency.
6	**OTHER AGENTS IN YOUR MARKETPLACE**	Another place to look for talent is in your own marketplace. Look for agents or office staff from other companies that have a solid reputation and might be looking for a career change. Possibly someone looking for: 1. Job stability with growth opportunities 2. Flexible hours 3. Training and experience (new agents)
7	**REAL ESTATE SCHOOLS**	Go teach, make presentations, and have "career opportunity" flyers at all the real estate schools or licensing schools in your area. Finding people brand new to the business has its advantages over hiring people with more experience—the new agents have no bad habits to break.

Figure 46

THE NINE MAJOR COMPENSATION OPTIONS

When you're trying to work out a compensation model that works for your staff and your market, you'll need to consider all your options. The Nine Major Compensation Options takes in all the ways you're likely to compensate your people. Most likely, you'll use a combination of two or more of the options. Let's quickly look at the fundamentals of each option before getting to our recommended compensation philosophies.

> *"The key to keeping great people is to pay them well and be flexible in their lives."*
> Jerry Mahan
> Millionaire Real Estate Agent
> Puyallup, WA
> Sales volume—$93 million

1. Salary

Salary will be the primary source of compensation for your middle office

The Nine Major Compensation Options:
1. Salary
2. Commissions
3. Pay Expenses
4. Bonuses
5. Profit Sharing
6. Retirement Plan
7. Insurance Benefits
8. Vacation Time and Sick Leave
9. Equity Opportunities
And Remember—
Reward What You Expect!

Figure 47

and back office employees. We always recommend being competitive within your local market. Most of your staff positions should be filled for between $25,000 and $50,000, depending on responsibilities and qualifications. Management positions will command more (between $36,000 and $100,000), but you can also be creative and use bonuses or profit sharing to keep your salaries competitive while minimizing your risk. It goes without saying that you need to make sure your bookkeeper is withholding income taxes and social security for all salaried staff members.

2. Commissions

Commission is probably the number one traditional method for compensating sales personnel; however, some companies have successfully experimented with a combination of salaries and either performance-based bonuses or profit sharing. In general, buyer agent commission splits should be 50/50. Should you need to adjust them, your options here include:

- Different commission splits for company-generated leads vs individual-generated leads
- Graduating the commission splits based on what the company earns
- Improving the commission split based on specific goals being met

Whatever method you choose, study it with care and move with caution. Market conditions can change, and talent can exceed expectations, and you never want to discover that your commission structure was so generous it hampered the financial growth of your business. Lastly,

The Millionaire Real Estate Agent

remember that with most commission-based compensation plans, your staff probably will be considered self-employed and neither taxes nor social security need be withheld.

3. Pay Expenses

Here's our rule of thumb on paying expenses: When salaried, pay all work-related expenses. When commissioned, pay some base expenses at most, although you may want to make exceptions for extremely productive staff members. Also, expenses should be approved in advance until your staff has a crystal-clear understanding of the budget, what expenses are acceptable, and what are not.

4. Bonuses

Bonuses can be paid monthly, quarterly, or annually. We favor the last. In March you don't have the luxury of knowing whether or not your year will be profitable. While it may appear to be wildly successful, a market shift could be just around the corner. Look at it this way, when you pay bonuses annually, you always have a firm grasp of your return on the business before paying out any bonuses.

You can base bonuses on criteria such as the staff members meeting their annual goals, helping the company reach its production or financial goals, or contributing to an increase in the company's net profits over the previous year. Whatever the case, bonuses should also be firmly based on a quantifiable goal, preferably one employees can impact directly. Bonuses should also be a preset, meaningful amount ($500, $1,000, $1,200, etc.) or a percentage of the employees' salary.

5. Profit Sharing

Profit sharing is a great method of supplemental compensation. Magical things can happen when your staff is as focused as you are on net profits. They tend to do without unnecessary expenses and police themselves on spending. However, what profit sharing absolutely requires is open books. You will need to disclose the books fully on a regular basis. If this makes you uncomfortable, then you should consider other options.

While profit sharing can happen on a monthly or quarterly basis, we strongly recommend an annual plan. Ideally, it should be based on a percentage of your net profits before or after tax. Staff members should also be with the company for six months or more before being allowed to participate in the program. It is hard to justify sharing annual profits with a staff member who has been with you for only a couple of months. It takes at least six months to make a significant contribution, especially when you are new to the business.

In the example outlined in Figure 48, you'll note that profit sharing caps at 50 percent of any staff person's salary. Keeping talent is important, but you also don't need to overpay. Paying someone 50 percent above market value can be an incredible recruiting and retention tool, but anything above that mark and you're simply being too generous. If someone deserves to make more than that in profit sharing, maybe you should consider option number nine, equity opportunities. Lastly, it is important that you clearly define the rules governing your profit sharing from the beginning. As with the example in Figure 48, rules should be clear and definitive.

6. Retirement Plan

Retirement plans are tricky because, with the exception of equity, it is one of the few types of compensation that lasts beyond the actual period of employment. We recommend starting small and simple because "take aways" are no fun!

As with profit sharing, an employee should be with the company for at least six months to qualify for the plan. Start with a nonmatching 401(k) or a simple IRA. Consider stipulating that any bonuses or profit sharing

A Profit Sharing Plan Example

Time period will be from January 1 through December 31 of each calendar year.

Must be with the company six months to participate in the plan.

Any loss carried forward applies indefinitely.

Losses are never forgiven.

Employee(s) may choose between their current bonus plan or the
profit share plan, but not both.

Profit share dollars not to exceed 50% of base salary.

Profit share dollars to be paid at year-end.

Should employee leave prior to year-end for any reason, the profit share
for that year would be waived.

Current company owners will not participate in the plan.

Creation of the Profit Sharing Pool

1st $100,000 net profits	=	0%	Profit Share
2nd $200,000 net profits	=	5%	Profit Share
Above $300,000 net profits	=	10%	Profit Share

Distribution of the Profit Sharing Pool

Each employee receives:

> 1 unit per year with the company
>
> 1 unit per $1,000 of salary

EXAMPLE:

a. John has been with the company 2 years	1 x 2 years	=	2 units
b. John makes $36,000 per year	1 x 36K	=	+ 36 units
c. John's TOTAL UNITS		=	38 units
d. Total units of all people in the company	380 units		
e. John has 10% of all the units	38 / 380	=	10%

f. John receives 10% of the pool, not to exceed 50% of his base salary.

EXAMPLE:

> $300,000 Profit = $10,000 = $1,000 to John
>
> $400,000 Profit = $20,000 = $2,000 to John
>
> $500,000 Profit = $30,000 = $3,000 to John

Figure 48

Earn a Million

will be considered contributions to the plan. Also consider delayed vesting and how nonvesting might occur on any company contribution. Vesting may also be affected by the legal structure of your company, so make sure you do your homework before putting anything in writing.

With retirement plans and insurance benefits, by far the easiest, most cost-effective way to provide these forms of compensation is to outsource them through a professional employer organization (PEO), which can offer excellent standardized retirement benefits. A PEO virtually "employs" thousands of employees and has the ability to negotiate high-quality investment, insurance, and retirement plans, which are almost always better than you can offer for a similar cost. They also provide a broad range of payroll and human resource administration while limiting your liabilities as an employer.

7. Insurance Benefits

As with retirement plans, we recommend exploring a PEO or other outsourced group to handle this aspect of compensation. PEOs can negotiate from a position of strength since they represent thousands of virtual employees. Most, but not all, will also have options for handling payroll, since deducting from salary is the preferred method of covering the discounted costs of these benefits.

No matter what route you go on insurance, we recommend a ninety-day period before employees can take advantage of this benefit. Lastly, the truth is, you never know how good a policy is until you have to use it, so be very careful when deciding on a plan. This is one area in which you don't want to cut corners or go bargain hunting.

8. Vacation Time and Sick Leave

Vacation time is a fairly standard form of compensation. Most companies give employees two weeks (ten days) of paid vacation each year. We recommend that employees be with the business for six months before being eligible for paid vacation. They will then get one week in the second half of the year. If this presents a problem for a new hire, you can work around it by granting time off without pay. (For most people the core issue is the time, not the pay.) You don't want to miss an opportunity to hire talent because someone has a trip to Disney World scheduled a couple of months after his/her hire date.

You can consider accruing vacation time on a monthly basis, as well. This is usually accrued in combination with sick leave and simply called PTO (paid time off). There should be a cap on vacation days that can be carried over from year to year. Employees will probably expect to be paid for unused vacation time when they leave, so plan for it and set your policy up front. Lastly, vacation time should increase gradually each year an employee stays with your company. Reward loyalty.

The standards for sick leave are a little more cut and dry. Generally speaking, employees need to be with you for six months to qualify and get six paid days of sick leave each year. You might want to let sick days accrue with a cap (eighteen days is fairly common), but you are not required to pay for unused sick days unless they are rolled into a PTO program.

Maternity and paternity leave (which is becoming more and more common) are options that should reflect your personal business. Some companies grant this specialized time off as time off without pay. Other companies pay a percentage of the employee's salary. You'll need to figure out what works best for your business in your market. Also, be sure approval of time off is obtained in advance (other than for emergencies). You need to know who will be available and when. This is how businesses are run.

9. Equity Opportunities

When we talk about equity opportunities, we're rarely talking about sharing equity in your main real estate sales business. Equity opportunities are usually about new ownership opportunities, real estate investments, or companies that may spin off of your business. Real estate investments are probably the most common form of opportunity you can offer your staff, but partnerships in other businesses like title and mortgage companies are not uncommon. Lastly, equity opportunities should not be handed out lightly. Team members should have to earn the right to participate through major contributions to your team over time.

SUMMING UP COMPENSATION

To wrap up our discussion of compensation we've supplied the following graphic (Figure 49), which should help you organize your thinking on these matters. You have three distinct areas of your business team, and each will demand a different kind of compensation. Just remember to hire talent, reward what you expect, and hold your investment in people accountable to results.

The fundamental principle behind the Organizational Model of the Millionaire Real Estate Agent is to find, hire, and retain talent. Looking for and identifying talent is always foremost in your people goals, no matter how spectacular your staff may be. This idea of the never-ending talent search is called "top grading"; you never know when you may lose talent in your organization, so whenever great talent becomes available, you would be wise to find a place for them in your company. More than once I've left a friend's office and said, "If you ever decide to part ways with _____, you let me know. I'll make room for you in my company!"

When you aren't having fun or are feeling overwhelmed, it is time to find someone to help with your "other" jobs. You don't have enough arms and legs to do everything all the time. Everyone should aspire to having an assistant to avoid burning out. And the leverage that talented people bring to your company is the fastest, surest way to continue up the path to becoming a Millionaire Real Estate Agent.

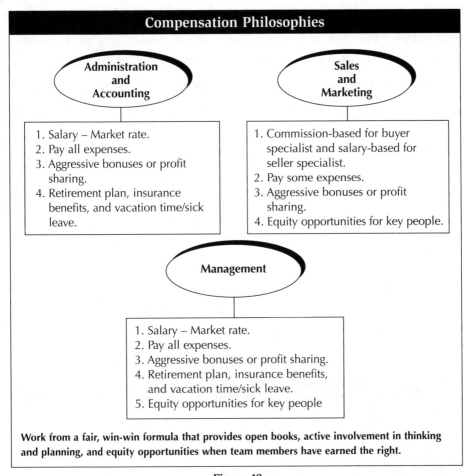

Figure 49

CONCLUSION

So let's recap what you've learned in Earn a Million. Together, we've walked through the four fundamental business models high-achieving real estate agents employ in their business—the Economic Model, the Lead-Generation Model, the Budget Model, and the Organizational Model. First, we took a high-level look at them for a general understanding of the guiding principles, and then we examined them in light of the specific goals of the Millionaire Real Estate Agent.

These models should be the foundation of your business. Like Buffett and his four volumes of *Security Analysis*, we encourage you to become a student of these models before you personalize them for your own style and market. Applying creativity from a position of experience is much more productive than adding creativity first and then seeing whether or not it will fly.

As mentioned previously, in our experience the transition between earning and netting a million is quite seamless. These Four Models of the Millionaire Real Estate Agent will continue to serve you as you move from earning to netting a million and beyond. What we hope you'll take away from Earn a Million is the need to plant these systems squarely at the center of your real estate sales business.

In the next stage, Net a Million, we'll address the sixteen primary issues that will affect your ability to ride these models all the way to your goal—a million dollars a year in annual personal income.

POINTS TO REMEMBER: The Millionaire Real Estate Agent Models

■ Earn a Million is just a step on the path to Net a Million. So begin with the end in mind and adopt the goals and models of Net a Million.

■ A team of highly trained specialists delivers a consistently and predictably higher level of fiduciary service.

■ The Millionaire Real Estate Agent Economic Model tracks GCI (gross commission income or revenue), COS (cost of sales), operating expenses, and net income.

- Your goals are to achieve: $2.4 million in GCI, $700,000 in COS, $700,000 in operating expenses, and $1 million in net income.

- Your average sales price (GCI per closing) determines the number of closed sales necessary to reach your GCI goal.

- Your conversion rates (appointments to listing agreements and listing agreements to sales) determine the number of appointments needed to achieve your closed sales.

■ The Millionaire Real Estate Agent Lead-Generation Model tracks the prospecting and marketing activities necessary to generate the appropriate number of leads and appointments.

- It is all driven by your contact database of Met and Haven't Met names.

- It should be marketing-based (leveraged activities) and prospecting-enhanced (relationship building) to achieve optimal results.

- Know your lead-generation ratios. With 33 Touch you can expect two closed deals (one a repeat and one a referral) for every twelve people in the Met portion of your database. With 12 Direct marketing, you can expect one closed sale for every fifty people in the Haven't Met portion of your database.

- Know your lead-generation costs. Each sale from the Met portion of your database will cost between $99 and $198 to generate. Each sale from the Haven't Met portion of your database will cost between $300 and $600 to generate.

■ The Millionaire Real Estate Agent Budget Model helps you track and evaluate the investments you make in your business.

- Know your cost of sale and keep it less than 30% of your GCI.

- Focus on the Big Two of operating expenses: Salaries and Lead-Generation. They account for more than 72% of your total expenses.

■ The Millionaire Real Estate Agent Organizational Model clarifies the division of labor and responsibilities on your team.

- There are three kinds of help: administrative, buyer (buyer specialists), and seller (listing specialists).

- Add administrative help first, then buyer specialists, and, finally, a listing specialist.

- Follow the Organizational Model to the 7th Level where you get to step out of the day-to-day business.

- Use the Seven Recruiting Sources —they all work.

- Understand the Nine Major Compensation Options you have and be sure to reward what you expect.

NET A
MILLION

"All things are difficult before they're easy."

Thomas Fuller

Figure 1

The thought of big success is exciting. The thought of the challenges that might be encountered along the way to big success can be frightening. And, frankly, even paralyzing. Interestingly enough, for many people it's quite possibly this fear of the unknown that sometimes holds them back. It's as if they don't know what they don't know, and it's this lack of knowledge that throws them for a loop. On your way to implementing your four business models, you will discover that things don't always go as planned. Understanding these models is one thing—successfully implementing them is another. Models tell you what to do and how to do it, but they don't always address the challenges you'll face as you try to implement them. This chapter is about the sixteen issues you're likely to face as you build and live with these models. Our hope is that, by making you aware of these issues, the aspect of fear can be removed, and you can get excited about the journey you're on. We've discovered that when you get clarity about what you will encounter and how to handle it successfully, your fear and anxiety will be drastically diminished. In fact, you could simply say, "When I get clear—I lose my fear." With this theme in mind, let's jump into the issues you will likely come across on your way to earning and ultimately netting a million.

IMPLEMENTING THE MODELS

As we pointed out earlier, the transition from Earn a Million to Net a Million is fluid. Both stages drive off the same fundamental models. Following and implementing those models will get you to Earn a Million; however, it's the mastering of these models that can take you all the way to Net a Million. And for someone who can successfully implement and master these models, business can get very thrilling because they'll soon discover they have no known achievement limits for their career.

The ability to conquer these sixteen issues makes all the difference for those who want to lift their business to the Net a Million stage. In this section we not only identify those issues, we also explore the best ways to deal with them. In Figure 2, the Issues In Between, we categorize these sixteen key issues into their five principle areas.

Three of the five areas—Leads, Listings, and Leverage—should be familiar to you by now as the Three L's. The issues highlighted under these three are golden and represent disciplines that can help your business at any stage. The fourth, Money, delves into budgetary disciplines that can help you be more businesslike and consistently bring more to the bottom line. The last area, You, addresses two specific challenges that you will have to overcome on a personal level to reach your greatest potential.

The Issues In Between Earn a Million and Net a Million

Leads

1. Sustaining a solid lead-generation program that emphasizes marketing and consistently increases the number of leads.
2. Tracking and converting leads through others.
3. Protecting your lead-generation focus time.
4. Weighing your options—the process of discovering what works and doesn't work for you.

Listings

5. Knowing the minimum number of seller listings you must list each month.
6. Listing the minimum number each month.
7. Getting sellers to accept the team concept.
8. Consistently marketing your seller listings for more leads.

Leverage

9. Making the time to learn and implement R/T/C/K (the Recruit/Train/Consult/Keep process).
10. Hiring "capacity" vs "cul-de-sac" talent.
11. Achieving accountability to the right standards.
12. Creating teamwork with "Rock and Role."
13. Combining quality service and quantity service.

Money

14. Sticking to the Budget Model and controlling your costs.

You

15. Staying focused on the 20 percent.
16. Counterbalancing your life to maintain your energy at a high level.

Figure 2

LEADS

As you move toward mastering lead generation, you will encounter four issues that may become obstacles between you and your highest levels of success. When you overcome these four challenges, there should be no limit to how many leads your real estate business can generate.

1. SUSTAINING A SOLID LEAD-GENERATION PROGRAM THAT EMPHASIZES MARKETING AND CONSISTENTLY INCREASES THE NUMBER OF LEADS

> *"I anticipate the market, not just react to it. I have learned marketing techniques and learned what pulls better."*
>
> Gregg Neuman
> Millionaire Real Estate Agent
> San Diego, CA
> Sales volume—$113 million

The biggest challenge you will face in building your sales business to a high level is continuing to focus on lead generation no matter how many leads you have or how busy you become. Once a high number of leads is being generated, there is a tendency to settle for that number and then devote more time and energy on servicing that business. This is a fairly common situation. Agents and their teams become stretched trying to handle their existing business and simply "take their eye off the ball" and neglect their lead-generation program.

You could view the idea of lead generation as being something like a shark. For one thing, in the ocean of real estate sales disciplines, lead generation is most definitely at the top of the food chain—there is nothing that has greater potential to impact your business. But lead generation is also like a shark in that it can never stop. As you may know, in order for most sharks to breathe, they must keep moving, which forces water through their gills. If they stop, they drown. Similarly, a lead-generation program must always be active; when it is idle for any length of time, it tends to lose its strength. In our experience, many agents who shift their focus between generating leads and servicing the leads tend to go through an up-and-down cycle of activity and cash flow. When they have lots of business and their income seems secure, they focus on service and administration. And when there is not enough business and their income is at risk, they shift their focus back to lead generation and try to re-create the momentum that caused them to shift their focus in the first place. Simply put, this is not a formula for long-term stability and success.

Millionaire Real Estate Agents never lose focus on lead generation. For them, lead generation always comes first. They understand that, to be most effective, lead generation needs to be systematic, consistent, and sustained. It never stops and never rests. Dealing with today's business should never take precedence over growing tomorrow's business.

Since time is a critical issue (especially for top-producing real estate agents), it is best to shift lead-generation activities largely toward marketing. As we discussed in the Lead-Generation Model, marketing is simply more time-efficient and therefore more leveraged than prospecting. Marketing is at its best and most effective when it is database-driven. Databases are built through acquaintances, captured leads, referrals, or targeted lists. This is really a pragmatic approach. In a few hours a week, Millionaire Real Estate Agents can supervise and shape their marketing message, which reaches as many people as they can amass in their

> *"I used to just throw mud at the wall; now I've narrowed my promotions. When you track your leads, you know what is working and where to spend your money. When you try a new program, track it for six months or a year. You have to give it a chance."*
>
> Bill Ryan
> Millionaire Real Estate Agent
> Chandler, AZ
> Sales volume—$54 million

database. And if you're using the 8 x 8, 33 Touch, and 12 Direct programs previously outlined, you'll be able systematically to deliver that message to your chosen audience. Without a doubt, this is the most vital discipline for a prosperous real estate sales business. It must be done.

If prospecting is used to enhance your marketing (which we recommend), you can delegate most of it to others in your organization: telemarketers, listing specialists, and showing assistants or buyer agents. At the end of the day, however, the most consistent, efficient, and predicable results will be achieved through marketing. The Millionaire Real Estate Agent must become a master of creating and sustaining a marketing-based and prospecting-enhanced lead-generation program.

2. TRACKING AND CONVERTING LEADS THROUGH OTHERS

Once leads are generated, they must be followed up on and turned into appointments. Those appointments should generate a predictable number of signed buyer and seller representation agreements. Working under those agreements can then efficiently lead you to written purchase contracts that close. By this point in your career, you have well mastered this process of turning leads into closed business. You have an instinct for it and have enhanced those natural abilities by acquiring over time the appropriate scripts and skills. Furthermore, you have a sense of urgency when you go about it, a nose for opportunity, and a sense about timing and readiness. All these skills and abilities are born of your experience, learning, and enthusiasm for the work you do. Now, to navigate successfully the path from Earn a Million to Net a Million, you will need to get those same great results through your staff. And, while

> *"We now have a lead coordinator to handle, assign, and track all of our calls."*
> Ronnie and Cathy Matthews
> Millionaire Real Estate Agents
> Houston, TX
> Sales volume—$99.5 million

this is not an easy thing to do, it is being done every day by an increasing number of top agents.

It begins by believing that your results can, in fact, be duplicated through others. But you conquered that MythUnderstanding long ago, right? You understand that a talented team can actually provide better service systems and standards. Knowing this, your first task is to make sure the right people—true talent—are turning your leads into closed business. Taking the time up front to identify, recruit, and train talent is crucial to the success of your lead-conversion program.

But, understand this: Hiring talent is not your only issue. Ultimately, your ongoing responsibility in this regard will be to assure proper tracking and converting. And this brings us back to the engine that drives this process—your database. As the leads come in, you'll need a lead-tracking process in place that is consistently used and accurate. This process must ensure that the lead is captured (Who is it and how do we contact her?), sourced (Where did it come from?), assigned (Who will follow up on the lead?), and stored (Where can we find it?) in the database. It really doesn't matter who in your organization handles this, but it must be done.

With this system in place, you'll be able effectively to train and consult with your staff on lead conversion that meets your standards. With this data in hand, you can more easily set performance standards and hold your team members accountable to them. And the real beauty of this system is that you will always absolutely know what is happening in your business—who is getting the job done and who is not. When the numbers are always in the open, it is much harder to hide behind excuses.

Over the years, I've worked with hundreds of agents whose businesses were experiencing trouble, the cause of which the agents simply could not identify. What these agents discovered by assessing their systems was that they really didn't know who was performing and who was not. Because they didn't really know how many leads their people were handling, they had no system for accurately measuring performance. In the end, after putting a tracking process in place, many of these agents came to find out that some staff members were burning lead opportunities through inability, lack of focus, cherrypicking, or, in some cases, laziness. Needless, to say, once they discovered the power and benefits of tracking the lead-conversion process, these agents never turned back.

An agent once told us in a consulting call that she didn't have time to follow up on all the leads that were coming in. She said she had stacks of notes and lead sheets on her desk filled with names of people who had called. We suggested that she imagine those stacks as piles of money that were burning. It was her money in those piles, and she had just lit them with a match. She immediately got the picture, hired two buyer specialists, and had her marketing director put in place a lead-tracking and -conversion system. She no longer has stacks of money burning on her desk.

Careful attention to tracking and lead conversion is one of the core disciplines of the Millionaire Real Estate Agent. These skills are vital if you want to build the kind of high-performance team capable of making the journey from Earn a Million to Net a Million!

3. PROTECTING YOUR LEAD-GENERATION FOCUS TIME

While time really isn't money, it is convertible into money. Ultimately, lead generation is the most dollar-productive activity you can do for your real estate sales business. For those who are seeking real estate success at a very high level, lead-generation time must be considered the most important time on their calendar. And as such it will need to be jealously guarded and protected. Because life seems to love to offer up the unexpected, guarding this time is never as easy to do as it may seem.

As your business grows, you will begin to sense that you have become its CEO. Well, in truth, you are. The problem with being a CEO is that you might be pulled back into

> *"My goals are fueled by my dreams. I defend and protect those dreams from distractions and from interruptions from other people."*
>
> Tim Wood
> Millionaire Real Estate Agent
> Big Bear Lake, CA
> Sales volume—$38 million

and entangled by day-to-day administrative, service, and personnel issues. If allowed to, people and problems can chew up your time and drain your energy. And then you will find yourself in the trap of managing your business instead of leading and building it. When this happens, one of the first things always to hit the back burner for most agents is lead generation. Why? Because when people don't truly understand the importance of lead generation it can masquerade as an "optional activity" rather than as the core foundational discipline it is. In my opinion, having learned from my own errors and the mistakes of thousands of agents I've worked with, this is something you should never allow to happen.

To avoid this pitfall, you need to make a commitment to block off substantial, regular time in your calendar and devote it to lead genera-

> *"My goal is to do more volume in less time with a better net. The key for me is to be disciplined in my time management and lead follow-up."*
>
> John Toye
> Millionaire Real Estate Agent
> Westland, MI
> Sales volume—$39.2 million

tion. This is the time you use to prospect, follow up on existing leads, and develop and implement marketing plans. To be able to do this, you must hold others accountable for handling the administrative, service, and personnel issues wherever possible. Delegate, train, and consult, but let others handle all the details. This will allow you time to focus on what is ultimately most important for your business—lead generation.

4. WEIGHING YOUR OPTIONS— THE PROCESS OF DISCOVERING WHAT WORKS AND DOESN'T WORK FOR YOU

Our experience and research has taught us that almost any form of marketing or prospecting can be effective—just not everywhere or for everyone. Lead generation is an art as well as a science. Successful lead generators pay attention and become very knowledgeable over time about what

> *"Use your strengths and natural abilities to build your business. I was in radio and TV for years, so I write my own copy and do my own radio commercials."*
>
> Russell Shaw
> Millionaire Real Estate Agent
> Phoenix, AZ
> Sales volume—$50.6 million

works and what does not work for them in their market. This is seldom initially obvious. Their understanding is the by-product of much learning, practice, and, most important, attention to results. Lead-generating success is not purely creative. Like so many other aspects of this business, it requires a system.

So many agents do spur-of-the-moment, idea-of-the-month marketing and prospecting. They adopt new lead-generation programs from the latest, greatest, best-and-most-creative-idea-ever seminar, or else they reinvent their program based on some can't-miss, pays-for-itself instant success program. Then they are off and running, spending money, discarding previous strategies, and going whole hog on their latest inspiration. While I understand this kind of behavior—marketing can be fun and exciting and downright entertaining to explore—it is simply not the way Millionaire Real Estate Agents go about their lead generation.

They always begin with the tried and true. They do that first. And they do it with a plan, a budget, a message, and a target audience. They don't discount a program that does not yield immediate results nor do they fall wholeheartedly in love with one that does. The ones who look like marketing and prospecting geniuses do it consistently over time and meticulously track and source their leads. They then weigh the costs of their plan against their net results so that they can get a clear sense of their cost per lead. Tracking, sourcing, and costing over time provides the information needed to judge accurately the merits of a particular method. Only after the Lead-Generation Model has been practiced and analyzed do they start adding creativity and tweaking the model according to their past results and new information. Their goals are simple. They want to discover the formula in a particular market that yields the greatest number of leads for the most reasonable amount of money. For all its creativity and art, the part of marketing and prospecting that is science always rules. This sort of system, when applied to a variety of techniques over time, will help you discover the best ways to promote the strengths of your business in your particular area.

Millionaire Real Estate Agents are willing and continuous students of the Lead-Generation Model and their local lead-generation game.

> *"For me, it has to be quality. I only advertise in color. I track my results and as soon as I started advertising in color I got 28 percent more responses to the same ad in color vs black and white. That has remained steady."*
>
> Gregg Neuman
> Millionaire Real Estate Agent
> San Diego, CA
> Sales volume—$113 million

LISTINGS

Millionaire Real Estate Agents know, without any doubt, that seller listings are the name of their game. Seller listings bring exposure, buyer leads, and more seller listing leads. In moving to Net a Million, understanding the power of seller listings and how to leverage it becomes more and more important. To help you take the seller part of your real estate sales business to the highest level, we've identified four key challenges you are likely to encounter. First, you'll have to know the minimum number of seller listings you need to list each month; then you'll have to organize your business approach to accomplish that feat; next, you'll need to get your seller clients to accept the team concept; lastly, you must consistently market your seller listings to get more leads.

5. KNOWING THE MINIMUM NUMBER OF SELLER LISTINGS YOU MUST LIST EACH MONTH

The Economic Model of the Millionaire Real Estate Agent shows how to work backward from your desired net income to your GCI goals. From there, it shows you the number of listings you'll need to close and even how many appointments you'll need to make to reach your goals. However, the real estate business is cyclical and markets shift. So while the fundamental Economic Model remains sound, the key numbers are usually in a state of flux. What this means is that it will take on your part considerable attention to current market trends and conditions to know how many listings you'll need to take in any particular month to meet

> *"I got very serious about listing in the early '90s. I became the top lister in my area, and it has been the foundation of my growth.*
> *Our target is to take at least twenty listings every month."*
> Rachel DeHanas
> Millionaire Real Estate Agent
> Waldorf, MD
> Sales volume—$52 million

your goals. In the classic words of Wayne Gretzky, you must "skate to where the puck will be."

The variables you must watch are made very clear from the model: the percent of appointments that will generate a listing and the percent of listings that will in turn sell. For example, a hot sellers' market generally leads to a higher percentage of listings that sell in less time and for a better price. But it may also create more FSBOs (For Sale By Owner) and entice more agents actively to work the listing side of the business, which can undermine your listing efforts. Some of this is predictable across the board, but most of these factors are driven by local market conditions that you will need to understand as fluently as your native tongue. If you stay on top of those key conversion ratios (appointments to listing agreements and listings taken to sales), you'll be better prepared to anticipate and react to market shifts. And you'll also be able to take the appropriate action (increase the number of listing appointments, for instance) to keep your income steady. The length of time the average home sits on the market will also have a telling effect on your net income if it is not accounted for in your goal tracking. When homes stay on the market longer, you may need to take more at the "right price" to keep your income on track. If listings are selling quickly, you'll have to speed up your marketing so you have the time to get the desired additional leads that marketing your listings usually provides. All of this adds up to an emphasis on attention to the key variables in your business. As many a Little Leaguer has discovered the hard way, when you take your eye off the ball, it is as likely to hit you in the nose as it is to land in your glove.

6. LISTING THE MINIMUM NUMBER EACH MONTH

What distinguishes the highest real estate sales business achievers from the rest is their insistence on hitting their goals. Now that they know what the number is, they know they have to hit it. They bring amazing urgency, persistence, and tenacity to their efforts. For them, there are no excuses, no hiding places, and no "victim behavior." Goal pursuit, for them, becomes very black and white—goals are met or they are not met.

Vince Lombardi summed it up well when he said, "Winning is not a sometime thing: it's an all-the-time thing. You don't win once in a while; you don't do the right thing once in a while; you do them right all the time. Winning is a habit. Unfortunately, so is losing." For high achievers, reaching their seller-listings-taken goals is the only habit they'll accept.

These real estate agents deal with failure as a temporary setback on the path to reaching and exceeding their goals. They don't ignore failure; they learn from it and make a commitment not to repeat next time around the same mistakes that may have caused it. This kind of tough-minded approach is the stuff of uncommon accomplishment.

When you know the right number, hitting that mark becomes the focus of the entire team. I believe in sharing goals because when your team shares your goals, synergy and teamwork begin to show up. So get into the habit of communicating your seller listing goals loudly, committing to them openly, tracking progress toward them with your team on a regular basis, and, not to be forgotten, celebrating your victories. Millionaire Real Estate Agents understand the power of making your goals public and then celebrating them as a team. One agent related, "My goal last year was $100 million in sales volume; we hit that, so I took sixteen of my staff on cruises!" She decided to set that expectation again the next year and reported that halfway through the year, even though the market had slowed down, her numbers were up over the previous year. That's the power of setting goals as a team and celebrating them together.

On the opposite side of the coin is accountability. When performance lags and seller listing goals are not being met, these high achievers maintain their standards and hold their staff accountable to their goals. After lead generation (the first L), meeting your monthly seller listing goal (the second L) is the most critical aspect of your business, and this is one area where high achievers allow themselves actively to step back into the day-to-day business if that is what it takes to make things right. When the game is on the line, they jump in and lead by example.

Meeting your monthly seller listing goal is a critical priority and a major preoccupation. Your personal tenacity, your public commitment to those goals, and your willingness to reward people and hold them accountable for those goals are the keys to getting the number of seller listings necessary to achieving your net income goals on a consistent basis.

7. Getting Sellers to Accept the Team Concept

Historically, the real estate business for so long was a personal sales enterprise with service being delivered by an individual agent. Consumers have come to expect real estate agents to deliver the "personal" service themselves, and the industry is still largely focused on real estate service delivered in such a way. The truth is that the concept of the buyer and seller being serviced by a team of individuals, instead of a single agent, has come in and out of fashion in the industry. Whether it is in or out, our experience has taught us that the best real estate sales businesses employ sales teams with specialized administrative support. If you remember the conclusions drawn from the "my clients will work only with me" MythUnderstanding, you understand that, if they know what to do, these specialized teams can actually deliver a higher standard of service and do it more consistently than a single real estate agent forced to operate as a generalist. Knowing this to be true, your team's job becomes to prepare the proper scripts and dialogues for all seller listing presentations that, when used, will convince the seller of the benefits of the team concept.

Your value proposition then becomes that of the surgeon who, surrounded by qualified specialists, appears only when needed. Would you really want a surgeon who, in addition to performing the operation, handled your check-in at the receptionist desk, processed your insurance paperwork, and called you to remind you of your next visit? Lawyers, doctors, and most professionals all tend to work from the belief that the best services are provided by a team of specialists led by the head specialist. What you and your team must communicate to your clients is that they can enjoy this same level of professional service and attention from your team.

The scripts and dialogues you use for this should be part of your training. Everyone on your team who is part of the lead-generation process needs to understand how to communicate effectively this team approach as part of your value proposition. Your team will in essence hand off the client to the next specialist as the transaction moves along. It then becomes a matter of organizing your team so that they all have a backup when help is needed, and that the client has a primary point of contact to give them a sense of continuity during the process. The ultimate goal of all this is not simply to satisfy your clients' expectations; rather the specialized team should focus on regularly "wowing" clients and generating the kind of word-of-mouth testimonies that drive a strong referral business.

8. Consistently Marketing Your Seller Listings for More Leads

Leveraging the marketing of your seller listings to generate buyer listings can sometimes be forgotten in a hot sellers' market. After all, the primary reason we market the listing is to have it sell for the appropriate price in the right time frame. And we have powerful tools to do this with: yard signs, advertisements, just listed postcards, etc. Through Multiple

Listings Services (MLSs), the real estate industry has established a powerful marketing infrastructure where information on new listings can be quickly and efficiently shared with every licensed real estate agent member. Having complete information about your seller listing disseminated to all the active agents in your market leads to more showings and the greater likelihood of that listing selling.

However, in order to meet your big financial goals, the proper marketing of seller listings cannot just be about getting these listings sold. It is extremely important that this marketing also generate more buyer and seller leads, which you then capture and follow up on in a systematic fashion. When real estate markets get hot and listings sell in a matter of days, rather than weeks, many agents tend to focus entirely on getting their listings sold and forget that the listing is also a marketing vehicle. It is an easy mistake to make when you're receiving multiple offers in a short period of time and focusing on representing the sellers' best interests. This is when your systems need to protect you from your own get-the-house-sold-as-quickly-as-possible instincts.

As we've already covered, every house you list should have a marketing checklist attached (see Earn a Million, Figure 17) that you and your team follow regardless of the market. This marketing process should continue all the way through the offer-pending period and will, at times, even serve to protect your sellers with backup offers. Even if that marketing generates inquiries after the sale of the house, those leads can be captured, handed off to your buyer assistants, or redirected to your other listings. Remember, in the Economic Model of the Millionaire Real Estate Agent, half of your business could be composed of buyer leads you capture from your seller listing program. This acquisition of buyer leads needs to be thoroughly systematic and absolutely consistent in your business. Why? As we discussed earlier, your marketing machine never stops and never rests. Because if it does, it loses its effectiveness, and your business becomes too vulnerable to market shifts.

LEVERAGE

On the road to earning and then netting a million, you're going to experience a variety of leverage issues. Hiring people is easy; however, bringing talented people into your business to work with you is never as easy as you might think. When taking leverage to the highest level, here are the five issues you're most likely to confront: making time to learn and implement R/T/C/K (the Recruit/Train/Consult/Keep process); hiring "capacity" vs "cul-de-sac" talent; achieving accountability to the right standards; creating teamwork with "rock and role"; and combining quality service with quantity service.

9. MAKING THE TIME TO LEARN AND IMPLEMENT THE R/T/C/K (RECRUIT/TRAIN/CONSULT/KEEP) PROCESS

The biggest people challenge you'll have is this: As busy as you are, you'll still have to find time to learn and put into place the R/T/C/K (Recruit/Train/Consult/Keep) process. If you are going to hire someone, learn to hire the absolute right person for the job. Someone who can do the job, solve difficult problems, and think at a high level. If you're going to hire a truly talented person, you'll also need to learn how to train and consult that individual to be effective. And if you're going to hire, train,

> *"Delegating and letting go was difficult in the beginning, but I really like it now. Jack and I take trips for two or three weeks at a time. The business keeps going, and no one knows we are not here."*
>
> Rachel DeHanas
> Millionaire Real Estate Agent
> Waldorf, MD
> Sales volume—$52 million

and consult someone, then you've invested a lot of time and energy in that person's development and you'll surely want to learn how to keep him/her. There are ample courses out there on how to do this effectively, but your challenge will be making the time to go take them.

Remember the old truth we quoted earlier, "If you don't have an assistant, you are one?" Well, there is another adage that goes hand in hand with that one, "If you have an assistant who can't get the job done, you'll eventually get the job back." When you learn R/T/C/K correctly, you don't get the job back.

Surprisingly, working with agents over the years, I've witnessed amazing mental gymnastics as agents tried hard to justify not having time to learn R/T/C/K. It takes time to learn something, more time to implement it, and even longer to approach mastery of it. Period. End of discussion. The irony is that R/T/C/K are the kind of skills that, once learned, can save you an enormous amount of time over the rest of your life. When you are able to recruit and retain talented individuals, you will no longer be faced regularly with the number one headache for real estate employers—turnover! The turnover rate in our industry is simply phenomenal, and when you consider that it takes at least three to four months to find and recruit good people (and longer to get them performing to your standards) justifying anything less than mastery of R/T/C/K becomes very hard to defend. If this doesn't ring true, please revisit our discussion of talent in Earn a Million, specifically Figure 21 and Figure 22: The Cost of a Bad Hire and The Opportunity of a Great Hire. Can you really afford not to master R/T/C/K?

And be prepared; the truth is, during this R/T/C/K learning and implementing period of your life, your world will be a little out of balance—no way around it. Why? You will not only be doing all your work but also learning a completely new set of skills. Then, after learning it, you will be doing all your work and then actually R/T/C/K-ing a new person. Is it worth it? Yes. If you will stay diligent and really learn the skills and then really apply what you know.

The worst possible result of not mastering R/T/C/K is what I call "turnover turmoil." When you haven't properly learned or implemented R/T/C/K, your business will be subject to the same turnover rates that we so often see in the real estate industry at large. And when people come and go, it creates an atmosphere among your team of "you don't know what you're doing around here," and eventually everyone leaves. This type of turmoil is all too common and can just plain wear you out along with everyone you're associated with. When you recruit and retain talent in your key positions, your organization gets grounded in their stability.

As we've said before, talent has a way of paying for itself. It pays for itself in terms of your time and your money invested. R/T/C/K pays for itself in the same way. When you invest time and energy to learn and implement it, you'll be rewarded in spades.

So remember these key points:

1. Learn to recruit talent (the right person for the job).
2. Learn to train them to do the job.
3. Learn to consult them to do the job at a high level.
4. Learn to keep them.
5. Invest time to R/T/C/K so your investments of time and money pay off with excellent leverage and the growth that will follow.

"The important thing is to hire good staff. I hire slowly and very carefully. I'm looking for attitude, integrity, and skill. I can teach skill, so I really focus on attitude and integrity."

Cristina Martinez
Millionaire Real Estate Agent
San Jose, CA
Sales volume—$136.3 million

10. Hiring "Capacity" Talent vs "Cul-de-sac" Talent

Although it would be natural to assume that talent is talent, you would be mistaken if you thought that. Talent is not just talent. As you begin to hire more than one person for your team,

> *"The biggest mistakes we make are to hire too quickly and take too long to fire. You really can't change people."*
>
> Allan Domb
> Millionaire Real Estate Agent
> Philadelphia, PA
> Sales volume—$135 million

you will soon discover that there are broadly two types of talent: "capacity" and "cul-de-sac."

"Capacity" talent is someone who can do not only the current job really well, but who also has the desire and ability (thus the capacity) to learn and take on new tasks and responsibilities. The person has the desire and ability plus the intelligence to grow beyond the basic job description. He/She can "plus" it.

"Cul-de-sac" talent is someone who can do the current job really well, but who does not have the desire or ability (thus the capacity) to learn and take on new tasks and responsibilities. This person does not have the desire, ability, or intelligence to grow beyond the job. Thus, the individual is like a cul-de-sac. (A cul-de-sac doesn't take us anywhere farther.) He/She doesn't "plus" the job.

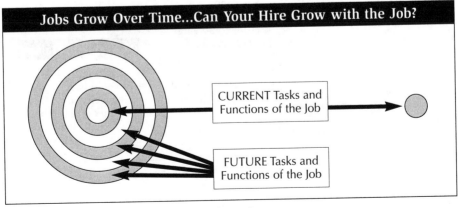

Jobs Grow Over Time...Can Your Hire Grow with the Job?

CURRENT Tasks and Functions of the Job

FUTURE Tasks and Functions of the Job

Figure 3

All jobs have two levels to them. One level is the current job's tasks and functions. The other, higher level consists not only of the current job's tasks and functions but also the tasks and functions that will exist in the future as the business grows.

If you intend never to hire more than one person, this really may not be an issue for you; however, once you decide to allow your business to grow through people leverage, you will see the need to hire as much "capacity" talent into your business as possible.

Let's say you have the chance to hire two very talented people for an administrative position; one is "capacity" talent and the other is "cul-de-sac" talent. Look at the diagram below to see the difference between the two.

After studying this diagram, which person would you want working with you in your business if you had a choice?

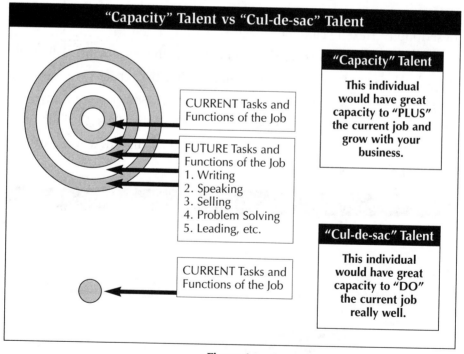

Figure 4

The Millionaire Real Estate Agent

The thought I want you to consider is this: "Capacity" talent might "plus or improve" the job, or someday even replace you on many additional tasks and functions you currently do. "Cul-de-sac" talent won't be able to. "Capacity" talent is not only support talent, but also "plussing or improving" talent (able to replace you by thinking or doing). "Cul-de-sac" talent is only support talent.

In other words, replacement talent will push you and free you up by not only taking "doing" off your shoulders, but also by taking some "thinking" responsibilities as well. Support talent will, more than likely, just take the "doing." This is why, at the end of the day, if your assistant is just support talent, you will get a lot accomplished and still feel mentally tired. The weight of the problems and solutions more than likely still reside with you.

"Capacity" (or replacement) talent has the desire, ability, and intelligence to do a good job and to make a big difference. "Cul-de-sac" (or support) talent has the desire and ability to do a good job. "Cul-de-sac" talent says, "I did what you said to do." "Capacity" talent says, "I did what you said to do plus what seemed to be needed. I heard what you asked and saw where you were going." The bottom line is that "capacity" talent has the ability to support you really well and replace you in some capacity—some combination of thinking and doing. "Cul-de-sac" talent has the ability to support you really well. The truth is, if you want your business to grow big, you really need to hire "capacity" talent.

"Earlier, I shared with you the story of Ebby Holliday and Mary Francis Burleson. Mary Francis was clearly not only talent—she was capacity or replacement talent. Can you imagine what Ebby's business life might have been like if she had hired "cul-de-sac" or support talent? Now, think for a moment about your business situation and ask yourself the same question, "What will my business life look like if I hire 'capacity and replacement' talent instead of 'cul-de-sac and support' talent?" Millionaire Real Estate Agents hire "capacity" talent.

11. Achieving Accountability to the Right Standards

Webster's defines a standard as a means of determining what a thing should be. When we speak of standards of performance, we typically are referring to performance meeting a predetermined level of acceptance. If standards define what we will accept, then in no small measure our standards define who we are. In the same way, our business standards will define our business.

What Customers Want

Many agents think that their customers use them because of the level of service they provide. While that is generally accurate, it is more precisely true that their customers use them because of the standard of service they expect and receive. When we draw a bead on the real reasons why, we understand that our standards really define the service experience our customers receive and are what keeps them coming back for more. We also then understand the truth that any standard that can be defined can, almost certainly, be duplicated by another.

Hence, it boils down to an issue of how successfully to document and communicate those standards to your staff so they are able to emulate your behaviors and level of service. You'll have to define how you want something done; explain the "why, when, where, and who" of it; train to the standard, and then hold your staff accountable to following your lead. However, until a process has been documented, you haven't "standardized" it, and you can't really expect someone else to be able to do it in your "standard" way. Quality service that is not defined and documented so it can be consistently duplicated is just a hollow slogan. At best, it becomes a promise you just can't make. Most agents have slogans about quality, but Millionaire Real Estate Agents have simple documented standards of quality. Thus, most agents are able to deliver high-quality service when they do it personally, but the quality suffers dramatically when someone else is asked to do the work. If you plan to enjoy the benefits of People Leverage in your real estate sales business, you'll have to make sure your team defines and documents what your customer's experience should be.

The most common mistake agents make when trying to teach and promote standards is when they pursue the follow-me-and-watch-what-I-do approach without any documentation in the mix. What tends to happen is the employee observes the agent for a few days or weeks until things get busy and then that person is pushed out of the nest and told to "ask me if you run into trouble." It is no wonder that so many agents have bad experiences hiring and training help, and then getting them to do things right.

The best possible way to get documented standards for your business is to have the first person you hire document the way you want things to get done. This doesn't require a specialist or consultant. With your guidance, you and your administrative hire can methodically document your standards until you have the equivalent of an operations manual that merely needs updating from time to time. In fact, in the next few pages we'll outline the Systems Documentation Model of the Millionaire Real Estate Agent.

Early and Often

The secret to succeeding this way is to start the documentation process early, work on it often, and never stop. As early in your career as possible is ideal, but it is imperative to begin when you make your first hire. In fact, documenting your systems will be an essential component of your first hire's job description. Documenting new systems and updating the old on a regular basis should also be integral to what your assistant does.

Like so many others, I had to learn about the importance of documentation the hard way. Early on in building one of our companies, we brought in a programmer, Bob Carter, to build a proprietary operating software program. It was an enormously complex project, and the first iteration was far from the final version. Over the next few years, Bob continued to tweak the system, fixing bugs and adding features. Then, in the mid-1990s, Bob was diagnosed with terminal cancer and given a short time to live. What we subsequently discovered was that, while the first version of the program was comprehensively documented, many of the fixes and features added along the way had been documented only in shorthand—no one but Bob Carter could easily (if at all) administer or upgrade the system. Bob appreciated what was at stake for the company he'd helped us build, and his integrity showed through. With the help of a consultant, Bob systematically documented years of system changes in between chemotherapy sessions up until his last weeks. His amazing commitment inspired the Bob Carter Inspiration Award that we give each year to the person in our company who has shown extraordinary unselfishness and service in the face of adversity.

Bob Carter's story is an extraordinary one. But this story plays out every day in real estate agents' sales businesses across the nation when key personnel leave unexpectedly. Replacing these individuals is often hampered by a lack of proper documentation; thus, valuable time and money are lost deciphering personal methods of doing this or that. Systems documentation is an ongoing process. It is never complete. Endeavor to start early and review your systems on a regular basis.

The Systems Documentation Model of the Millionaire Real Estate Agent

Even agents who understand the importance of documenting their methods may not follow through because of the perceived difficulty involved. Writing a manual is something they've never done and usually appears to them to be very difficult. It's not difficult, it just takes time—time that could be spent listing and selling homes. The truth is that documentation does require some patience, persistence, and organization. That's why we advocate that you enlist the help of your first hire (administrative help) to get you successfully through the process with a minimum of lost sales time.

But generally you can't just say to someone, "Document my systems," and expect to get a quality product in return. You'll need to give them a model for building a manual and provide ample input from your position of experience. After all, up until this point, no one but you knows exactly how you do business and how you expect it to be done by others. The Systems Documentation Model of the Millionaire Real Estate Agent (Figure 5) provides an overview of the documentation process.

Step one of the process will be almost completely led by you, unless your assistant has prior real estate experience. You must also realize that this is a process, not a project. Your first pass at trying to list all the things you do will doubtless be full of holes you will want to plug later. The point of the process is really to get a working operations manual in place and then add to it and improve it constantly over time. For example, you'll come back to your office after a particularly brilliant listing presentation and say to your assistant, "I just realized that we've left out an important aspect of my presentation. I almost always spend the first five to ten minutes touring the property with the client, but what I'm also doing is getting a sense of the homeowners, what kind of people they are and what kind of service they are likely to expect. . . . Please add those elements right at the beginning of the 'Listing Presentation' process, and then we'll review it together. . . ." Of course, that is just one example. The point is to drill down over time and don't take any of your processes for granted. It is much easier to cut steps out when feedback from your future staff helps you understand which aspects are necessary and repeatable vs which aspects are just a function of your personality. And here's the greater truth: As well as you personally do something, it can be improved upon. And the fact is that unless you write down how you currently do it, you won't really be able to improve it.

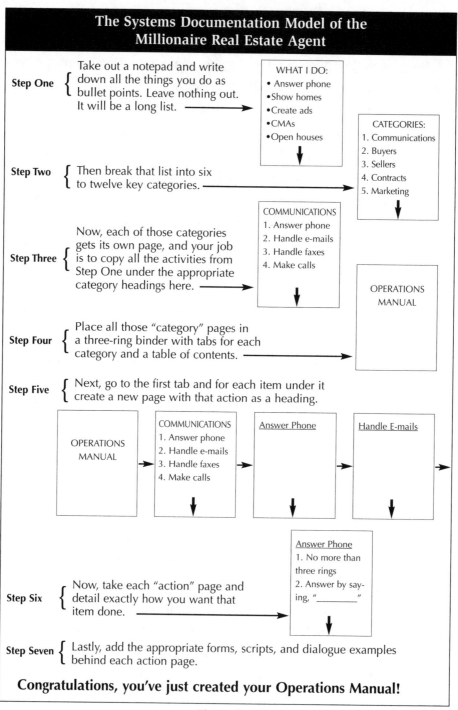

The Systems Documentation Model of the Millionaire Real Estate Agent

Step One { Take out a notepad and write down all the things you do as bullet points. Leave nothing out. It will be a long list. ⟶

WHAT I DO:
- Answer phone
- Show homes
- Create ads
- CMAs
- Open houses

CATEGORIES:
1. Communications
2. Buyers
3. Sellers
4. Contracts
5. Marketing

Step Two { Then break that list into six to twelve key categories. ⟶

Step Three { Now, each of those categories gets its own page, and your job is to copy all the activities from Step One under the appropriate category headings here. ⟶

COMMUNICATIONS
1. Answer phone
2. Handle e-mails
3. Handle faxes
4. Make calls

OPERATIONS MANUAL

Step Four { Place all those "category" pages in a three-ring binder with tabs for each category and a table of contents. ⟶

Step Five { Next, go to the first tab and for each item under it create a new page with that action as a heading.

OPERATIONS MANUAL

COMMUNICATIONS
1. Answer phone
2. Handle e-mails
3. Handle faxes
4. Make calls

Answer Phone

Handle E-mails

Answer Phone
1. No more than three rings
2. Answer by saying, "_____"

Step Six { Now, take each "action" page and detail exactly how you want that item done. ⟶

Step Seven { Lastly, add the appropriate forms, scripts, and dialogue examples behind each action page.

Congratulations, you've just created your Operations Manual!

Figure 5

Accountability

Different aspects of your operations manual will serve as components for the detailed job description you give your staff. If answering the phone is part of their duties, then your expectation and standards for doing so should be clearly detailed in the manual. The key then becomes to hold your staff accountable to meeting your standards. I've found that the best process for building accountability into your business is to:

1. Set weekly appointments with the individuals who report to you
2. Work from a specific job description
3. Work from a very specific goal worksheet

You can refer to our template for the Consultative Interview (Earn a Million, Figure 26) if you need guidance about the process of these meetings. The importance of having your standards defined for your staff cannot be underestimated. It allows you to hold actions accountable, something that is definitive and objective, vs holding people accountable for "being a certain way," which is personal and subjective. I've also found that performance for any person has the best chance to improve when the ambiguity about what she should be doing is removed from the equation.

Finally, it is important that you use your operations manual as well. As we discussed in point number eight, "Consistently marketing your seller listings for more leads," these checklists can help you combat the urge to skip steps or drop the ball when you are feeling stressed or fatigued. Before long, the systems can be committed to memory and, through repetition, transformed into Big Habits that can boost you on your way to the highest levels of real estate sales success.

12. Creating Teamwork with "Rock and Role"

As you include additional people in your business life, teamwork will become an issue. Your ability to get people to work together and to create synergy among differing personalities can generate momentum in your business or stall it altogether. The latter happens all too often as

> *"Everyone on our team knows their role. We all practice scripts. We are focused on becoming grand masters at what we do."*
>
> David and Judie Crockett
> Millionaire Real Estates Agents
> Concord, OH
> Sales volume—$53 million

staff members all pull in their own directions instead of pulling together. While the problem is common, it is also fairly easy to remedy. The solution is what we fondly call a focus on "rock and role."

To achieve teamwork, you need to do two things:

1. Articulate clearly the key goals of your business. These are what we refer to as the "big rocks" of the business. For example, your main business goal might be to reach $80,000,000 in closed production. That is now the team's "rock."

2. Ensure that each team member understands exactly how his role (job description) contributes to the achievement of your business goal (big rock). For example, if your business goal is $80,000,000 in closed production, one of your buyer specialists might have a goal of $10,000,000 in closed production toward that goal. And that is his "role."

Make it clear that if the business is not on target to hit the "big rock" then everything about the business is in jeopardy of being reevaluated, including individuals and their roles. No one is protected if the business goals are not met. This may sound hard-nosed and even antithetical to creating a teamwork atmosphere, but one of the truest ways to hamstring synergy is for accountability to be perceived as lax or, worse, not even-handed. Just don't forget to balance accountability with ample recognition and reward when goals are met or exceeded. So while you are going to be very tough on accountability to standards and goals, you'll also celebrate and reward great results.

Adding an individual to a team does not necessarily make him a team player. It's like my wife says, "Being in the garage doesn't make you a mechanic." And just because people get along well doesn't make them productive in the way true teams are. Try not to confuse camaraderie with teamwork. What an individual contributes directly to your goals will define whether or not he is a part of the team. A team player work-ing with other team play-ers toward a common goal is what defines a team. I believe in the old sports aphorism that "everyone gets along when they're winning." In the realm of professional sports, we've seen this acted out year

> *"Operating a team is like being in a family—there are ups and downs, and there are different personalities. Your job is to help everyone stay positive and appreciate one another's role."*
>
> John Toye
> Millionaire Real Estate Agent
> Westland, MI
> Sales volume—$39.2 million

after year. High-achieving players come together despite personal differ-ences or even animosities because of a common overriding goal—to be champions, to be the very best.

In our experience, the solution is to "rock and role." To build a team, you need the "rock"—the big goal of your business. Everyone shares that "rock" and works toward it together. It is in working toward it that we get our "role." Everyone on the team has a contributing "role," from the person answering the phone to the person going on listing appointments.

Group	vs	Team
1. No clearly stated goals.		1. Clearly communicated goals in writing—big rocks.
2. Daily assignments and tasks.		2. Clearly written job descriptions—roles.
3. No sense of urgency.		3. Healthy sense of urgency with specific accountability.
4. One person feels responsible for success or failure.		4. Everyone feels responsible for team success or failure.
5. Competition within the group.		5. Teams take on outside competition.

Figure 6

When people know their "role" and how they must contribute to the big "rock," all you need is accountability to have the makings of a high performance team. Without either, all you're left with is a group.

The Group vs Team chart (Figure 6) helps illustrate the basic differences between being a group and being a team. The bottom line is this: When you do everything yourself, you're just a technician. When there are a bunch of technicians, you've got a group. When everyone has a "role" he's accountable to perform in order to achieve the big goal or "rock," you've got the basis for a team. So your motto should be to "rock and role" every day, all the time. It is the music of high performance.

13. COMBINING QUALITY SERVICE AND QUANTITY SERVICE

As you strive to build a sales business that does a large number of transactions, you will most certainly face the quantity versus quality issue. The question is, "What is 'quality service' and how much time does it take to deliver it." One common perspective holds that the more time an agent spends with the client, the better the quality of the experience for the client. The belief is that customer satisfaction is most effectively achieved by personal contact and lots of time spent doing it. However, our experience with top agents doing high volumes and servicing large numbers of clients provides another perspective on this. These agents achieve high marks in service and enjoy an abundance of word-of-mouth referrals, yet they spend less time with their clients than the average agent.

"Whatever you do, focus on the consumer benefits you provide."
Russell Shaw
Millionaire Real Estate Agent
Phoenix, AZ
Sales volume—$50.6 million

Just how do they do this? Well, here's what they've told us: "Be a minimalist with great communication." What they mean is that doing what matters most and doing it efficiently while staying in touch and keeping the client informed is what creates high levels of customer satisfaction, not time spent together. In fact, they say, taking too much time can create less satisfaction, more frustration, and a reduced sense of professionalism. The more refined, efficient, and timely you can make your services, the higher the perceived quality of service likely will be.

In our experience, the consistency and clarity of your communications are extremely important to customer experience. Knowing when they expect to hear from you and how then to communicate with them quickly and efficiently is part of the challenge. Communicating with your clients in a planned and purposeful manner is much better than a lot of communication just thrown at them. In this instance, timeliness with purpose is more important than time.

Because highly successful real estate agents concentrate their personal contact to these "moments of truth" during the buying and selling process, top agents and their teams can handle more volume and keep quality standards high. If you intend to take your business from Earn a Million to Net a Million, you'll have to master being a "minimalist" with great communication and great timing. As with so many other aspects of the Millionaire Real Estate Agent business, the difference between "big" and "really big" is how you manage your time and focus. Achieving the same or better results with a smaller investment of time is a big part of the Net a Million game.

MONEY

In business, money is always an issue, whether you have too little and even if you have more than you expected. Your quest as a real estate sales businessperson is to increase your revenues, control your costs, and, at the end of the day, increase your net income. Part of the battle is to become familiar and proficient with your Economic Model and your

Budget Model. Much of the difference between having a business that earns a million and one that nets a million is often centered on two monetary disciplines: sticking to the Budget Model (harder than it looks) and controlling costs (easier than it sounds).

14. STICKING TO THE BUDGET MODEL AND CONTROLLING YOUR COSTS

One of the hardest tasks you will have to address is sticking to your Budget Model. Unless you have owned other successful businesses or are among the few real estate agents with formal business or accounting training, you may be challenged in this area up front. Budgeting is not so much a matter of specialized professional expertise as it is about a little know-how, some experience, and some discipline. It is not that difficult to understand an income (profit and loss) statement or to prepare a budget. It just takes a little repetition with someone who is comfortable with these tools. Usually, your sales manager or broker will have this experience and skill. If not, he can point you in the right direction. Whether you or your personnel office manager handles the budget, you will ultimately be responsible for reviewing it and authorizing any unbudgeted expenses. This means you need to understand your Budget Model and your Economic Model, basically the relationship between all the variables from your gross revenue to your net income. It doesn't require a Herculean effort, just some time to get up to speed. It is your money, and taking care of it supports your future.

> *"If we work hard to make it . . .*
> *we need to work doubly hard to keep it."*
> Mike Mendoza
> Millionaire Real Estate Agent
> Phoenix, AZ
> Sales volume—$60 million

The bigger your business gets, the more detailed your budgeting process can and should become. This is one reason we stress the importance of implementing the models on the front end of your career—before things have a chance to get overwhelming. Strive to put the

Budget Model and systems in place as early as you can; then, over time, you'll become more and more proficient with them. In this way, by the time things start getting more detailed, you'll feel comfortable and capable of handling the more challenging issues as they arise.

But keep it simple. You don't need to rush out and enroll in an MBA accounting program. Do an annual budget, stick to it, review it monthly (or weekly), and pay serious attention to any variances. Identifying variances early is very important. This level of awareness will help you make more accurate cost projections and know where your money is going sooner. Don't treat your budget lightly, and don't alter it easily. Make it difficult for you and others to justify spending outside the budget. Always look for areas where you can reduce expenses. Trial and error can sometimes be quite effective. Try living without something and if you find you can't, you'll know it was important. But when all is said and done, the true financial disciplines are learning to say no and are learning to ask why. Casual spending and the phrase, "This is only the cost of a commission from one more sale," are the bane of a Millionaire Real Estate Agent. Stick to your budget and when you have to spend outside of it, make sure the move is absolutely justifiable.

These truths and principles sound simple, but they are actually a little difficult to do over time. In our experience, inattention to the money and overspending are the norm. If you are truly going to Net a Million, you will have to fight those natural tendencies. Oddly enough, those of us who have the most confidence in our ability to generate money often have the greatest difficulty in keeping it!

When you build in systems and processes, they tend to serve two purposes: First, they help you keep your good habits and do the right things; and, second, they make it very, very difficult to regress into old bad habits and do the wrong things. In this way, your budgetary systems should be geared to keep you focused on "following the money" and to prevent you from losing control of your expenses.

One easy example of this is to separate your deposit account from your operating account. Only transfer enough into your operating account to cover that month's budgeted expenses. Then set a business standard (for you and your staff) to avoid exceeding that amount. And if it appears you need to exceed your budget, require a variance justification (a written form) that must be reviewed before the money can be transferred to the operating account to cover those additional costs. At the very least, this makes you aware of every item that exceeds your budget allowance. And awareness is half the battle.

Another good technique is to have someone else (a CPA, a financial consultant, even a knowledgeable peer) hold you and your business management accountable and then schedule monthly consultations with you. But remember, they need to be empowered to be critical and to get answers to their questions. Otherwise, their consultation will have little ability to keep you on track.

As a general rule, you should request a detailed budget for any new marketing plan, equipment purchase, or staff position. For each proposal, insist on a complete Economic Model—how it will increase income or save expenses or cause higher productivity. This is Red Light, Green Light at a high level. Make it a habit to question a new expense until you are confident it makes economic sense to do it. Then let it rest for a couple of days and see if it still makes sense! It may sound like overkill, but when you allow the habit of impulse or even urgent spending outside the bounds of your budget, you are sounding a death knell for your net income. Listings and lead generation are urgent matters; however, spending money should always be a deliberate enterprise! Some agents simply take their projected net income off the top of every commission check. Then, when unexpected expenses arise, they become very aware that they are reaching into their own wallet to cover them. It is probably a good idea always to think of unbudgeted expenses in this way.

The Millionaire Real Estate Agent

Acquiring this perspective on controlling costs and making it a habit is essential to your success as a businessperson at any level. But it is most apparent when you are attempting to take your real estate sales business to the highest levels, to Net a Million and beyond.

You

When you get down to it, your Millionaire Real Estate Agent business will ultimately be a reflection of you. If it is to change, improve, and grow, you will have to, too. In fact, your growth will actually come before the growth of your business. Your ability and willingness to work on yourself will in large part determine how far you and your business go. The high achievers we've worked with and interviewed dedicated significant money and time toward personal development. In fact, for many, personal development—being their best—is their Big Why. Self-improvement is a high priority and is tracked along with all their other goals. Time and experience have helped us identify two particular areas of personal development that will have a significant impact on your ability to reach greater success: your ability to maintain your focus on the 20 percent of the business that matters most, and your ability to maintain some sense of balance in your life so you will always have the energy you need to pursue your goals.

15. Staying Focused on the 20 Percent

On the road to building your Millionaire Real Estate Agent business, you will constantly be faced with the issue of distractions. As soon as you are able to delegate a responsibility, it seems, you will get pulled right back into it to advise, consult, or simply make an executive decision. It will increasingly become a challenge to stay focused on the cornerstones of your business—Leads, Listings, and Leverage. The busier you get, the busier you get: this is a truth you will definitely come up against. One way you'll handle this will be to train your team to respect your time by teaching the 80:20 Rule and helping them understand which activities are truly dollar productive.

Instilling those principles in your team members will, first and foremost, give them the ability to pursue their goals with focus and, as a by-product of that focus, help sustain the productivity of your business. It's really about having goals, knowing priorities, and doing the important things first. Although this can truly be a mental discipline, I've found that there are also simple methods that can serve to bolster and aid

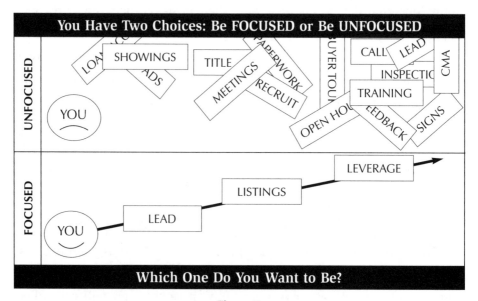

Figure 7

you and your team in your attempts to recognize your 20 percent and prioritize it properly.

It all begins by recognizing you really only have two choices regarding focus: to be focused or to be unfocused.

To be successful at high levels, being focused is the *only* way to be. One method you can use to gain focus for you and your team is a process called The Goal-to-Action 20 Percent System. This is a very simple four-step process that can give your business the focus it must have to achieve big.

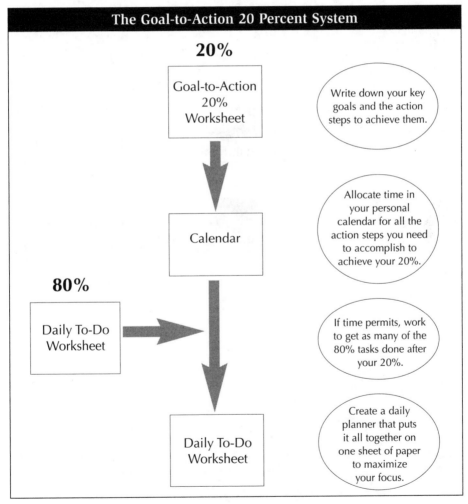

Figure 8

The three questions it will answer are:

    1. What do I/we want? (goal)

    2. When do I/we want it? (date)

    3. What has to happen for me/us to have it? (action steps)

Here are the four steps in this system:

The Goal-to-Action 20 Percent Worksheet	
Name:	Date:
GOAL	
Accomplishment Date	
Action Steps	

Figure 9

Master Task List–80 Percent

Figure 10

Daily Worksheet	Date:
Business Tasks	**Messages and Notes**
1.	1.
2.	2.
3.	3.
4.	4.
5.	5.
6.	6.
7.	7.
8.	8.
9.	9.
10.	10.
Personal Tasks	11.
11.	12.
12.	13.
13.	14.
14.	15.

Appointments	
5:30 AM	2:00 PM
6:00 AM	2:30 PM
6:30 AM	3:00 PM
7:00 AM	3:30 PM
7:30 AM	4:00 PM
8:00 AM	4:30 PM
8:30 AM	5:00 PM
9:00 AM	5:30 PM
9:30 AM	6:00 PM
10:00 AM	6:30 PM
10:30 AM	7:00 PM
11:00 AM	7:30 PM
11:30 AM	8:00 PM
12:00 PM	8:30 PM
12:30 PM	9:00 PM
1:00 PM	9:30 PM
1:30 PM	10:00 PM

Figure 11

The forms you and your team can use to follow this system are in Figure 8, Figure 9, Figure 10, and Figure 11.

Focus becomes increasingly possible in direct proportion to how clear you are about what you want, when you want it, what you must do to get it, and how well you have blocked out the time in your calendar so you can do it. And the same applies for anyone working with you. Focus is a real issue you can effectively accomplish through a simple system you and your team can adopt.

16. COUNTERBALANCING YOUR LIFE TO MAINTAIN YOUR ENERGY AT A HIGH LEVEL

The idea of having a balanced life is actually more idealistic than it is practical. I've found that it is healthier to attempt to lead a counterbalanced life where the issue isn't that you got out of balance, but how long you stay there.

> *"Last year I was diagnosed with cancer. I didn't work for the bulk of the year. We did 383 sales and over $50 million in volume. So I wasn't there, and I had my best year ever."*
>
> Russell Shaw
> Millionaire Real Estate Agent
> Phoenix, AZ
> Sales volume—$50.6 million

Implicit in the label is an acceptance that, at times, your life will be out of balance. And, frankly, for Millionaire Real Estate Agents, life can seesaw quite dramatically from balance to imbalance, so it is very important to acknowledge this so you can then deal with it. The ruling factor of living a counterbalanced life is to allow imbalance when key goals are at stake, but not to dwell in that state for too long. Why? Because when you allow yourself to live in imbalance for too long, you cannot maintain your energy, and you risk burnout.

To become a Millionaire Real Estate Agent, you'll need not only to maintain your energy, but to maintain it at a high level. High energy is not something that can be forced for any length of time. You can "get up" for the big moment, but maintaining that level ultimately comes from living your life in the most self-actualizing, personally fulfilling way.

You'll be counterbalancing between or among all the vital areas of your life: work, family, health, spiritual pursuits. It's mind, body, heart, and soul. The best counterbalancing formula is something that is unique to each individual. No one else can determine how neglecting or overemphasizing an area will impact your enthusiasm and your drive.

For high achievers, the counterbalancing challenge lies between the work and nonwork aspects of your life. The truth is, there will be times when work is the priority and you will have to "make hay while the sun shines." But if you stay overworked and out of balance for too long, you must understand that your energy level will sink and the risk of burnout increases. "Redlining" your career for too long is unhealthy for you, your family, and also your business. Sadly, this happens to far too many people, especially in the real estate business. When you feel this energy drop,

> *"By building a staff, we have bought back some of our time."*
> Jill Rudler
> Millionaire Real Estate Agent
> Westerville, OH
> Sales volume—$58 million

you need to recognize the need to counterbalance your life. Devote yourself to other aspects of your life (family, friends, education, hobbies, etc.) and "right the ship" as quickly as you can.

I sometimes illustrate counterbalancing by comparing it to skiing, specifically mogul skiing. If you've every seen mogul skiers on television, you understand that—despite all their athleticism, grace, and the appearance of controlled balance—for about 75 percent of the descent from mound to mound, from bump to bump, the skiers are airborne, off balance, or out of control. They have learned how to counterbalance, avoid crashing, and adjust course while maintaining their speed to the bottom of the run.

Leverage, such as hiring talented people, setting standards, and implementing systems and tools can help make counterbalancing easier in your work life. However, the time and focus needed to put these things in place while still doing the business is difficult to achieve and may, in fact, throw you out of balance. Just don't lose sight of how this leverage, once it is finally in place, actually helps restore balance and stabilize your life. Leverage is an essential key to leading a counterbalanced life. And counterbalancing is absolutely essential if you plan to take your real estate sales career to the highest levels and maintain your success for the long term.

When you see a successful person who appears balanced, please realize it is an illusion. What you're seeing that appears to be balance is really fast and timely counterbalancing. Counterbalancing done this way is just as healthy and fulfilling as the so-called "balanced life."

CONCLUSION

Recognizing and working on the issues in between Earn a Million and Net a Million can make all the difference in your career. It goes without saying that the earlier you turn your focus on them, the sooner you'll reap the benefits and the more seamless will be your transition from Earn a Million to Net a Million. These issues affect the core areas of your professional life: Leads, Listings, Leverage, Money, and You. Endeavor to understand them and implement the lessons learned in your life.

The next transition, from Net a Million to Receive a Million, may, in fact, be the most difficult to achieve. It requires a fundamental shift in your thinking, the difference between working in a business and owning one. But the rewards are amazing! If you're ready to explore the possibilities of taking passive income to the ultimate level, then let's move on to Receive a Million.

■ Net a Million is the natural outcome of fully implementing the Four Fundamental Business Models of the Millionaire Real Estate Agent. In our experience, there are sixteen issues that must be addressed to successfully make the transition. You must:

1. Sustain a solid lead-generation program that emphasizes marketing and consistently increases the number of leads.

2. Track and convert leads through others.

3. Protect your lead-generation focus time.

4. Weigh your options and discover what works and doesn't work for you.

5. Know the minimum number of listings you must list each month.

6. List the minimum number of listings each month.

7. Get sellers to accept the team concept.

8. Consistently market your seller listings for more leads.

9. Make time to learn and implement the R/T/C/K (Recruit/Train/Consult/Keep) process.

10. Hire "Capacity" vs "Cul-de-sac" talent.

11. Achieve accountability to the right standards.

12. Create teamwork with "rock and role."

13. Combine quality service with quantity service.

14. Stick to the Budget Model and control your costs.

15. Stay focused on the 20 percent that matters.

16. Counterbalance your life to maintain your energy at a high level.

RECEIVE A MILLION

"Train up a fig tree in the way it should go, and when you are old sit under the shade of it."

Charles Dickens

Figure 1

WHEN YOUR MONEY WORKS FOR YOU

Like so many other kids, my first real job was mowing yards. I canvassed the neighborhood with my signature flyers (with the tag line "You Grow It—I Mow It") and quickly had eight or nine yards to mow, edge, and trim each week. Well, summer rolled around, and our family had a weeklong vacation planned, so I recruited a friend down the street to take over my business while I was away. My friend was eager to help, and had let drop several times that he'd be happy to take over any yards I was "tired" of mowing. Well, I capitalized on his eagerness and gave him all my yards for the week for $10 each. The deal was this: I'd let the clients know; he'd mow the yards; I'd collect the money and then pay him when I got back. We high-fived on it, and everyone was happy. Especially me. You see, what I didn't tell him was that I got paid $15 per yard. My mother chided me a bit for this, saying that the deal was fine but that I should have told my friend. She was right, and I learned a good lesson about integrity in business. But I also learned a huge lesson about leverage and passive income. I wasn't mowing a single yard that week but would still make about $40. My aha—I needed to go out of town more often!

What has become so crystal clear through the teachings of Robert T. Kiyosaki, Robert Allen, Mark Victor Hansen, and others like them is that there are broadly only two routes to acquiring money and financial wealth: You can either earn it, or you can receive it. And although there are multiple paths to earning and receiving, you can still divide them into two neat categories. Either "you work for money" or "your money works for you."

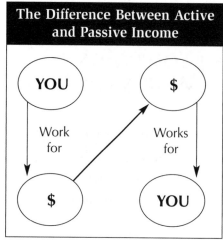

The Difference Between Active and Passive Income

Figure 2

It is the difference between active and passive income. Active is where you work for your sales business and passive is where your sales business works for you. Most real estate agents work for their businesses, and always will, which is why we wrote a chapter entitled Receive a Million. The goals of this chapter are to teach and encourage you to grow and organize your business in such a way that someday your business will work for you. This is the powerful opportunity of passive income and the theme behind Receive a Million.

As surprising as it is, I've learned that most real estate agents really don't understand, respect, or aggressively pursue passive income. For some reason, if they are earning $50,000 a year, they think that $5,000 a year in passive income is nothing to get excited about. Likewise, if they are earning $100,000 a year, then $10,000 a year in passive income isn't significant enough to raise their eyebrows. What they fail to appreciate is how much and how long they'd have to earn and save (after taxes) to achieve these passive income numbers.

For example, if we assume a conservative 5 percent rate of return on your savings, you'd need $100,000 in the bank to earn $5,000 per year in passive income. Now, to save that much, you would actually have to earn (and not spend) a total of $149,253, which, when you take out taxes (33 percent) amounts to $100,000 in the bank. Even a disciplined agent who sets aside $10,000 a year before taxes would still have to wait fifteen years to amass $100,000 in total after-tax savings.

Saving for Passive Income?			
$149,253 Gross Income	x 33% Tax Rate	= $49,253 taxes	
$149,253 Gross Income	− $49,253 taxes	= $100,000 in Savings	
$100,000 in Savings	x 5% Interest Rate	= $5,000 Passive Income/Year	

Figure 3

So, incredible as it may sound, you can see that $5,000 in passive income really represents at least fifteen years of work and disciplined money management. That's no small feat! And if you hoped to earn $10,000 a year in pretax passive income, you'd have to save for thirty years to accumulate the necessary $200,000 in savings after tax. Now, if you quantify it in monthly terms, it looks like this:

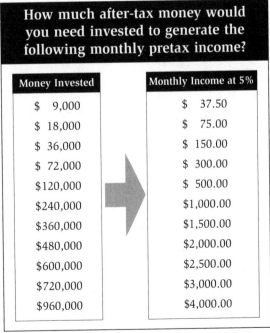

How much after-tax money would you need invested to generate the following monthly pretax income?	
Money Invested	**Monthly Income at 5%**
$ 9,000	$ 37.50
$ 18,000	$ 75.00
$ 36,000	$ 150.00
$ 72,000	$ 300.00
$120,000	$ 500.00
$240,000	$1,000.00
$360,000	$1,500.00
$480,000	$2,000.00
$600,000	$2,500.00
$720,000	$3,000.00
$960,000	$4,000.00

Figure 4

Are you getting a sense of the investment in time and money that wealth building through totally conservative and conventional means requires? Even if you invest your money in the stock market, which has historically generated about a 10 percent return in any seven-year period dating back to the 1930s, you'd still be looking at a significant investment of money over time to generate meaningful passive returns.

We believe that as you build your sales business, you have another option for generating wealth through passive income—through business ownership. In fact, we believe that turning your self-employed real estate sales job into a business is the most straightforward path you can take to building financial wealth and passive income. Our point of view is that when you accomplish this, you will have created for yourself a business-based source of passive income, which has the potential to generate a substantially higher rate of return.

WORKING "ON" THE BUSINESS INSTEAD OF "IN" THE BUSINESS

For you to "receive" a million dollars a year from your business without having a job in the business, two things must happen first:
1. You must gross a lot more than $1 million a year.
2. You must hire someone who can run the business at the level you did.

Those are the two basic prerequisites if you want to achieve the passive income of the Millionaire Real Estate Agent.

But you should know that you don't necessarily have to net a million dollars to make the move to business owner and passive income. For example, if your business were netting you $200,000 a year and you could hire someone to run it for you for $100,000 a year, you'd have a business that netted you $100,000 a year. That is nothing to sneeze at!

In fact, if you were looking to retire or move on to some other endeavor, turning your $200,000 job into a $100,000 per year passive income source is a wonderful way to attain the freedom to make those choices. In other words, turning your real estate sales business practice into a business that generates passive income to you is one way to move from your work life into your life work.

Before I can introduce you to the four issues of Receive a Million, I need to point out that as a business owner you will be challenged to work ON your business instead of working IN it. So what's the difference? As Michael Gerber explains in his book *E-Myth*, IN is when you are doing the actual day-to-day work of the business, and ON is when you are doing the work of planning and building the business. If it helps you to remember the difference, try thinking of it this way: The difference between IN and ON is the difference between a focus on "I" (what "I do" to achieve the goals of the business) and a focus on "O" (what "others do" to achieve the goals of the business). Figure 5 provides a nice illustration of the path you're likely to go through on your way from IN to ON.

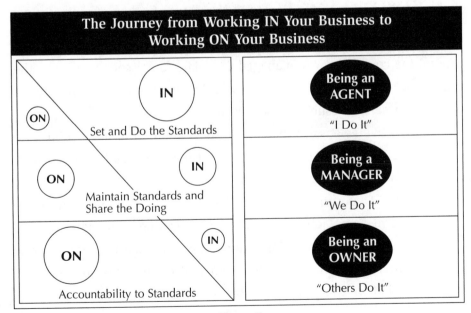

Figure 5

This diagram really shows how you progress from "I do it" to "We do it" to the final stage where "Others do it." As much sense as it makes to transition from IN to ON, the act of letting go and letting others run the business is a difficult challenge for most. We hope that, by learning about and understanding the four issues of Receive a Million, you will be able to make this transition as painlessly as possible.

THE FOUR ISSUES OF RECEIVE A MILLION

"It took me twenty years to have $1 million in the bank, but only two more years to have $3 million—and another two years to get to $5 million."

Tim Wood
Millionaire Real Estate Agent
Big Bear Lake, CA
Sales volume—$38 million

From our experience working with and interviewing top agents around the country, we've managed to isolate four issues that make the difference when you're jumping from business owner to Receive a Million. These four issues can be summarized as follows:

1. Active vs Passive Income—Understanding that passive income is not truly "passive." Your business will still require your involvement and attention, just in a different way.
2. The Opportunity of the 7th Level—As difficult as it is to transform your job into a business, exiting your job through conventional investing requires just as much mastery and can be just as tough. Turning your real estate sales business into what we call a 7th Level Business is a better, wiser option.

3. The Three Key Hires of a Millionaire Business—It takes three magnificent hires to create the foundation for a Millionaire Real Estate Agent business. Your job is to recruit, train, consult, and keep (R/T/C/K) these three extraordinary "capacity" talented individuals.

4. Your Role and Responsibilities—As a Millionaire Real Estate Agent, you have one role—accountability. Your success will hinge on your ability to hold your team accountable in three areas: leadership, people, and capital.

The first two issues are really about the understanding and awareness that will aid in your transition. And the last two are about the actual steps you'll need to take and your ongoing role in your business. Let's take a close look at the pivotal issues that stand between you and receiving a million.

1. ACTIVE VS PASSIVE INCOME

Active income (where you work for money) and passive income (where money works for you) actually represent opposite ends of the spectrum. On one side you have a job and are paid directly for the work you do. And on the other end is ownership income, sometimes called "mailbox money," where money comes to you from your business or investments. But here's the rub: As passive as it may appear, even "mailbox money" requires your active involvement. For example, even dividends from a stock you purchased required your attention at some point when you selected and purchased the stock. And you have to keep your eye on that stock, too. Obviously, in this example, the return on your time investment can be so significant as to make it virtually "passive" money. The key word is *virtually*—you still had to do some work to get it. Likewise, business ownership still requires your attention and involvement, just on a smaller scale and in a different way. The truth is, unless you are the beneficiary of a trust fund, there is actually no such thing, in a practical sense, as completely passive income!

Dollars per Hour

There is an interesting economic concept that might help you get a better grasp on just how passive your income really is. It's called "dollars per hour." Basically, if you take your net income and divide it by the hours you spend earning it, you can measure your progress toward higher levels of business passive income.

> *"I bring focus to my work, and I seek to create cash flow and passive income from businesses and projects I own."*
>
> Don Zeleznak
> Millionaire Real Estate Agent
> Scottsdale, AZ
> Sales volume—$77 million

For example, if as a real estate agent you net $300,000 per year and work sixty hours a week, fifty weeks a year to earn it (3,000 hours), your dollars per hour is $100/hour ($300,000/3,000 hours = $100 per hour). When you've built a business that nets the same amount but you're working only forty hours a week for forty weeks (1,600 hours), your dollars per hour look like this: $300,000/1,600 hours = $187.50 per hour. Now, were it to become a business where you spend ten hours a week for forty weeks (400 hours) a year working ON the business, your dollars per hour looks like this: $300,000/400 hours = $750 per hour.

In the Millionaire Real Estate Agent model it is possible, with the right people and the right amount of leads, to earn $1 million in the same 400 hours. In dollars per hour, that's $1,000,000/400 hours = $2,500 per hour in business passive income. Now that's a goal worth striving for!

> *"In my business, I want to work fewer hours and make more money."*
>
> Cristina Martinez
> Millionaire Real Estate Agent
> San Jose, CA
> Sales volume—$136.3 million

Productivity is the key to this equation. If, over the course of your career, you can focus your time on the dollar-productive actions of Leads, Listings, and Leverage, you'll find your "dollars per hour" will steadily climb. Your transition from Net a Million to Receive a Million will then be, in part, a reflection of your mastery of the Three L's.

Connect vs Disconnect

So be wary of how you view business "passive" income. It is not so much passive as it is highly leveraged. As a business owner, your active participation will still be required; however, the nature of that involvement will be dramatically different from when you held a "job" in the business. As the Millionaire Real Estate Agent, your primary role will be to make sure that the right people are doing the right things and meeting your standards. But your role is active—not passive.

> *"I have learned to stick with what I know—residential real estate."*
> Bill Ryan
> Millionaire Real Estate Agent
> Chandler, AZ
> Sales volume—$54 million

Unfortunately, many people don't get this subtlety and take the position that business ownership frees them to devote all their attention elsewhere. They mistake "business passive income" for "pure passive income." As a result, their businesses often suffer from that neglect. Here is an interesting business point you must not miss: "Active is active" and "passive is active" in business. They are both active. In business, "active" is working IN the business and "passive active" is working ON the business. Be warned: Absentee ownership usually equals business demise. Owners who wish to be absent, to have no active role, should simply sell. The same principle of entropy that applies to the universe applies to your business—"Anything left alone eventually falls apart." So anytime you feel as if you've earned the right to be AWOL from your business for a while, revisit that point. You just don't know what you might come back and find.

2. The Opportunity of the 7th Level

As we discussed earlier, as your business grows you will discover seven distinct and separate levels you can progress to or move through, depending on your goals and your ability to master your current level. These levels are really seven potential models of people leverage. At level one, it's just you doing it all, and at the other extreme, at level seven, it's an entire team of people, and you're just working on it. Interestingly, these levels are not just about money. Although it is more common to find the Millionaire Real Estate Agent operating at levels six or seven, we have, on occasion, met Millionaire Real Estate Agents operating at levels three, four, or five. They're just working more in it and therefore have more jobs than they would if they were operating at level six or seven.

> *"If you don't treat it like a business, it won't become a business. Now that I have a real business, I work because I want to, not because I have to."*
>
> Bill Ryan
> Millionaire Real Estate Agent
> Chandler, AZ
> Sales volume—$54 million

The reality is if you don't choose to turn your self-employed job into a 7th Level business that runs without your having a job in it, then you will obviously have to master investing in order to achieve passive income in your life. This is the dilemma of every person in the real estate sales industry. Because there is typically no retirement plan set aside for them, they must create their own. Sadly, most do not.

While the real estate industry provides great freedom, flexibility, and the opportunity for a high income, it does not provide for the financial security of its independent agents. These two realities—unlimited earning potential and no security structure—represent two of the most compelling arguments for and against working in real estate sales. The fact is, independent practitioners must fend for themselves and provide for their own financial future.

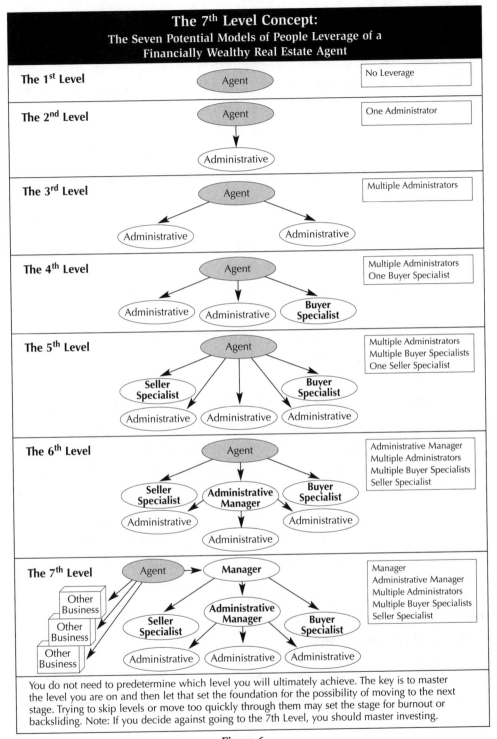

The 7th Level Concept:
The Seven Potential Models of People Leverage of a
Financially Wealthy Real Estate Agent

The 1st Level — Agent — No Leverage

The 2nd Level — Agent → Administrative — One Administrator

The 3rd Level — Agent → Administrative, Administrative — Multiple Administrators

The 4th Level — Agent → Administrative, Administrative, Buyer Specialist — Multiple Administrators / One Buyer Specialist

The 5th Level — Agent → Seller Specialist, Buyer Specialist, Administrative, Administrative, Administrative — Multiple Administrators / Multiple Buyer Specialists / One Seller Specialist

The 6th Level — Agent → Seller Specialist, Administrative Manager, Buyer Specialist, Administrative — Administrative Manager / Multiple Administrators / Multiple Buyer Specialists / Seller Specialist

The 7th Level — Agent → Manager → Administrative Manager → Seller Specialist, Buyer Specialist, Administrative; Other Business, Other Business, Other Business — Manager / Administrative Manager / Multiple Administrators / Multiple Buyer Specialists / Seller Specialist

You do not need to predetermine which level you will ultimately achieve. The key is to master the level you are on and then let that set the foundation for the possibility of moving to the next stage. Trying to skip levels or move too quickly through them may set the stage for burnout or backsliding. Note: If you decide against going to the 7th Level, you should master investing.

Figure 6

If real estate agents do not build their own practice into an asset-based business that can generate business passive income, they will have to find some other means to take care of their financial needs when they stop listing and selling homes. They will need to have invested a significant share of their earned income over a period of many years. And they will need to have wisely placed that money in investment vehicles from stocks and bonds to CDs and real estate to achieve sources of future income. Those real estate agents will then have to master those forms of investing or pay someone to do it for them.

With this in mind Millionaire Real Estate Agents choose to provide for their own future by moving their income-generating real estate job into a business that can eventually provide them an ongoing stream of passive income long after they cease personally selling and listing homes. Mastery of other forms of investment is not necessary. Their whole career has been about the pursuit of mastery (of being their best) in real estate. Taking their business to the 7th Level is just an extension of that mastery. Long before they chose to shift from Net a Million to Receive a Million, they had an exceptional grasp of their Economic, Budget, Lead-Generation, and Organizational Models. They followed a normal progression from sales productivity to business leadership. In the end, they built a business that can be productive and profitable without their sitting in the driver's seat day in and day out. They leveraged themselves into financial security.

When you reach this level, you will have an asset that can financially sustain you, one you can continue to own or choose to sell. You can continue to reap the benefits of your wise decisions or, at some point, simply cash out. Having a 7th Level business gives you choices. Sadly, most agents don't have this choice.

> *"It is a mistake not to delegate as much as you should. I've made that mistake and tried to do all the details."*
>
> Glen Calderon
> Millionaire Real Estate Agent
> Ozone Park, NY
> Sales volume—$73 million

3. THE THREE KEY HIRES OF A MILLIONAIRE BUSINESS

One of the great business truths is that it doesn't take a lot of people to make a lot happen. Yes, by the time your business reaches the 7th Level, there will be a lot of people involved. But in any well-organized company of any size, the leader has only to focus on a few key personnel who make all the rest happen. We call this the Three-Foot Rule, which demands that we make sure everything within our reach (usually three feet) is magnificent. Applying the Three-Foot Rule to your organization means that the people who report directly to you should also be magnificent. When you surround yourself with "capacity" talent, then everything else falls into place. If you do not have "capacity" talent, no amount of work by you is going to salvage it. From the president of the United States to the neighborhood paperboy, no one succeeds by himself.

History shows great success is achieved when working through a few great people who then in turn work through a few great people, and so on.

> *"The key is to hire good staff."*
> Cristina Martinez
> Millionaire Real Estate Agent
> San Jose, CA
> Sales volume—$136.3 million

So here is a huge truth that most real estate agents might miss: You are probably no more than three hires away from being a Millionaire Real Estate Agent. If you look at the Organizational Model of the Millionaire Real Estate Agent (see Figure 42 in Earn a Million on page 197), you'll notice that when completed there are three people at the top:

1. The lead listing specialist
2. The marketing and administrative manager (who also moves up at the 7th Level to become the business manager)
3. The lead buyer specialist

Everyone else in the chart reports to one of these three people, who, in turn, at any level below the 7th Level, report to you. So when you have those three people in your life and they are magnificent talent, the rest will begin to fall into place. Agents who understand this at a gut level turn their sights toward finding those three key people without hesitation. These three key people will be real "capacity" talent at their jobs. They will see themselves staying for a long time. And they will count on building their careers inside the business of and through a lasting relationship with the Millionaire Real Estate Agent.

You should make note that it is not at least three—it is only three. The key is to have only these three people within your "three feet" and taking your time. The rest of the growth of your company is their job. They will be responsible for recruiting, training, and enforcing standards with the rest as needed to fulfill their job descriptions, departmental goals, and the Big Goals of the team. (Once again, "rock and role" should be playing.) If these three people are not truly capable, then you'll get pieces of their jobs back and some of their people in your space and time.

Five-Year Commitment

When you are looking for these three people, it is extremely important that you seek at least a five-year commitment from them. They need to see the position you are offering them as having serious potential to be their life's work. No matter how great the candidate, don't settle for anyone who

> *"Retention is critical!"*
>
> Glen Calderon
> Millionaire Real Estate Agent
> Ozone Park, NY
> Sales volume—$73 million

can't convincingly demonstrate that level of enthusiasm for your business. Why? You want keepers for life. You need three magnificent people who see themselves in a business relationship with you for a long time.

Big Goals and a clear understanding of what it takes to achieve them will be the real keys to attracting this kind of talent to your organization. Big Goals are like recruiting magnets. They will not only pull you through, they'll attract key talent to you. If there is one thing talent enjoys, it is a big vision of the future and the challenge of getting there. If talent perceives your goals to be too low, you may find that person questioning them from the start. "Why not $2.4 million in GCI?" The positions you're hiring for will not be easy. In fact, they will be full life-expanding challenges, and you don't want to present them as anything less. Low goals and minimal job descriptions actually tend to attract less-ambitious people who look for jobs that will neither push them nor force them to grow. And if those kinds of people are running your business, you should not expect it to grow either. Anything short of magnificent talent need not apply!

Weekly Meetings

So you've found your three key people, managed to recruit them, and are reaping the benefits of bringing real talent to your organization. You must now dedicate time to meet with these key people, strategize, and work on goals and accountability. Open your calendar and pick two hours during the week and reserve those blocks of time every week for the year. One hour will be dedicated to meeting with the person who runs the business. The other hour will be spent with this person as well as the other two key personnel. This second meeting is like an executive staff meeting.

These meetings should always start and end with a discussion of your business goals, whether or not the business is on track, and how to get it on track or keep it there. Ask them to bring their individual goal worksheets that have their personal long-term, one-year, one-month, and weekly goals. You don't need agendas for these meetings—your company goals and their individual goals are the agenda. What else would you need to talk about? Nothing. The rest is all 80 percent stuff. These meetings are consultative; they are about accountability, but they should also be rich with idea sharing and exploration of new directions for the business. If these people are magnificent talent, they will not only identify new areas for growth in your business, but will also serve as excellent sounding boards for your ideas.

Hiring

Not only is it your responsibility to hire the person who will be managing the day-to-day business, but it will also be your responsibility to oversee and be as involved as necessary in the hiring of the other two key personnel. If you've recruited the right person to manage your business, she will likely identify excellent candidates for the other two positions. But don't be lulled into passivity by the magnificence of your first primary hire. You must be actively involved in the hiring of the other two and make absolutely sure they are right for the job. There is simply too much at stake. In the end, hiring and staying in business with these three key people become your total people focus. When done right, they'll hire, train, and consult the rest. When done wrong, you'll get it all back and you'll be busier than you've ever been in your life. Interestingly, the more you focus on making sure your team has the right three key people, no matter how many people you ultimately have, your life becomes and stays less stressful and less complicated than before. It all becomes much more manageable.

The big thought here is this: The way to build a great big business is to build a great small business first. And, in our experience, the way you build that great small business is to build it around three magnificent people. When you get out of their way, provide accountability, and avoid placing limitations on their growth, the great big business will come.

4. Your Role and Responsibilities

The role of the Millionaire Real Estate Agent in a 7th Level business is very clear. It is the same role that every successful business owner has—accountability. You're never released from this responsibility until you decide to sell the business and pass the mantle of accountability to the next owner. At the end of the day, the buck stops with you. It is your business, and you are accountable for its financial success. You may be able to spend less time on the business (when it is achieving goals), but you can never step off the accountability bus.

Accountability is both a mind-set and a skill set. The mind-set is about clarity in setting standards and a tough-minded determination to meeting those standards. The skill set is, on the one hand, about planning and goal setting and, on the other hand, about keeping track and holding others responsible for hitting those goals. You must be able to set standards and goals, clearly communicate them to your team, and then be attentive and persuasive enough to hold people to those standards and goals.

As an owner, the role of accountability is focused on three key areas: leadership, people, and capital. No matter how much time it may take, the Millionaire Real Estate Agent never loses focus on these three aspects of their 7th Level business. These three areas keep the business growing and profitable at a high level. Inattention to them may lead to backsliding, loss of personnel, and loss of profitability.

Leadership Accountability

Visit the business section of any bookstore, and you'll probably find more books on leadership than you can carry to the counter. Having read more of those books than I could list here, I can tell you that while most have great information on how the leader should act, think, and interact in the arena of the business world, they often overlook what the leader must bring to an organization. I've come to believe that as important as personality, drive, and experience are to leadership, the key lies in bringing five things to your venture: mission, vision, values, beliefs, and perspective. We call this the MVVBP of your business, or, as one person put it, the

> *"It's my job to run the business and oversee the marketing—to bring us business."*
>
> Russell Shaw
> Millionaire Real Estate Agent
> Phoenix, AZ
> Sales volume—$50.6 million

DNA code for leaders. In our experience, leaders are attuned to and bring clarity to these five issues:

1. **Mission**—What is our purpose? Why are we in business?
2. **Vision**—What does the world look like during and after we've achieved our mission? What is the journey and the end we have in mind? What are the short-term goals (vision) that will lead us to our long-term goals (mission)?
3. **Values**—What is important to us? What do we value? What is the "why" behind our business? What are our priorities?
4. **Beliefs**—What are the rules and guidelines we will follow as we work together?
5. **Perspective**—What is our current situation? What is the reality of where we are right now?

Basically, leaders are constantly thinking along these lines and communicating and reinforcing their MVVBP in their organization. This is a big part of their responsibility. They bring focus, clarity, and reality to the business. At any meeting, they are the ones who ask: "Where are we going? What will the business look like when we're done?"—mission; "What are our short-term goals?"—vision; "What are our priorities?"—values; "What rules and standards will we follow?"—beliefs; "Where are we right now?"—perspective. They are following a classic formula for leadership. Your business needs leadership, and you must provide it. MVVBP is one formula you can follow to provide direction to your key people.

People Accountability

As we have pointed out, you may be only three hires away from having a Millionaire Real Estate Agent business. However, be forewarned, making great hires is just the beginning of the process. Even with "capacity" talent in place, you cannot sit back and allow them to take your business in any direction they choose. Absentee ownership, as we've said, is a slippery slope that can lead to disaster. People accountability is how

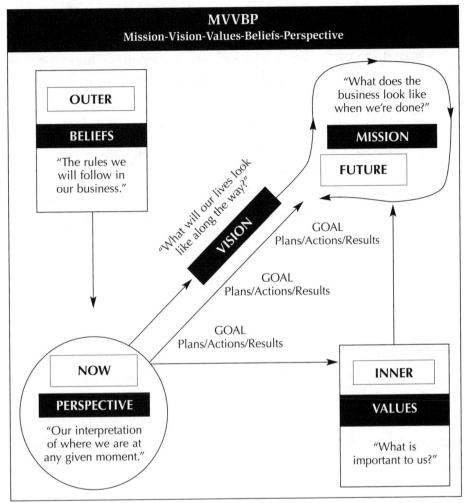

Figure 7

you, as the owner, help your best people grow and meet the standards you have set. In the end, people accountability is how you help them take your business to the highest level possible.

While we have already outlined the methods for achieving accountability (weekly meetings and the consultative interview) and the system for quantifying goals and standards (the goals-to-action worksheet), what you must take away from this section is an understanding and acceptance that "people accountability" will always and ultimately be your responsibility. When you have the right three people in place, accountability is an easy and often uplifting experience. Talent, after all, tends to overshoot the mark. When you are lacking talent in these three positions, accountability will take more of your time, be more stressful, and accomplish less. Just remember, as stressful as it can be to hold someone accountable for a broken standard or unmet goal, accountability is not nearly as stressful as losing the business or having to get back into the day-to-day work of the business.

Our experience with accountability has shown that tough-love accountability with people who are not true talent eventually leads to a mutual parting of the ways or a reduction in their responsibilities. And then you will need to find a truly great hire to replace them. If your other two hires have been great, they will help you make this transition in a way that forces you to step back into the business and completely take over the missing person's job. But you've got to be prepared to do this at any time, if that is what is necessary to preserve the business and get it back on track. It's like James Stewart's character, George Bailey, in *It's a Wonderful Life*, who, on his wedding night, jumps behind the counter to save the family business, the Bailey Bros. Building and Loan, from a potentially disastrous bank run. Business ownership is never really passive, and sometimes it requires sacrifices on your part. Holding your people accountable to standards is the way you improve the odds of not having to jump behind the counter and back into your business.

Beyond this, you are tracking and making sure your key staff members are holding their people accountable to the same standards. Accountability is a skill you want to nourish and develop in them. You'll also be helping them constantly to improve the performance of the team and upgrade talent among the team whenever possible. It goes without saying that the better you are at people accountability, the better your key three will be at hiring talent and upholding standards, and the higher the success of your business.

Capital Accountability

The final area of responsibility for the Millionaire Real Estate Agent business owner is capital accountability—the financial side of ownership. As the owner of a business, you are responsible for providing the financial resources the business needs to survive and grow. You are also ultimately responsible for ensuring that ongoing obligations are fulfilled (you pay the bills) and new systems or hires are funded (you invest in growth and improvement). Owners follow their money, evaluate results seriously, and hold their dollars accountable to appropriate results. Again, we are saying you need to play the Red Light, Green Light game to make sure your return on investments is better than "dollar for dollar."

Fundamentally, this means you are approving all budgets and reviewing your monthly P&Ls (profit and loss statements) with your three key people. It means having every budget variance justified to ensure fiscal accountability. As explained in the Controlling Your Costs section of Net a Million, a handy trick for making sure you are involved any time expenses exceed your budget is to:

1. Separate your deposit account from your operating account;
2. Authorize only yourself to write checks or move money from your deposit account; and
3. Place in the operating account at the start of each month only enough money to cover budgeted and approved expenses.

In this way, when expenses run over, your bookkeeping team member will have to come to you to transfer the difference into the operating account. Half of the battle of accountability is awareness. (Incidentally, we've also seen that this method drastically reduces the risk of embezzlement and financial mismanagement—a lesson too many top agents have learned the hard way.) In a similar way, you'll be insisting on economic justification for any new lead-generation ideas, equipment or furniture purchases, or staff hirings. You'll be evaluating whether these proposed costs will generate enough new profit to justify the money spent.

The goal of all of these measures is not just to say no. Besides being the ultimate keeper of the budget, your role is to teach budget accountability to your team. Getting people to understand how to evaluate costs in light of potential benefits, rather than current needs, is invaluable and makes your job much easier. You will be a financial teacher. And as the owner, budget accountability will be a primary area of focus until the day you sell the business.

CONCLUSION

One of the reasons we chose to compare the path of the Millionaire Real Estate Agent to climbing Mount Everest is because so few people have thus far been able to accomplish either feat. Of the thousands of real estate agents we've worked with, only a small number have actually achieved a 7th Level business of the Millionaire Real Estate Agent. But we believe this is more a reflection of the fact that the path to the summit of the real estate sales business has only recently been identified. As with Everest, once the route is clearly marked, more and more high achievers will find they have the desire, the means, and the ability to make the journey themselves. There are thousands of top agents across the country who are perfectly positioned to make the move to Receive a Million, and more who could quickly get themselves on the path. This book is that path.

We firmly believe that once you have taken your real estate sales business to the Net a Million level and have identified the person who can and will take over the management of the business, you have only to focus your attention on the mastery of a handful of issues to reach Receive a Million.

1. Active vs Passive Income—Understanding that passive income is not purely "passive" when we own a business. Your business will still require your involvement and attention, just in a different way.

2. The Opportunity of the 7th Level—As difficult as it is to transform your business into a 7th Level business, exiting your job through conventional investing requires just as much mastery and can be just as tough. Turning your real estate sales business into a 7th Level business is a great option.

3. The Three Key Hires of a Millionaire Business—It takes three magnificent hires to create a Millionaire Real Estate Agent business and take it to the 7th Level. Your job is to recruit, train, consult, and keep these three extraordinarily talented individuals.

4. Your Role and Responsibilities—As a 7th Level Millionaire Real Estate Agent, you have one role—accountability. Your success will hinge on your ability to hold your team accountable in three areas:

   a. Leadership—Part of the measure of your ability to lead your business to a high level of sustainable success will be determined by your ability to bring MVVBP to your business. A true leader is the standard-bearer of the business.

   b. People—Through regular meetings, goal worksheets, and a tough-love insistence on meeting standards, you must bring accountability to your key people and, through them, accountability to your business as a whole.

   c. Capital—As much as you are the ultimate keeper of the budget, you must also bring others to understand the importance of budget accountability.

Part Three:

STAYING ON TOP

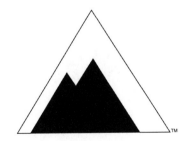

PUTTING IT ALL TOGETHER WITH FOCUS

*"Even if you are on the right track,
you'll get run over if you just sit there."*

Will Rogers

THE $64,000 QUESTION

"No horse gets anywhere until he is harnessed. No steam or gas ever drives anything until it is confined. No Niagara is ever turned into light and power until it is tunneled. No life ever grows great until it is focused, dedicated, disciplined." These words were written by Harry Emerson Fosdick, and ever since I heard them, I can't get them out of my mind. After spending most of my adult life working with successful real estate agents, I am convinced that they succeed through the power of narrowing their focus. You see life doesn't just happen to you. Business success or failure doesn't just happen to you. It's all about choices—choices about what you focus on and how you maintain that focus.

In a PBS interview, Sonny Fox, a former host of the popular game show *The $64,000 Question*, related an interesting story about the tenacity of a young woman determined to appear on the show. Although the young lady had a degree in psychology, she was staying home with her first child while her husband pursued his internship. This was in the fifties. The couple watched *The $64,000 Question* regularly and, eventually, the young woman decided to audition for the show. Even though she had expertise in her field (one of the prerequisites of the show), she was turned down. A young housewife who was a psychologist didn't seem to inspire their imagination. They were looking for "dramatic juxtapositions," like a fisherman who was a mathematician or a pilot who catalogued butterflies. Determined to make the show, this young woman struck upon the idea to fashion herself into a boxing expert. So she began studying in earnest, checked out every book she could find on boxing, and started going to matches.

After a year, she sent in another application with her picture and listed her avocations as "Housewife, Psychologist, and Boxing Expert." She got on the show. And went on to win $64,000 and celebrity. But the story doesn't end there. She used the winnings to complete her doctorate degree in psychology and leveraged her game show celebrity status to kick-start what has become a tremendously successful career. You may know her as Dr. Joyce Brothers. Sonny Fox had this to say about her, "One thing you have to know about Joyce is she's absolutely purposeful in her life. I mean, if she wants something, she goes after it."

Dr. Joyce Brothers knew what she wanted, focused on it, and achieved it. She proved that today's focus could ultimately manifest itself as tomorrow's reality.

FIVE SIMPLE STEPS

At the outset of this book, I made it clear that we believe high achievement may be simpler than you might think. Not easy—just simpler. What we meant by simpler is that what you need to do is clear and it is absolutely possible for anyone to do it. However, when we say "anybody can succeed," we do not mean "everybody can succeed." There is a big difference. It is our belief that anybody can succeed at a high level, but not everybody will. Why? Focus. We don't know why people are unable to achieve focus, we just know that it is the little difference that makes the big difference in their lives. The great thing about your sales business is that it's not about what everyone can do, it is about what you can and will do. It is about opportunity, not averages.

The future of your real estate business depends directly on your ability to focus it in the proper direction. Obviously, the direction you aim determines the targets you can hit. Aim low and you will probably only have the option of hitting a variety of low targets. Pull your aim higher and you'll probably have the option of hitting higher targets. Just remember that when you aim low only a stray bullet hits a high target.

Big can be great, but only if you narrowly focus your business on the simple issues that make big happen in a great way. The bigger you want your business to be, the narrower your focus will need to be on what matters. In the end, the size of the business or staff isn't really your main concern—the focus is. Stephen McKenna once observed that "all good is gained by those whose thought and life are kept pointed close to one main thing, not scattered abroad upon a thousand." With this in mind, I want to suggest five simple steps that can lead you to great focus and open up a world of possibilities in your business and in your life:

1. Create a personal plan and make process your focus.
2. Time block to get your focus.
3. Get accountability to keep your focus.
4. Make sure your environment supports your focus.
5. Keep your energy to maintain your focus.

1. CREATE A PERSONAL PLAN AND THEN MAKE PROCESS YOUR FOCUS

The first thing I want you to do is set high goals in key areas. Anton Chekov taught that "man is what he believes." I want you to think and believe big. Big Goals require Big Models, and that's what I'm really after.

> "Everything I do is thought out and planned in advance. By four or five P.M. I have my next day planned."
>
> John Toye
> Millionaire Real Estate Agent
> Westland, MI
> Sales volume—$39.2 million

I want you following a big plan that is built from a Big Model. What I know for sure is that the achievement of Big Goals is only possible when the plan you are following is built from a Big Model and you make the implementation process your focus. An amazing truth is that process brings focus even when we ourselves feel unfocused. Call it a trick of the trade if you want, but it's true. When you concentrate on the process of implementing a plan that comes from a Big Model, big achievement becomes not just possible but much more likely. Now this doesn't mean that simply because you follow a big process, you'll hit the Big Goal. What it does mean is that it won't be possible to become your very best if you don't. The truth I have come to know very clearly is that seeking mastery is a process and a path, not an event. Therefore, staying on the path and working from the process becomes your focus.

AIM HIGH

It is appropriate here to reiterate the opening concept of the book—aiming high matters. Aiming high empowers big accomplishment. On the one hand, knowing the minimum income you need to make to live your life the way you desire is important. On the other hand, letting that number become the driving force for your business plan will always hold you back. Can you see that now? Goals are an end point, a finish line. And what do we do when we cross the finish line? We stop. We express our relief at having made it or cry for joy, and we stop. The thing you must be careful about with goal setting is to avoid letting your goals become ceilings to your future achievement. Low (even moderate) goals are limiting. At best, we stop for a while, realize we still have gas in the tank, and go about setting new goals to motivate us to keep moving and growing. Time is lost and opportunities are missed. A much better path is to set goals that place the finish line far, far away and then allow ourselves to pause to catch our breath or celebrate our progress along the way. Big Goals keep our feet moving and lead us closer to our highest possible potential.

The Big Model will tell you when your plan needs focus. And your plan will always be about taking action. What I hope this book has revealed to you is that this action plan must always focus on the three big rocks:

1. Leads—Use a database-driven approach with a focus on seller listing leads.
2. Listings—Get the number of seller listings you must get and market those listings systematically to gain additional buyer and seller leads.
3. Leverage—Recruit "capacity" talent with an emphasis on your three key hires, and require the talent to implement systems and tools.

Stay focused on these three things and you will take your business to the highest possible level. Try to get past the natural tendency to judge whether you can or can't do it and commit yourself to the pursuit of excellence. Then focus on the process of implementing and growing into the Big Models.

T.R.Y.

Not to be cute, but rather to be instructive, I would ask you to view the word try as an acronym for The Real You. Through years of teaching, we know for a fact that most people will never know who they really are or what they can really achieve because they fear to try. The Real You can show up only when you try. So don't be left high and dry—just aim high and try!

2. TIME BLOCK FOR FOCUS

The next thing I want you to do is begin to time block. The second step in making your business success happen is focusing on making sure the key things get done. Time blocking will help you with this. Think of it this way: If everyone has the same amount of time, then success at a high level isn't about how much time you have, but rather how you use that time.

> *"I do my calls first and my need-to-dos second. My get-to-dos come last."*
> John Toye
> Millionaire Real Estate Agent
> Westland, MI
> Sales volume—$39.2 million

BUSINESS VS BUSYNESS

All real estate agents have a choice—they can either be in business or in "busyness." Most are in busyness. Why? Their time is not focused on what really must be done to drive their business at a big level. They are not clear about their models, so they are not clear about the activities and priorities on which they should focus their time. Millionaire Real Estate Agents are just the opposite. They don't have a "to do" list—they have a "have to" list. Through time blocking, they make sure that the "have to" gets done before the "to do." They know what has to happen, and, at the beginning of each year, month, week, and day, they open their calendar and "block off" the appropriate amount of time to get those things done. Everything else—their "to do" list—gets scheduled after and around the "have to" activities.

When you give every activity equal importance, prioritization happens only when deadlines and problems force you to react to them. Let's face it, the stuff that matters most isn't always the most fun. This leads people who work off of "to do" lists to act like children picking at their food—they start with the favorites and save the veggies for last. So by the time they get to them, their "business veggies" (read: tasks that would have been easier or more effective if done earlier) are cold and hard to get down, or they may be full (read: worn out) and not have room (read: energy) for more.

High achievers are sensible enough to prioritize activities according to their ability to make the business grow and then time block their calendars to ensure they have time to do them. They look first to take care of lead generation with a focus on seller listings. Only when these important items get done, and done well, do they turn their focus to other, less important activities. It is the difference between business and busyness. It is the difference between productivity and activity. It is the difference between the Millionaire Real Estate Agent and everyone else.

BUDGET YOUR TIME

Many, many years ago, I learned a basic truth about time blocking: Until your goals consistently hit your calendar—you won't consistently hit your goals. This truth makes your calendar an achievement power tool, just as your budget is your financial power tool. In fact, time blocking can just as easily be thought of as a way to budget your time. That

> "I have a peaceful morning to start my day. I work out three times a week. I end my work day at six or six-thirty p.m., and I take no phone calls at home."
>
> Valerie Fitzgerald
> Millionaire Real Estate Agent
> Los Angeles, CA
> Sales volume—$160 million

is, you are going to your calendar and setting aside in advance enough time to accomplish the activities that will drive and build your business to its highest potential (Leads, Listings, and adding Leverage). In much the same way you hold the dollars you spend accountable for producing appropriate results, you will be holding yourself accountable for focusing your energy where you've budgeted it for as long as you've budgeted it or until the task it completed. If you set aside an hour each morning to make ten prospecting calls to your allied resources, then you'll hold yourself accountable to making all ten calls, even if the first nine were spectacular, and even if you run long and have to bump other items off your calendar. Time blocking is for your 20 percent and is a skill that absolutely must be learned, practiced, and turned into a key productivity business habit. It will become, over time, one of the most important business habits you ever acquire. Agents who never acquire the time-blocking business habit end up with time-wasting busyness habits and fall short of their potential.

FOCUS YOUR TIME BLOCKING

Let's get a little clearer. The habit is not about blocking off all your time. That would be too rigid and impractical. The idea is to block off enough time for your key 20 percent activities. Time blocking up front is actually easy. Just go to your calendar and do it. The real challenge is to honor the system by protecting the time you've set aside and utilizing it with absolute focus in the face of the inevitable barrage of false priorities and interruptions that appear each day. You have to remind yourself that nothing—let me repeat—*nothing* is more important to your business than your focus on lead generation, listings, and the pursuit of leverage through talent. If you take care of these core issues, you will experience what is possible. Lose your focus on these key issues, and you'll experience the low ceiling of limitations and the feeling of what is not possible.

In the end, time blocking is a process, a system to help you maintain your focus. It opens the door to focused activity and the high accomplishment that focus makes possible.

3. GET ACCOUNTABILITY TO KEEP YOUR FOCUS

Working with and observing agents over the years has taught us a few things. Everyone has habits, behaviors, biases, and skills that, at some point, create a natural ceiling of achievement for them. All agents reach a point where they say, "I'm doing my best, and this is the best I can do." That's what we call a hard achievement ceiling, and no matter who you are, you will hit one. Breaking through it will require your focus on the key areas and maintaining that focus over time.

> *"I've always learned from others. Allan Domb taught me to focus my market and make better use of my time."*
>
> Gregg Neuman
> Millionaire Real Estate Agent
> San Diego, CA
> Sales volume—$113 million

LONG-TERM FOCUS

Getting focus is easy. Keeping it over time is not. Acknowledging that focus is difficult to keep is a great place to start. How good are you at maintaining your focus? Honestly? Do exercise regimes and nutrition plans remain a part of your life, or do you pursue them just long enough to get results? The core models, systems, and issues of high success are clearly identified in this book, but to be your best you'll have to focus on them daily for as long as it takes. And by virtue of the fact that they are very Big Goals and Big Models, it may take a long while. As far as your focus is concerned, staying the course is critical.

Just why is long-term focus so hard to achieve? First, prolonged focus on the same issues can feel like routine, and routine can lead to boredom. When boredom sets in, attention drifts. And when your attention drifts, the craving for novelty creeps in and doing something new starts to appear more and more appealing. Think back to when you were a kid and set out to singe a leaf or burn lines in a wooden plank by hovering your magnifying glass above it. For the technique to work, you had to hold your magnifying glass perfectly still to focus the sun's rays on a tight spot and then keep it there until the leaf or wood crackled and burned. You learned quickly that moving the magnifying glass around too much didn't have much effect at all. One approach creates fire—the other brown spots. One required long-term focus—the other did not. One was hard—the other wasn't.

If focus brings results, then long-term focus brings long-term results. Everyone can focus on something for some period of time. The trick is to learn how to focus on something day in and day out for the long haul. Long-term results require that you focus your efforts on the smallest number of key activities that will, in turn, generate the greatest results. No other principle is violated more in the real estate sales business than the basic principle of long-term focus. In no other industry that I know of do people change strategies so often. This is due in part to intense competition and also to the extraordinary number of differing opinions about what real estate practitioners should be doing with their time. This is unfortunate since all our experience points to a simple path of beginning with a proven Big Model and riding that jumbo jet as far as you can go.

Realistically, you can't have total focus in everything you do, nor maintain it all the time on any single thing you do. Acknowledging the limits of your ability to focus is important because it allows you then to choose carefully what you need to focus on and then find ways to help you maintain that focus at a high level over time. One of the best ways to do that is to bring some accountability into your business life.

ACCOUNTABILITY FOR REFOCUS

Accountability is an empowering process for continuous focus and refocus. Let's pull together some of the points we've made thus far in our quest to get you powerful and prolonged focus: First, we created a personal plan (Big Goals and Big Models) and made the implementation process of that plan our focus. We have focus. Next, we time blocked so our time to do the key activities was always protected. This gave us short-term focus by allocating our time to fit our focus. Then reality hits! We discover it's hard to keep our focus over time, even with time blocking. We discover that time blocking alone won't keep us focused over time. We need help. The solution is accountability.

Unfortunately, most people have a warped understanding of accountability and little to no appreciation for how empowering it can be in their life. Insofar as your focus is concerned, accountability picks up where time blocking leaves off. And you get the best accountability through a relationship that follows a process to refocus you regularly. It sharpens you over time. Accountability shapes and reshapes your focus. It is a learning loop for seeing clearly what you should be focusing on and a feedback loop for refocusing when your attention slides.

THE ACCOUNTABILITY PROCESS

Basically, accountability is a process you do with someone else. It's hard over time to hold yourself accountable to tough goals. To be effective, it relies on your ability to accurately track your activities and the results you get. If you open up your dictionary to the word *accountability*, you'll see that it is derived from *account*, which means "to furnish a justifying explanation." It means "to answer for." Accountability is about defending your activities to an objective observer. It is funny how, when you are asked to explain why you are doing something, you can immediately see the foolishness of actions that seemed perfectly logical at the time. I think spouses provide a heavy measure of accountability in our idle time, and that takes the form of, "Honey, what the heck are you doing?"

Kidding aside, you do need someone else to hold you accountable, but you also have to keep track of your numbers. Your goal numbers may be the target, but they mean nothing if you are not taking regular measurements of your progress toward them. Monthly and weekly goals need to have monthly and weekly progress assessments to be meaningful. At any point in the game, you've got to know the score and how far ahead or behind you may be; otherwise, you'll never be in a position to make meaningful adjustments. Real estate agents who do not keep track of their lead generation, sales productivity, and financial performance will be hard-pressed ever to sustain high-level results.

With your numbers in hand, accountability is about getting and using feedback. This means to take time on a regular, planned basis to meet with whoever is holding you accountable, look at your business numbers, and refocus your efforts. This is the essence of the accountability feedback loop—set goals, do the key activities, measure the results, evaluate the process, and make adjustments (refocus) when necessary. The more often you go through this process, the better your ability to maintain your focus on the activities that yield the best results.

Make no mistake—you cannot effectively do this alone. You must involve someone else to hold you accountable. Some people may be more disciplined or have greater focus, but no one can successfully and continually hold themselves accountable. Existentialist philosopher and playwright Jean-Paul Sartre in his masterful play *No Exit* shows how hard it is to discover the truth. You see, our perceptions of our own actions are forever colored by our intentions, and others see only our actions without the benefit of knowing what we really intended. The truth, of course, lies somewhere in between. Having an outside perspective helps strip away the excuses so you can see your actions and results in a very honest, unblinking manner. It takes another person or a group of people to hold you accountable and get you refocused. That is why nearly all high achievers have coaches and consultants. Even the best of the best—Mia Hamm, Tiger Woods, Marion Jones, and Michael Jordan—all have a coach or coaches to keep them focused and on track to their Big Goals. Accountability is the relationship of choice for champions.

So the key to accountability is to select a person (coach, consultant, mentor, or peer partner) or a mastermind group, and then meet on a regularly scheduled basis to review your goals and results. The same rules apply to your accountability sessions that apply to your sessions with your staff. You need to bring and share your goals worksheet, an accounting of your business plans and activities, and an accurate summary of the results you have achieved to date. You've got to avoid rationalizations and hiding places and just deal with your actions and results. Accountability is not just about maintaining your focus; you will find it can empower you to build more effective habits and awareness of when you are and aren't on track. When you don't have accountability in your life, failure often comes as a total surprise. This is not a good thing.

Accountability is the most powerful tool for achieving Big Goals and long-term success. We like to say, "Keep track and feed it back." That, in fact, could be the focus motto of the Millionaire Real Estate Agent. In the end, it is not only a refocus tool for themselves but also for their key people. As we pointed out in Receive a Million, accountability is the key to achieving high performance and success through others.

One final thought on accountability—frequency matters. The more you try to achieve or the greater the personal growth you seek, the more frequent your accountability will need to be. In business, a monthly review of activities, production, and financial performance is the minimum. For personal performance accountability, we recommend a more rigorous weekly or biweekly schedule of review and accountability. Some top performers have daily meetings (in person or by phone) with their coach or consultant. Over time, you will learn what frequency of accountability works best for you. The obvious truth is this: Just do it.

4. MAKE SURE YOUR ENVIRONMENT SUPPORTS YOUR FOCUS

Environment is one of the most underrated, catch-you-by-surprise issues of success. Whether or not you are aware of it, your business environment and your personal environment matter. They matter a lot. In fact, your environment matters so much that it may be one of the most important focus support issues you ever have to deal with. While people may join companies for a lot of reasons, they usually stay or leave for one—the environment and its impact on them. We believe strongly that your environment is a critical issue to your success and that it must clearly support your goals.

The first time I ever experienced this was when I first entered management. In my first year, I encountered a surprising number of women who one by one ended up in my office in crisis and, often, in tears. They were dealing with frustration over their situation. These women where in their late forties and early fifties and, after raising a husband and a family, had reentered the working world. After years of sacrifice in the name of family, this was to be their time for professional self-expression. And they were each having a serious challenge. Why? Because the deal their family had cut with them was this: "We'll support your work as long as dinner is still on the table at six and our lives are not disrupted or altered by this 'career phase' you're going through." I was in shock. These women were in situations where they were in deep psychological and physical turmoil because a key aspect of their personal environment—their family—was not supporting them. Let me rephrase that: A key aspect of their personal environment was pretty much working in direct opposition to their goals. That was when I realized that our environment absolutely must support our goals.

Look, most of us just try and adapt to our environment. We make the best of it. Sometimes we get frustrated and complain about it. But we seldom see our environment as something we can control, as something we can change. So rather than attempt to shape our environment, many simply choose to abandon it. That, or we soldier on and continue to live in an environment that does not support our focus to become our best.

THE CHIEF ARCHITECT

Your environment has an impact on you constantly. It either builds you up and supports you, or it tears you down and fights you. Sometimes this is obvious right up front. Other times it creeps up and takes you by

> *"Calm down and organize yourself. When you organize your life and your mind—that voice in your head—you get very calm inside and you get more productive outside."*
>
> Valerie Fitzgerald
> Millionaire Real Estate Agent
> Los Angeles, CA
> Sales volume—$160 million

surprise. The more you are aware of the power of your surroundings to affect your life, the sooner you can address it and become the chief architect of your own environment. By being the chief architect, you reduce the risk of becoming a victim of it. As chief architect, there are two important design issues you must deal with: your physical environment and your people environment.

Your Physical Environment

The key issue of your physical environment is productivity. That is, does your office space, furniture, equipment, and tools support your productivity goals. This is basic stuff from the ergonomics of your chair to the quality of your office lighting. Either they support your efforts to keep you focused, or they distract you with an aching back and irritated eyes. Likewise, your equipment needs to be up to the task. You don't need an IBM mainframe for your basic real estate computing needs, but you will need a reliable desktop, with updated software that isn't prone to crashing. Your systems are also a part of your physical environment. How the phones are answered, messages taken, or calls directed; what, how, and where records are stored; how easily forms and data can be found and used—these are all physical systems that can enhance or reduce your ability to be productive.

One of the key elements to reach your full potential is your physical environment and how well it matches up to, supports, and focuses you in your endless pursuit of productivity. It is surprising how many people choose to tolerate a poor physical environment rather than take a little time or money and fix it. In truth, your physical environment is much easier to alter than your people environment, so don't forget who the architect of your life is—*you*!

Your People Environment

The other main environmental issue is people. If your physical environment is about productivity, then your people environment is about energy and synergy. Your people environment is composed of three groups: the people you are in business with (your team, your company, and other agents); the people you do business with (your clients and vendors); and the people outside your business (your family and friends). What most fail to realize is that you are the gatekeeper and you can control who you let into your world, thus becoming an architect of your people environment.

> *One of the keys to my success has been masterminding and associating with other high-achieving, optimistic agents."*
> Mary Harker
> Millionaire Real Estate Agent
> Dallas, TX
> Sales volume—$52 million

In our experience, high achievers tend to associate with energizers and synergizers—the people who support their goals and work well with them to achieve those goals. People who consciously or subconsciously don't support them, who drain energy and disrupt synergy, are isolated and weeded out. Just like your mom told you, the "kids you hang out with" make a difference in your life.

This is where recruitment of talent plays yet another significant role in your life. The better you are at this, the better your people environment, the better your support, the better your focus, and the less time you'll have to spend at the unsavory task of weeding out the bad. You can either purposely choose to associate and let into your life the people who will support your goals, or you can just use the "wing and a prayer" approach. But, at the end of the day, if the people in your life are not in synergy with your goals, you'll end up negotiating and compromising and feeling less focused.

Your environment can make you or break you—it's that important. And while it may take more grit and courage to alter your people environment than your physical environment, you are ultimately responsible for both. Don't leave the architecture of your environment to chance— shape it, craft it, and make it one that helps you fulfill your promise.

5. KEEP YOUR ENERGY TO MAINTAIN YOUR FOCUS

The fact is that your ability to maintain your focus at a high level over time will largely depend on whether or not you can stay consistently enthusiastic and energized. Getting and sustaining enthusiasm and energy are a bit of a mystery. High achievement requires big energy, but, paradoxically, achievement can also be a source of energy and enthusiasm. So which comes first, the energy or the achievement? Honestly, I don't know. What I do know is that you can't reach Big Goals without a big, sustained effort. And a big, sustained effort requires big, sustained energy. High achievers (certainly all the Millionaire Real Estate Agents I've met) have big energy. The trick is learning how to get it and keep it, too.

Life is energy. For all its applications and complexities, when you boil Einstein's $E = mc^2$ down to the basics, all it says is that everything is energy. Everything is energy, even our physical bodies. After some reflection, I've come to the point of view that what you do with your life and how you do it either adds energy to or subtracts energy from your life. The energy you have at your disposal—the fuel for your life— is determined by the choices you make.

Metaphysics aside, there are some very specific things you can do to increase your energy and thereby maintain your focus. First, I recommend taking a long look at the five energy areas and the Millionaire Real

Estate Agent Energy Plan (Figure 1) outlined in the next section. This section basically describes five kinds of energy in your life and how to get them. Second, I'd ask you to consider the power of learning-based living. In the end, having the energy necessary for Big Goals and sustained achievement is, for us, about two essential habits: the habit of launching your day with energy and the habit of constant renewal through learning.

THE MILLIONAIRE REAL ESTATE ENERGY PLAN

Early in my professional career, I discovered a simple program to harness energy for my life and pull me through the day. It is deceptively simple, but it is also one of the most powerful things I've ever done in support of my goals. Having a steady supply of positive energy is invaluable for the entrepreneur! I call it the Millionaire Real Estate Agent Energy Plan—a big plan for big energy!

The Five Energy Areas

There are five areas in which I need energy. Most likely, they are much the same for you. I need spiritual energy, physical energy, emotional energy, mental energy, and business energy. My simple formula is to "block off" my time such that I can be assured I will be able to pull a lot of energy into my life every day. What I've learned is that the world doesn't really get going until about ten-thirty to eleven A.M. That means, if you really want to get something done with a minimum of interruptions, you'll do it before eleven A.M. when the phone starts ringing and people start popping by. My energy routine is designed with an eleven A.M. end time in mind.

Here is what I do: I get up every day by six A.M. and meditate and pray—for spiritual energy. Then, I exercise and eat—for physical energy. Afterward, I hug, kiss, and laugh with my family—for emotional energy—

and try to do it so that I get to spend time with all of them and still get to the office between eight A.M. and nine A.M. (Most people plan for emotional energy time only in the evenings or on weekends, when it can do little for their daily pursuit of Big Goals.) I then plan and calendar my day—for mental energy—and spend my first, most energized hours in the office working hard on lead generation and recruiting talent—for business energy. I never slack off before eleven A.M.

It is funny, but those early hours of intense focus tend to pull me through the rest of the day. You can get so much going that it takes you the whole afternoon just to wrap things up. That's positive energy creating amazing momentum in your life! Even when I am less structured in the afternoon, I still tend to be phenomenally productive because my earlier actions have dictated my priorities. I truly believe that those first few structured hours of each day make all the difference.

The Millionaire Real Estate Agent Energy Plan
1. Meditate and Pray—Spiritual Energy
2. Exercise and Eat—Physical Energy
3. Hug, Kiss, and Laugh—Emotional Energy
4. Plan and Calendar—Mental Energy
5. Lead Generate—Business Energy

All by Eleven A.M. Every Day!

Figure 1

Renewal Through Learning

Energy matters. How energy is used also matters. Learning is how we come to understand the most powerful and productive ways to use our

"We're education junkies. We talk to others, and they help us realize what is possible."

David and Judie Crockett
Millionaire Real Estate Agents
Concord, OH
Sales volume—$53 million

energy. When we observe people who have achieved a high level of mastery in any endeavor, their actions seem almost effortless, and it appears as if they could do it forever. That is sometimes very much the truth. When people have highly developed skills or great awareness, what they do actually requires less energy and effort. They are simply more efficient and know how to get more of their intended results from their actions.

The illusion is in how "natural" this appears. Sure, a minuscule percentage of us are naturally gifted with extraordinary energy, focus, and skills, but the truth is, most people who appear naturally gifted had to work very hard to achieve that. Jack Nicklaus, in a post-tournament TV interview, once said, "Some people tell me they are amazed with how easily I hit the golf ball so consistently straight and far. I just tell them that if they had been watching me hit hundreds of golf balls every day for all those years, they wouldn't be so amazed."

My point here is this, if you are committed to achieving Big Goals, you must be committed to learning-based living. Learning is both empowering and energizing. It is about gaining new knowledge and new skills. It's also about renewal. And renewal is fun.

So, learning is about gaining knowledge and skills. It allows you to do more with the energy you have, and it is the foundation of proactivity—taking charge and being in control. Being learning-based gives you a great advantage in business over those who are not—by default they have less energy and are spending more of it to do the same things you do easily. For them, ignorance is not bliss.

For you, learning is leverage, and it provides you with three important advantages: wisdom (knowing what to do), competence (knowing how to do it), and foresight (knowing when to do it). Not only does this leverage allow you to avoid wasting energy and to get more done with less energy, it actually brings more energy to you. Honestly, we're not sure why this is true. We just know that it is. Maybe it is in the fact that wisdom, competence, and foresight bring with them healthy confidence, which, in my opinion, is a very energizing emotion. Maybe it is the excitement that comes from doing something really well. The energy may also stem from the mental and spiritual lift that comes from greater awareness and insight. Or maybe it simply comes from personal satisfaction at taking on a new challenge, having the courage to try it, and then realizing you can now do it. Whatever it is, wherever it comes from, this learning-based energy renewal is very real and very powerful.

Whether you are learning by doing or by studying, you'll find that they are both valid and crucial to achieving the highest level of productive energy and using that energy most efficiently. Learning by doing leads to greater skill and competence. Learning by studying leads to greater wisdom and foresight—doing lends experience and study borrows the experience of others who have lived before us.

The Millionaire Real Estate Agents we know read books, listen to tapes, watch videos, and attend seminars and classes regularly. In fact, many spend as much as 10 to 15 percent of their work time pursuing learning. They call it an investment in themselves and a necessary one on the path to big achievement. We agree. It is both a good business strategy and a great life strategy.

Once you accept the challenge of lifelong self-improvement and the path of mastery, you will be humbled by how much you don't really know. A bottomless pit of learning awaits us all. And this is not a negative awareness, it is an exciting and challenging discovery. It will energize you to learn more and never stop. It is perhaps one of the most energizing and uplifting aspects of the path to Big Goal achievement and will hopefully become a big part of your Big Why. It is not just "live and learn"—it's "live to learn!"

CONCLUSION

Focus is really the linchpin in your pursuit of excellence. If we've done our job with this book, you should now know where your focus needs to be today, tomorrow, and for the rest of your career. Leads, Listings, and Leverage may be the cornerstone issues between you and great real estate sales, but if you can develop the kind of intense focus necessary to become a Millionaire Real Estate Agent, that same powerful focus will be yours to apply to other areas of your life. Let focus drive your dreams into reality.

Finally, if we've learned anything, we've learned that

> *"Our systems and our expectations are in place. We can build this business to a very high level. It is a living entity, and I don't see it ending."*
>
> Mary Harker
> Millionaire Real Estate Agent
> Dallas, TX
> Sales volume—$52 million

when you think big, you think possibilities. You think, "What could I possibly do if I really tried? What is possible in my life?" When you think possibilities at this level, you seek out Big Models and processes and then make them your focus. The Big Models and Big Goals will pull you up through smaller goals to your highest achievements possible. You end up living larger, achieving the most you could achieve, and becoming the best you could become.

POINTS TO REMEMBER: Putting It All Together

- In the end, the distinguishing characteristic of high achievers is their ability to maintain their focus over time. We are all capable of great focus, but this personal discipline must be fostered and nurtured in our lives.

  - Create a personal plan and make process your focus.
  - Time block for focus.
  - Get accountability to keep your focus.
  - Make sure your environment supports your focus.
  - Keep your energy to maintain your focus.

- Our admonition to you is to believe in and seek the possibilities your life holds!

Think Big

Act Bold

Live Large

Become the Very Best You Can Become!

REAL-LIFE MILLIONAIRE REAL ESTATE AGENTS

REAL ESTATE ROLE MODELS TO LEARN FROM

Throughout this book we have quoted the words and shared the wisdom of many high-achieving real estate agents. These agents represent—in their real-life accomplishments—what we are endeavoring to teach. We are deeply grateful to all of them for their willingness to give of their time and their wisdom. It is important to note that even though these agents represent all the top national real estate companies and many of the strong regional ones, they all chose to share their knowledge without hesitation or qualification. Like us, they see real estate not in terms of individual companies, but rather in the sense of a family composed of all real estate agents. With that in mind, we chose not to identify their "larger" real estate company affiliations. The truth is their names and personal reputations are their actual "brands"—just like it should be!

In this "real-life" section of the book, we'll share sixteen of their profiles. Because we could not include them all, we selected those whose businesses, in our opinion, are most reflective of the broad base of real estate agents: the listing and sales of existing single-family homes. We hope you will enjoy getting to know them better, just as we have. Their beginnings are varied, and their stories inspirational. Their comments and observations provide both guidance and reassurance. In the end, they show us what is possible on the journey to the highest summit of real estate sales success. Enjoy!

SNAPSHOT OF A MILLIONAIRE

CHRIS CORMACK
Ashburn, VA

Experience—14 years
Before Real Estate—Fashion designer and owner of a custom leather boutique

2001 Production

Transactions—212
Sales Volume—$70 million
Gross Commission Income—$1.9 million

The Team

Sales—Listing specialists, buyer specialist team leader, and nine buyer specialists (with three more candidates pending)

Support—Chief financial officer, closing manager, listing coordinator, executive assistant and marketing director, multimedia specialist, and two runners

Quick Takes

Keys to Success—Today my team is composed of specialists who collaborate to make a well-oiled machine. Our product is designed to create excellence in our marketing, sales, and service. I applaud the professionalism of each team member and am particularly gratified to be working with my son, who is a successful buyer agent.

The benefits of working with a team of specialists are contact quality and expansion.

Training plays a huge role in the success of our team. When a buyer agent joins the team, they go through CC Boot Camp, a two-to-three-week process. In the boot camp, they are trained how to sell real estate at our level of excellence. We have high standards, and they have to learn to play our way and at our pace. They are required to preview five homes every day and meet with the team leader in weekly accountability sessions.

Lastly, we think and act like a business. From our titles to our organization structure, everything reflects a professional business culture. We track our goal, statistical, and budget numbers on a weekly, monthly, and annual basis. Because we know precisely what is happening with our team and our marketplace, we can make solid, informed decisions.

Inspiration—My immediate family. We grew up outside of Washington, D.C. My dad was an incredible salesman who sold to the government. So I learned my selling skills at the dinner table. He was always talking about his current sales. My mother worked for the CIA, which was inspiring. My grandmother was an awesome entrepreneur. She started nursery schools in the days of the Depression, when women didn't really work, and she bought investment real estate. Before that, my great-grandmother came over on a boat, an Irish immigrant. She had been a servant but learned to do bookkeeping and went on to grow her business.

To my two daughters, I am passing on a legacy of being a successful entrepreneur in any field they choose.

Lead Generation—Our primary source of business is marketing. Marketing makes my phone ring. We advertise heavily, and the other portion of my business comes from the Internet. Maybe 20 percent comes from referrals. Overall, we budget 8 to 10 percent of our projected gross for marketing. This year, it's $148,000, and we're on budget. The most effective form is newspapers. We do a full-page ad that's mailed to 50,000 houses. We do this every week. We have a quarter-page ad we run in the local paper. The biggie is CC News. We do a custom full-color newspaper with a market review and all our listings. Our circulation is 22,000, and we even sell ad space. The cost is $7,200 per month before ad sales.

Other Business—A founding member of eFROGG, an interactive Internet system for agents, buyers, and sellers.

Next Year and the Future—For 2002, we're on track to do $2.4 million in GCI. That's our goal, and we're on track for it. We've got 178 transactions on the books. These are our numbers through July. Our goal is 300 units, and we're at 54 percent of that goal. Our volume is 100 million, so we're 53 percent of the way there as well.

SNAPSHOT OF A MILLIONAIRE

David and Judie Crockett
Concord, OH

Experience—24 years
Before Real Estate—Chemist and homemaker

2001 Production

Transactions—306
Sales Volume—$53 million
Gross Commission Income—$1.6 million

The Team

Sales—Three listing specialists (Judie, their daughter, and their son)

Support—Office manager/escrow manager, client service (listing) manager, advertising manager (part time), and an administrative assistant (part time)

Quick Takes

The Beginning—Judie started in 1978 and became a top producer in the area. I left my industry job in 1984 and became manager of the largest office in our area. In 1994, we formed the Crockett Team: Judie, me, our daughter, Melissa, and our son, Todd.

Keys to Success—I'm a strong believer that listings make the business. They make the phone ring. Nobody knows who the selling agent was, but everybody knows who listed it! The best source of leads is the yard sign.

Our business is set up on a systems basis. We set it up so everybody on our team has a special focus. We want them to develop their experience and become a grandmaster of what they do. Then we systematize everything—it's got to be repetitive, it's got to be automatic. It's always documented, and it all goes into our operations manual.

Inspiration—We are education junkies. We attend an awful lot of these things, and we're instructors at many of them.

The real secret to success for Realtors is recognizing what's possible out there. You won't find it looking up and down your street. You need to go out and talk to other people and learn from them.

Lead Generation—We mail postcards to our database of clients four times a year. We send out between 250 and 300 cards around each listing and each sale. We negotiated a very good deal on our Yellow Pages ad (a hard tab in the middle of the book), and we advertise in our regional newspaper.

The mistake that most Realtors make is they love every idea they see. And they're all over the place. You need to define what you want to be and run with that. The typical short, spotty, little campaigns are essentially useless.

We have focused recently on lead tracking. We know where they come from, and we have increased our speed of response and our conversion rates.

Advice—You have to start with good basic people who are likable right away. You don't need anyone who's in any way dysfunctional. Are they motivated? Do they have goals? Are they willing to work as a team? Do they understand how business works? Do they have common sense? If I were a client, would I like this person right away?

Next Year and the Future—We're forming a limited liability company with the four of us being equal partners. We'll have a buy-out program so our children can benefit from what we've built.

SNAPSHOT OF A MILLIONAIRE

Rachel DeHanas
Waldorf, MD

Experience—20 years
Before Real Estate—Secretary for the Board of Education

2001 Production

Transactions—246
Sales Volume—$52 million
Gross Commission Income—$1.5 million

The Team

Sales—Listing specialist (daughter-in-law), buyer and relocation specialist (daughter-in-law), and two buyer specialists

Support—Bookkeeper and property management (husband), marketing and advertising manager (son), computer specialist (son), contract manager, client care manager, a contract specialist, and a contract assistant

Quick Takes

The Beginning—We've lived here since 1969, so I saw the marketplace become the marketplace. My husband, Jack, has had his license since 1976. He talked me into it in the early eighties, and I got my license in 1983. I had a nine-to-three job. We had four sons, and we decided that once we had them raised, I could do something different. That schedule worked very well for me as a mother, a working mother, and allowed me to earn some income outside the home. I also owned a ceramics business where I was a teacher three nights a week. I had about a hundred students. So I operated that business three nights a week in addition to working the school secretarial job, raising four children, having dinner on the table at five, and all that good stuff. And in the early seventies, before I got into the ceramics business, I sold Tupperware. I was a manager for Tupperware and had about eighteen salespeople under me. . . . So I've always held two or three different jobs at the same time.

Keys to Success—The systems. Having systems in place and being able to capture the buyers. The Internet also. We're getting probably 47 percent of our buyers from the Internet. I have listings. I'm the top lister in the area, and I have been. We get buyers because we have listings.

In the early nineties I started looking at it as more of a business and hiring assistants. After the first assistant, I saw how much more volume I could do. It seemed like every time I added a person or did something different, it freed me up to concentrate on the important things. It is a steady increase.

Lead Generation—We have a monthly newspaper. It's bulk mailed, so it goes out to probably 50,000 to 75,000 households. We inserted it in our local paper, but the distribution was not good enough. Once we started bulk mailing it, we could tell a big difference in the number of calls we received.

We're about 47 percent Internet now. My signs are the next best thing. Since 1987 or '89, I've done a thirty-second spot on our local cable station. I don't know that you can track that. When we ask people when they call in, most of them say, "I just see you everywhere."

Other Business—Property management.

Next Year and the Future—DeHanas has targeted in 2002 to do more than 500 transactions, $75 million in sales volume, and $2 million in commissions. Her vision for the future: My vision would be to have a business my children can take over and pay me very well in my retirement years so I can live the life I'm accustomed to.

SNAPSHOT OF A MILLIONAIRE

VALERIE FITZGERALD
Los Angeles, CA

Experience—14 years
Before Real Estate—Fashion model

2001 Production

Transactions—57
Sales Volume—$160 million
Gross Commission Income—$3.2 million

The Team

Sales—Four buyer agents

Support—Office manager, marketing coordinator, a contract and escrow coordinator, and a personal assistant/call coordinator

Quick Takes

The Beginning—Having been a NYC-based world-traveling professional model, I moved to Los Angeles for a job assignment. It fell through, and I, as a single mother, needed to find a way to earn a living. A friend guided me into real estate.

I had no people skills, sales skills, or business experience, but I was determined to make it and make a life for my daughter.

I made a pest of myself until a builder gave me a break by letting me sell his $3 million home. I held it open every Saturday and Sunday and met many new people until it sold, and my career began.

Keys to Success—I make it my business to know the real estate and financial markets, and I give informed advice. Most people want you to lead them.

I'm a listing agent. Ninety-five percent of my business is listings. I do what I want to do—list, sell, and negotiate—and I hire people to do the rest.

Just take the leap of faith and hire someone. It will open you up and free you up.

I work with celebrities like Sly Stallone, Leonardo DiCaprio, Ben Affleck, Christina Aguilera, Bruce Willis, Demi Moore, Vanna White, and Holly and Rodney Peete, to name a few. In my experience, they are no different than anyone else—they are real people. When representing them, I create a comfort level for them.

Inspiration—I love this business. My motto is: If you shoot for the moon and miss, you're still among the stars.

I work out three times a week, and I have three coaches: a personal coach, a physical coach, and a business coach.

Calm down and organize yourself. When you organize your life and your mind (that voice in your head), you get very calm inside, and you get more productive outside.

Lead Generation—I do a lot of media public relations for television. I have done shows for *Entertainment Tonight* and for the following networks: CBS, NBC, HGTV, MTV, and E! Entertainment Television. But, most important, I am talking and being in front of people *all* the time. I do this by staying involved in charity events, political events, school programs, sporting events, social events, and religious activities.

SNAPSHOT OF A MILLIONAIRE

MARY HARKER
Dallas, TX

Experience—34 years
Before Real Estate—Symphony violinist, violin and
piano teacher, choir director,
gourmet food editor

2001 Production

Transactions—178
Sales Volume—$52 million
Gross Commission Income—$1.4 million

The Team

Sales—Listing and buyer specialists (sons Dan and Joseph) and a part-time referral agent

Support—Executive administrator, listing coordinator, a runner, and occasional
part-time staff

Quick Takes

Perspective—I've been in the business for thirty-four years helping relocating families
find a home and reconnect their fractured activity network.

Keys to Success—We've been successful because we started with great discipline and
focused on what we wanted to achieve. And that means putting our goals in writing.
In the beginning, I had high energy, a burning desire to succeed, and written goals,
but no training. By the end of the first year, I had earned $376! My dad told me,
"You can be anything you want to be if you really put your mind to it." Tapes and
books on success became my teachers, later many trainers added to that.

Mastering marketing and production took us only so far. Focusing on results, from written goals, implementing models, systems and procedures, and holding them accountable has led us to the next level. Being coached and consulted by Gary Keller is moving us from having a job to having a business through business skills and disciplines of profitability and leverage. It's been pointed out to me by other mega producers, "How in the world did we do so well, when we knew so little."

Inspiration—I surround myself only with people of matched values…those who are optimistic and positive. My mom lived to be ninety-five. Every morning I would ask her, "Are you going to have a good day?" She would always answer, "I choose to have a good day. I don't have enough days left in my life to have a bad one." She was right, she didn't. And neither do I!

Lead Generation—Teaching in Texas, across the United States and Australia for conferences, and also as a CRS faculty member, writing for publications, masterminding has led to incredible opportunities of building relationships. We have built a national agent-to-agent referral network that generates 84 percent of our repeat and referral business and has led to a database of 6,000 people. Every year a magnetic calendar including our picture is sent out. Because this piece generates over 2 million exposures to our name, no wonder we hear over and over, "It's hard to forget your face, Mary, when we see it every day." We believe in turning one sale into multiple sales through direct mail pieces of added value every twenty-one days followed by notes, phone calls, and face-to-face meetings.

We honor our customers and vendors by contributing a portion of our commission to children's charities and a Christian camp for children.

We give back to the community by sitting on advisory boards for developers and builders and boards of directors for Sky Ranch Christian Camp, and raising funds for Habitat for Humanity, Leukemia, and the Dallas Symphony.

Next Year and the Future—I see myself being able to walk out the door of our company and still have a residual income that will allow us a lifestyle we have enjoyed for the last twenty years. We are debt-free. That gives us a lot of options.

Joe Harker, my husband and best friend for more than 46 years, and I have endeavored to bring value to the lives of our three married children and eight grandchildren by teaching them balance and the importance of making a difference in the lives of people through teaching and service in the years to come. God, Family, Business—that is the legacy we want to leave.

SNAPSHOT OF A MILLIONAIRE

CRISTINA MARTINEZ
San Jose, CA

Experience—13 years
Before Real Estate—Chemical engineer in aerospace

2001 Production

Transactions—240
Sales Volume—$136.3 million
Gross Commission Income—$4.08 million

The Team

Sales—Two buyer assistants

Support—Office manager, broker, a listing service coordinator, three closing coordinators, and a bookkeeper

Quick Takes

Keys to Success—Number one is, I have a high regard for work—a very good work ethic. Number two is integrity. A good name is to be chosen over great riches.

I have a system that works for me. I have a great staff. I do all the negotiations. All listing and sales appointments are done in the office, as are all closings. I have my own mortgage company.

I know that if I have to run a business, it must be profitable. I track my expenses closely and I am operating at 60 to 65 percent profit. I do this in both my real estate and mortgage companies.

I work only four days a week, and I average ten sales a week. I have to maximize what I do. That's why I have created a system where everybody is proficient doing what they are supposed to do, as my extension of the business.

Lead Generation—My business comes 70 percent from repeat and referral. I send my past clients a calendar every year. After every closing we send them a gift. I do no advertising, no direct mail, and no geographic farming.

I just call. I have a schedule I follow. The first hour I call five clients, the second hour I do lead follow-up, and the rest of the day is appointments and contract negotiations. And, that's it.

I deal with a lot of investors. Last year, I did 300 deals, but I worked with only 100 people. I do multiple deals per person—about three deals per person in a year.

I turn my past clients into investors—I create a dream for them. I change their financial destiny.

Next Year and the Future—I see my business doing $10 million in income in 2003 and $15 million the following year. I plan to keep the profit margin at 60 percent.

The business success has allowed me to buy buses for my church so that we can bring children to Sunday School. We visit underprivileged kids on Saturday to see what they need, and then on Sunday we load them on buses and bring them to Sunday School. After we've fed them spiritually, we feed them physically before we take them home. I just donated $3.1 million for building Golden State Baptist College. I believe the key to my business is putting God first. If I'm right with God, I can be right with man.

SNAPSHOT OF A MILLIONAIRE

RONNIE AND CATHY MATTHEWS
Houston, TX

Experience—14 years
Before Real Estate—Owners of a plumbing and
utility business

2001 Production

Transactions —624
Sales Volume—$99.5 million
Gross Commission Income —$2.5 million

The Team

Sales—Three buyer agents and one listing specialist

Support—Three in the pending department, three in the listing department, one in general administration and technology, and one contract specialist

Quick Takes

The Beginning—In 1988, we closed the doors to our plumbing and utilities business. After building it to sixty-five employees in 1988, the Houston economy crashed, and many of our clients went out of business and never paid us. We ended up losing everything and having to start over.

I was a high school dropout, and Cathy had a year of college. We had nothing to fall back on. We had bought and sold some real estate, so we said, "Look, this sounds pretty good—let's try this." That's how we started. It caught on, and we have been pleasantly surprised.

Cathy and I have always done our separate things. We've worked together but always used our different talents and our different personalities. She worked with all buyers, and I was the listing guy. I've also run the business and counted the dollars.

At first it was tough to hire the people and invest the time to train them. But the business bloomed, and it grew. We'd add a person here, a person there, and something would just kick in and we'd grow 30 to 40 percent every year. Next thing you knew, we're at $100 million a year in sales!

Keys to Success—There are two or three basics to the real estate business. First, you have to realize you're in business for yourself. Most Realtors just don't understand that. Second, you've got to work harder and smarter than anyone else—particularly at the beginning. Third, you must always return a phone call, even when it's inconvenient. We've always made it a practice to return every single call every single day.

Lead Generation—I have never made a cold call, never knocked on a door, never called a For Sale By Owner. If you do your job right and you take care of people, they will spread the word. Everyone knows someone who is thinking of buying or selling a home. We just keep our name in front of them.

We have a client base of about 3,000 that we mail to every six weeks, generally a large four-color postcard. Then we have about 5,000 in our farm area, and we mail to them every three weeks. Asking for business is an important part of everything we do.

Next Year and the Future—I've worked a hundred hours a week for a lot of years. I've brought it down to seventy and then down to sixty. I'd like to get it down to twenty. I'm nowhere near ready to just quit, but we are starting to think about what we might do when we grow up.

I've started branching into some other things. I bought 130 acres about six years ago, and we've subdivided and developed that. In the past twelve months I closed on two separate fifty-acre properties. And now, I have a contract on another 170 acres. I own twenty or so residential income properties and a small office complex. The idea is to generate passive income from my properties and my business.

Anyone can be successful in our great country, but you have to earn it!

SNAPSHOT OF A MILLIONAIRE

MIKE MENDOZA
Phoenix, AZ

Experience—19 years
Before Real Estate—Professional Baseball Player
(Houston Astros)

2001 Production

Transactions— 348
Sales Volume—$60 million
Gross Commission Income – $1.79 million

The Team

Sales—15 licensed real estate agents

Support—Listing coordinator, transaction coordinator, administrative assistant, a relocation director, and an accountant

Quick Takes

The Beginning—Well, for me, real estate was really the first job that I considered working. I never considered baseball a job. I never made a ton of money playing baseball. The most I ever made in the major leagues was $32,500 a year, so it wasn't as if I had to replace a huge income. I see a lot of people today—they retire or change jobs and they want to start in real estate to try to replace that huge income. I looked at real estate as if it was my job. My father always worked hard. I sort of saw the way he did it. He was in sales. He worked for Wrigley Chewing Gum Company for thirty-some-odd years. He went to work early; he got his stuff done. It was a steady increase for me, but every year I made more money, every year it kept increasing. To be quite honest, I never fathomed I would make the kind of money I do through selling homes. I always thought if I was ever going to make a lot of money in life, it would come from baseball.

Keys to Success—I don't dictate to [my sales team whether they do listings or buyers]. I've always been an advocate of them being full-time real estate agents and doing both sides of the business. They operate under their names, although every time they list a house, it's "The Mike Mendoza Team." Everything's built around the team. We sell the team and support the team and sell the benefits of having more people working for you than just one.

I always tried to put somebody else in the position that enabled me to do the things that I enjoyed doing in the business. I started doing it a long time ago, and that's why I think my business grew more rapidly than most. I wasn't afraid to have additional staff doing certain things that created more business opportunities for me. It gave me more time to focus on the more dollar-productive activities that I do, rather than processing paperwork or something.

Lead Generation—I would say the bulk of our leads are generated from our listing inventory. We work the listings for other opportunities—if you have no inventory, obviously the phone's not going to ring.

I've always been a believer in treating people the way I want to be treated. Follow up with people, give people good service, and then people will enjoy working with you. My referral business is quite large now, and it should be after nineteen years. If it wasn't, there'd be something wrong. I've always been one to try to give a lot back to the community. I try to be very involved in the community and the local charities—the YMCA, the Chamber of Commerce, and things like that—because that is where I make my living.

Next Year and the Future—The Mike Mendoza Team, at the time of writing, is on pace to match or better our 2001 production. I'm forty-seven now, and I'd really like to take a larger step back from the business by the time I'm fifty-five and both my kids have gone through college and have their lives going. I'd like to be more involved in the regional business than I am in my personal business and do some more coaching and consulting. It's about trying to find the right person who can step in there and maybe wear my shoes a little bit more.

SNAPSHOT OF A MILLIONAIRE

GREGG NEUMAN
San Diego, CA

Experience—21 years
Before Real Estate—Professional bartender (fifteen years)

2001 Production

Transactions—356
Sales Volume—$113 million
Gross Commission Income—$3 million

The Team

Sales—His partner Jennifer and eight buyer agents

Support—Office manager/marketing director, two transaction coordinators, a listing coordinator, and a full-time courier

Quick Takes

The Beginning—I was a bartender for fifteen years. I went to one year of college. I knew the only way I could make a lot of money without a great deal of education was in sales . . . some larger ticket items . . . I thought houses would be it.

I actually tended bar for the first year and a half, at night, while I sold real estate during the day.

One night I was writing an offer for a million-dollar property and I was rushing so I could get down to the bar shift. I said, "Wait a minute! I'm going to make thirty grand on this transaction and I'm rushing to get to the bar to make a hundred bucks." So, I called my boss and told him I'd be late.

Keys to Success—Real estate has always been easy for me. I like making deals. I know how to overcome objections. I know how to overcome challenges. I know how to talk to people and make them feel good about giving up things they'd rather not give up.

I did everything wrong. . . . I wasn't good with money. I bought an office with no ownership experience; I merged it with another office. I was chasing all the money I had at the time. Finally, I found someone to unload it on and just became an agent.

I did ten sales, then twenty-three, and then thirty. Then I added an assistant and my business almost doubled. Back then, I worked ten hours a day, seven days a week. Now with my great team, I take off eight days a month, I never work Sundays, and I take three vacations. And last year the business netted over $1.6 million.

Inspiration—I've always felt there is no end . . . The opportunities in real estate are limitless. You can become whatever you want to be.

Lead Generation—I anticipate the market—not just react to it—and I have learned better marketing techniques. I do color ads (they pull better) with IVR commercials. I send out 200 cards around every listing and every sale.

Allan Domb is my hero. He taught me to focus my market and to make better use of my time.

SNAPSHOT OF A MILLIONAIRE

Elaine Northrop
Ellicott City, MD

Experience—30 years
Before Real Estate—Homemaker

2001 Production

Transactions—159
Sales Volume—$71 million
Gross Commission Income—$1.8 million

The Team

Sales—One buyer specialist

Support—Marketing director (husband), office manager, bookkeeper, listing coordinator, and an administrative assistant

Quick Takes

The Beginning—My husband left me with two small children; I played the victim. After six months I gave that up and just plunged in. . . . I sold $1 million in the next six months.

Keys to Success—I learned to use creative visualization. I saw my success. I pictured my life as getting much better. The more I made those pictures happen, the more I created a new life for myself.

I watched other agents who were doing well. I began to do what they were doing. Every year I set higher goals— "double it" was my motto, and it worked.

I got an assistant early. I love sales, not paperwork.

Inspiration—For me, real estate is not work, it's a way of life.

First, you must create success in your own mind. Then set goals and make them happen. Invest in yourself.

Lead Generation—I do extensive advertising. I take out ten to twenty pages in the home magazines and a full-page ad every Sunday in the local paper. I write a name and story for each house I have listed. Our ads are very creative and catchy.

I do 300 just-listed and just-sold cards, but no other direct mail. And I hold client parties.

SNAPSHOT OF A MILLIONAIRE

JOE ROTHCHILD
Katy, TX

Experience—21 years

Before Real Estate—Phone sales and apartment locating

2001 Production

Transactions—597

Sales Volume—$106.9 million

Gross Commission Income—$2.6 million

The Team

Sales—Three buyer agents plus a team leader (brother)

Support—Financial manager (wife), a listing manager, a marketing director, a customer feedback coordinator, two closing coordinators, two receptionists, and a courier

Quick Takes

The Beginning—I went directly from college into sales—phone sales. I have no fear about calling people or knocking on doors. It's how you make business happen.

I did some land sales and then apartment locating. Eventually, I would help people rent an apartment, then rent a house, then buy a house.

I wanted to have my own business, so I started Rothchild Realty and bought a franchise. I sold that and bought another one, and the office is very profitable.

Now I have nine staff and four buyer agents. My wife runs all of our financials and our apartment-locating operation. My brother leads our buyer agent team. I handle all the listings and go on three to five listing appointments six days a week.

Keys to Success—My keys to real estate are knowing my industry, knowing my product, adding value, taking care of my clients, focusing on systems, and building my local reputation.

I keep my thumb on my business. I watch everything like a hawk and make sure everyone's doing what they need to be doing. I hold them accountable.

I strive to be persistent and determined in everything I do. People tell me that my goals are unachievable, but that just makes me all the more determined to meet my goals and prove them wrong. I believe that persistence and determination are omnipotent, almighty, capable of anything—the sky is the limit.

Lead Generation—We get a lot of referral leads, but I have a broad marketing plan—newspapers, home magazines, and the Internet. Our office yard signs alone generate over 7,000 prospects a year.

I have always focused on local advertising media that I could dominate without spending too much money.

Next Year and the Future—Now I'm looking for more passive income. I have over thirty rental properties that I manage, including four commercial buildings. My goal is to receive a million dollars a year in passive income from these rental properties.

SNAPSHOT OF A MILLIONAIRE

BILL RYAN
Chandler, AZ

Experience—28 years

Before Real Estate—College and part-time retail

2001 Production

Transactions—281
Sales Volume—$54 million
Gross Commission Income—$1.4 million

The Team

Sales—Six buyer agents

Support—Office manager, transaction coordinator, listing coordinator, client care manager, and two people in property management

Quick Takes

The Beginning—I came right out of college into real estate. I'm a native of the area I live in. So I just kind of worked from the ground up. We had a population of 15,000 to 20,000 back then. Now it is 200,000. It's been my market niche, and it's just grown over the years.

Keys to Success—I have learned to be more businesslike. If you don't treat it like a business, it won't become a business.

I am high on education—CRS was great. I've learned to implement what I've been taught—to set goals and put systems in place. Now I enjoy teaching others how to be successful.

I've had an assistant for twenty-four years, but when I hired Kerri as my office manager four years ago, my business made a major leap. She's doubled her income, and I've doubled my business.

Lead Generation—I used to just throw mud at the wall, now I've narrowed my promotions. I stopped doing ads in home magazines and in the Yellow Pages. My business still grew, and I saved more than $40,000 in expenses.

When you track your leads, you know what is working and where to spend your money. When you try a new program, track it for six months to a year. You have to give it a chance.

I do a monthly newsletter to my 3,000 sphere of influence and to my 12,000 address farm area. I do 200 to 400 cards around my sales, and I've improved my Internet site.

Other Business—The 1986 Tax Reform Act hit me hard. I went from a plus $4 million net worth to a negative $2 million. I learned to stick with what I know—residential properties. I now own twenty and am adding two a year. I like equity buildup and appreciation.

SNAPSHOT OF A MILLIONAIRE

Russell Shaw
Phoenix, AZ

Experience—24 years
Before Real Estate—Insurance sales and radio and
TV broadcasting

2001 Production

Transactions—383
Sales Volume—$50.6 million
Gross Commission Income—$1.5 million

The Team

Sales—Two buyer agents and one listing specialist

Support—Two transaction managers, a listing manager, an office manager, and an administrative assistant; his wife assists with both sales and support management

Quick Takes

The Beginning—I came out of the insurance business, so I knew how to build a client base that would bring repeat business.

Keys to Success—At first I was an idiot at hiring. I've gotten better. The cleverest thing I've ever done is to delegate everything. My wife is better at hiring than I am. So I leave it up to her and my office manager. Now, I don't micromanage, and they actually do it better than I would have.

With the exception of one neighbor, I haven't worked with a buyer since 1993. Last year we took 519 listings from 912 listing interviews and I went on about twenty-five of them. And I don't present offers—my contracts manager does this.

I used to give away all of my buyers. I knew I was losing business. Now, with my sales team, we're doing a lot more business.

It's my job to run the business and oversee our marketing—to bring business to us.

Inspiration—Agents need to stop focusing on the deal they *almost* got and focus on *all the business* that is out there. If one wants to look at waste, the customers they never contacted in anyway represent the real losses—not the one that got away.

I had been diagnosed with cancer and I didn't work for the bulk of last year. My business did grow. I wasn't there, and I had my best year ever.

Lead Generation—Use your strengths and natural ability to build your business. I was in radio and TV for twelve years, so I do radio commercials and have a radio show. I write my own copy and I do comedy.

I have a 5,000-person database that I mail to every month. I highlight our solds and offer our information package.

Whatever you do, focus on the consumer benefits you provide.

SNAPSHOT OF A MILLIONAIRE

SHERRY WILSON
Purceville, VA

Experience—18 years
Before Real Estate—Middle-school teacher

2001 Production

Transactions—351
Sales Volume—$102.6 million
Gross Commission Income—More than $3 million

The Team

Sales—Six buyer agents (and two new buyer agents)

Support—Operations manager, listing manager, contract manager, executive assistant, a reception and advertising coordinator, special project coordinator, and two part-time runners

Quick Takes

The Beginning—In the middle of 1984, while still teaching school, I decided to get my license. I always enjoyed reading those real estate magazines and knew the market. We had just moved to the county, and real estate was something that was interesting to me. I figured that I could sell a house or two a year and help some people. I enjoy helping people, so that's what I did. While I was teaching school full time the next year, I was rookie of the year. And the next year, also while teaching full time, I was top in sales for the county. I was really scared that I was just lucky. I taught two full years after I had my license and then I gave it up. Every year since, I was either top producer in the county, top in sales, or top in listings.

Keys to Success—I always had help. Six months into the business I had a part-time assistant. I had help long before anyone had heard of the team concept. Before everyone started talking about assistants, I had help for the parts of the business I didn't enjoy.

I'm very consistent in everything that I do. My eye was always on tomorrow's business. And I never, never, ever—and I teach my agents that if they think this way, they too, will succeed—keep my eye on how much commission I make. My focus is and will always be helping others achieve their goals.

Lead Generation—A strong referral system and name recognition through advertising. No farm system. No direct mail. Where I am, I can walk into a grocery store, a restaurant, a movie theater, I can go anywhere and I will have people coming up to me from sign recognition, from ad recognition. My budget's pretty significant in advertising.

Other Business—I own a real estate company, a title company, a referral company, and fifteen investment properties. I was really scared that I wouldn't have a retirement, so I made it my goal for my first ten to fifteen years in the business to buy an investment property each year.

Next Year and the Future—I am ahead of my 2001 numbers by a tad. In 2001, my goal was to reach $100 million in sales volume. As a reward for helping me reach that goal, I took sixteen members of my staff on a cruise. Because the market has slowed down, I kept my 2002 goals at $100 million in sales volume. An increase in my average sales price from $292,000 to approximately $315,000 is keeping me ahead of my 2001 pace. It also helps that my staff knows that if we match or top our 2001 production, we'll get another cruise!

SNAPSHOT OF A MILLIONAIRE

TIM WOOD
Big Bear Lake, CA

Experience—27 years
Before Real Estate—Newspaper printer

2001 Production

Transactions—275
Sales Volume—$38 million
Gross Commission Income—$1.45 million

The Team

Sales—Two licensed real estate agents (one of whom is Wood's son) who handle approximately 25 percent of listings outright and support the 75 percent Tim works personally

Support—Staff of two for administrative and sales support; relies on mortgage and escrow companies, so no transaction coordinator is needed

Quick Takes

The Beginning—The first five years I focused on how much money I could make. I thought making $100,000 a year would make me a millionaire. I drove Porsches. I spent lots of money, all the material stuff. And I had tax problems. That was the first five years.

Keys to Success— Then, the last twenty to twenty-five years, I found that focusing on the money goals didn't necessarily wake me up in the morning. I found that, for me, it's about focusing on, internalizing, personalizing the emotions of my dreams and my vision—that's what wakes me up in the morning. That's what keeps me motivated.

That's what keeps me excited and on track.

My belief is that dreams and visions are much larger and more long-term than goals. Goals are strictly aiming points that, when accomplished, put you closer to your dreams and visions. Goals are simply the vehicle to your dreams, and dreams are the fuel of your goals.

Inspiration—What inspired me was my attachment to that day in the future when I would have total freedom. My idea of that day is: I'm riding down the road on a mountain bike, with hair down to my shoulders, no shirt, cut-off jeans, and I'm going to the post office to box 315. And I pull out a tan envelop with a green check for $100,000—for the day! Now that is a great day. That's why I get up at three-nineteen A.M.!

Other Business—Wood owns a real estate, escrow, and mortgage company.

Advice—Keep it simple. Making and earning a million dollars—most people make it much more complicated that it really is. You must be patient. The lack of patience is the hero of our demise. Everyone wants to earn a million dollars, but few can hang in there long enough to achieve it. Look, it took me twenty years to accumulate $1 million cash in the bank. Two years later, I had $3 million. And at the end of this year, I'll have $5 million. A lot of people don't understand what patience is. It is one of the final steps. It can't be sidestepped. It's either your ally or your enemy, and you need to know when it is and when it isn't.

Next Year and the Future—This year (July 2002), we've closed 275 sides and have over 500 projected for the year. Sales will be $50, $55, or $60 million, and we'll have around $2.2 million in commissions.

Tyler and Mike (the licensed real estate assistants) are twenty-seven and twenty-eight years old. My goal is to have these kids in position to retire, if they'd like to, when they are thirty-five years old.

SNAPSHOT OF A MILLIONAIRE

DON ZELEZNAK
Scottsdale, AZ

Experience—14 years
Before Real Estate—Apartment syndications/
financial planning

2001 Production

Transactions—491
Sales Volume—$77 million
Gross Commission Income—$2 million

The Team

Sales—One person, my son Ryan, who has been in real estate since 1997

Support—One person, Dee Ann, handles all the administration and transaction coordination

Quick Takes

The Beginning—In 1984, I moved from Minnesota to Arizona. I had done over $100 million in real estate syndications, but decided I would go into real estate sales. I grow my business by working with investors. I helped them find great buys and then invest in "no-qual" sales with wrap mortgages. Some would just buy and resell; others would improve the property and resell.

There are about one hundred people I stay in touch with as repeat investors. Two years ago, we moved into more traditional work with sellers and buyers. Our database is now at 1,000, but most of our business comes from referrals.

Keys to Success—I love the action, but I tend to take on too much. That's what my wife keeps reminding me.

I bring focus to my work and I seek to leverage cash flow and passive income from businesses or projects I own.

Hiring my first assistant was a big step. If you are going to get someone good, you have to pay them well.

I have a great accountant who understands business—not all accountants do. But I do all my own budgets, and I track my P&Ls closely.

Next Year and the Future—I will do about $80 million in sales volume in 2002, with about $2.2 million in GCI. But I will do that with half the transactions we did in 2001.

While my son Ryan does a lot of the listings and buyer work, I'm focusing on real estate development. I have seven commercial projects (mostly office condos) and a 3,000-lot subdivision that will take ten years to develop. It will be a great source of future buyers, sellers, and commission income.

APPENDIX A: SAMPLE PROFIT AND LOSS REPORT

SAMPLE PROFIT AND LOSS REPORT

Category	Monthly Total
Income	
4000 Residential Income	
4010 Listing Income	
4020 Resale	$0.00
4030 New Home	$0.00
4040 Relocation	$0.00
4050 Listing Income—Other	$0.00
Total 4010 Listing Income	$0.00
4110 Sales Income	
4120 Resale	$0.00
4130 New Home	$0.00
4140 Relocation	$0.00
4150 Sales Income—Other	$0.00
Total 4010 Listing Income	$0.00
Total 4000 Residential Income	$0.00

4200 Commercial Income	
4210 Listing Income	
4220 Existing	$0.00
4230 New	$0.00
4240 Listing Income—Other	$0.00
Total 4210 Listing Income	$0.00
4310 Sales Income	
4320 Existing	$0.00
4330 New	$0.00
4340 Sales Income—Other	$0.00
Total 4310 Sales Income	$0.00
Total 4200 Commercial Income	$0.00
4810 Residential Lease Income	$0.00
4815 Commercial Leasing Income	$0.00
4820 Referral Income	$0.00
Total Income	$0.00

Cost of Sales

5010 Commission Paid Out	
5020 Buyer Specialist	$0.00
5030 Listing Specialist	$0.00
5040 Miscellaneous COS	$0.00
5050 Commissions Paid Out—Other	$0.00
Total 5010 Commissions Paid Out	$0.00
5200 Concessions	$0.00
Total Cost of Sales	$0.00

Gross Profit	$0.00

Expenses

6919 Accounting and Tax Preparation

6020 Advertising

6040 Newspaper	$0.00
6050 General Magazine	$0.00
6060 Proprietary Magazine	$0.00
6070 Radio	$0.00
6080 TV	$0.00
6090 Billboard	$0.00
6100 Internet	
6110 Design Work	$0.00
6120 Website Maintenance Fee	$0.00
6130 Home Page/Access/E-mail	$0.00
6140 Internet—Other	$0.00
Total 6100 Internet	$0.00
6140 Giveaway Items	$0.00
6150 Business Cards	$0.00
6155 Signs	$0.00
6160 Flyers	$0.00
6165 Direct Mail	$0.00
6170 Telemarketing	$0.00
6175 1-800 Number	$0.00
6177 IVR Technology	$0.00
6020 Advertising—Other	$0.00
Total 6020 Advertising	$0.00
6180 Automobile	
6185 Interest Portion of Payment	$0.00
6190 Gas	$0.00
6195 Maintenance	$0.00
6199 Automobile—Other	$0.00
Total 6180 Automobile	$0.00

6200 Banking

6205 Checks	$0.00
6210 Service Charges	$0.00
6215 Banking—Other	$0.00
Total 6200 Banking	$0.00

6215 Charitable Contributions	$0.00
6220 Computer MLS Charges	$0.00
6225 Continuing Education	$0.00
6230 Books	$0.00
6235 Newsletters	$0.00
6240 Tapes	$0.00
6245 Seminars	$0.00
6250 Magazine Subscriptions	$0.00
6255 Continuing Education—Other	$0.00
Total 6225 Continuing Education	$0.00

6260 Contract Labor	$0.00
6270 Technology Support	$0.00
6280 Consulting	$0.00
6290 Contract Labor—Other	$0.00
Total 6260 Contract Labor	$0.00

6290 Copies	$0.00
6300 Credit Reports	$0.00
6310 Customer Gifts	$0.00
6315 Depreciation/Amortization	$0.00
6320 Dues	
6330 MLS	$0.00
6340 NAR	$0.00
6350 Other Dues	$0.00
6355 Dues—Other	$0.00
Total 6320 Dues	$0.00

6360 Equipment Rental

6370 Copier	$0.00
6380 Fax	$0.00
6390 Computer	$0.00
6400 Cellular Phone	$0.00
6410 Pager	$0.00
6420 Other Equipment Rentals	$0.00
6425 Equipment Rental—Other	$0.00
Total 6360 Equipment Rental	$0.00

6430 Interest	$0.00

6440 Insurance

6450 E & O	$0.00
6460 Property	$0.00
6470 Car	$0.00
6480 Equipment	$0.00
6485 Insurance—Other	$0.00
Total 6440 Insurance	$0.00

6490 Legal	$0.00
6500 Lock Boxes	$0.00
6510 Meals	$0.00

6520 Office Supplies

6530 Paper	$0.00
6540 Other Office Supplies	$0.00
6545 Office Supplies—Other	$0.00
Total 6520 Office Supplies	$0.00

6550 Photography	$0.00
6560 Postage/Freight/Delivery	$0.00
6570 Printing (Nonadvertising)	$0.00
6580 Professional Fees	$0.00
6590 Rent—Office	$0.00

6600 Repairs and Maintenance

6610 Office	$0.00
6620 Computers	$0.00
6630 Fax	$0.00
6640 Copier	$0.00
6650 Other Repairs	$0.00
6660 Repairs and Maintenance—Other	$0.00
Total 6600 Repairs and Maintenance	$0.00

6670 Salaries

6680 Management	$0.00
6690 Listing Specialists	$0.00
6700 Buyer Specialists	$0.00
6710 Staff	$0.00
6720 Runners	$0.00
6730 Other Salaries	$0.00
6735 Salaries—Other	$0.00
Total 6670 Salaries	$0.00

6740 Telephone

6750 Phone Line	$0.00
6760 Long Distance	$0.00
6765 Pager	$0.00
6770 Cellular Phone	$0.00
6775 Voice Mail	$0.00
6780 Answering Service	$0.00
6790 Fax Line	$0.00
6800 MLS Line	$0.00
6810 Computer/Internet Line	$0.00
6815 Telephone—Other	$0.00
Total 6740 Telephone	$0.00

6820 Taxes	
6830 Payroll (FICA)	$0.00
6840 Payroll (FUTA)	$0.00
6850 Payroll (SUTA)	$0.00
6869 Federal Income Tax	$0.00
6880 State Taxes	$0.00
6890 Taxes—Other	$0.00
Total 6820 Taxes	$0.00
6900 Travel/Lodgings	$0.00
Total Expenses	**$0.00**
Net Ordinary Income	**$0.00**

Other Income

7000 Other Income	
7100 Profit Sharing	$0.00
7110 Interest Income	$0.00
7120 Miscellaneous Income	$0.00
7130 Other Income—Other	$0.00
Total Other Income	$0.00
Other Expense	$0.00
Net Other Income	**$0.00**
Net Income	**$0.00**

APPENDIX B:
SAMPLE BALANCE SHEET

SAMPLE BALANCE SHEET

Category	Monthly Total
Assets	
Current Assets	
Checking/Saving	
1010 Business Checking Account	$0.00
1020 Business Money Market Account	$0.00
Total Checking/Savings	$0.00
Accounts Receivable	
1300 Accounts Receivable	$0.00
Total Accounts Receivable	$0.00
Other Current Assets	
Total Current Assets	$0.00
Fixed Assets	
1600 Computers	
1601 Computer Cost	$0.00
1602 Computer—Accumulated Depreciation	$0.00
1603 Computers—Other	$0.00
Total 1600 Computers	$0.00

1610 Automobiles

1611 Automobiles—Cost	$0.00
1612 Automobile—Accumulated Depreciation	$0.00
1613 Automobile—Other	$0.00
Total 1610 Automobile	$0.00

1620 Furniture and Fixtures

1621 Furniture and Fixtures—Cost	$0.00
1622 Furniture and Fixtures— Accumulated Depreciation	$0.00
1623 Furniture and Fixtures—Other	$0.00
Total 1620 Furniture and Fixtures	$0.00

1630 Equipment

1631 Equipment—Cost	$0.00
1632 Equipment—Accumulated Depreciation	$0.00
1633 Equipment—Other	$0.00
Total 1630 Equipment	$0.00

Total Fixed Assets	$0.00

Other Assets

1700 Refundable Deposits	$0.00
1710 Prepaid Expenses	$0.00
1800 Start-Up Costs	$0.00
Total Other Assets	$0.00

Total Assets	**$0.00**

Liabilities and Equity

Liabilities

Current Liabilities

Accounts Payable

2010 Accounts Payable	$0.00
Total Accounts Payable	$0.00

Credit Cards

2020 Credit Cards Account	$0.00
Total Credit Cards	$0.00

Other Current Liabilities

2100 Federal Withholding Payable	$0.00
2110 FICA Withholding Payable	$0.00
2120 State Withholding Payable	$0.00
2130 FUTA Payable	$0.00
2140 SUTA Payable	$0.00
2200 Federal Income Tax Payable	$0.00
Total Other Current Liabilities	$0.00

Total Current Liabilities	$0.00

Long-Term Liabilities

Note Payable

2710 Note Payable	$0.00
Total Long-Term Liabilities	$0.00

Total Liabilities	$0.00

Equity

3000 Opening Balance Equity	$0.00
3100 Common Stock	$0.00
3900 Retained Earnings	$0.00
Net Income	$0.00
Total Equity	$0.00

Total Liabilities and Equity	**$0.00**

ABOUT THE
AUTHORS

GARY KELLER

Gary has excelled as a real estate salesperson by teaching clients how to make great home buying-and-selling decisions. As a real estate sales manager, he's recruited agents through training and helped them build their careers the same way. As cofounder and chairman of the board, he built Keller Williams Realty International from a single office in Austin, Texas, to the #1 position as the largest real estate company in the United States by using his skills as a teacher, trainer, and coach. Gary defines leadership as "teaching people how to think the way they need to think so they can do what they need to do when they need to do it, so they can get what they want when they want it."

An Ernst & Young Entrepreneur of the Year and finalist for *Inc.* magazine's Entrepreneur of the Year, Keller is recognized as one of the most influential leaders in the real estate industry. He has also helped many small business owners and entrepreneurs find success through his nationally bestselling Millionaire Real Estate series. A book, after all, is just another way to teach, but one with an infinitely large classroom. As a business coach and national trainer, Gary has helped countless others realize extraordinary results by narrowing their focus to their own ONE Thing.

Unsurprising to those who know him, Gary believes that his single greatest achievement is the life he's built with his wife Mary and their son John.

DAVE JENKS

A passion for helping people realize their greatest potential has led Dave Jenks to inspire thousands of top real estate agents, as well as entrepreneurs from many other walks of life. A consultant and trainer with more than 30 years of experience in real estate, he's taught for the Dale Carnegie Institute and Keller Williams University, where he is co-author on several books in The Millionaire Real Estate series with Gary Keller and Jay Papasan.

JAY PAPASAN

Jay is the executive editor and vice president of publishing at Keller Williams Realty and president of Rellek Publishing. He attempted to write his first book on an electric typewriter in junior high and was hooked. At least one high school teacher thought his writing had promise and circulated one of his essays to the entire staff. Jay paid the bills in college by working in a bookstore. He got his undergraduate degree in writing and later, his Master's. After graduation, Jay took a job in publishing. During his years at HarperCollins in New York he worked on bestselling titles like *Body for Life* by Bill Phillips and *Go for the Goal* by Mia Hamm. More recently, in the ten years he's worked with Gary, Jay has coauthored numerous award-winning or bestselling titles, including the Millionaire Real Estate series.

Jay is passionate about sharing the ideas in his books and regularly speaks at conventions and training events. He is a member of the Keller Williams University International Master Faculty.

Outside of work, Jay co-owns a successful real estate investment business and sales team with his wife Wendy. They enjoy life in Austin, Texas, with their children Gus and Veronica.

MY NOTES:

MY NOTES:

MY NOTES:

MY NOTES:

Reap the benefits of thinking big and aiming high! Visit us at **www.KellerInk.com** and expand your possibilities as part of a growing community of top performers.

- Explore blogs and additional commentary written by the authors of KellerInk books.

- Browse our ever-growing content including a variety of videos, latest trends and "Market of the Moment" commentary, as well as audio interviews with innovative industry leaders and rising stars.

- Utilize free downloads and other business-building resources.

- Purchase KellerInk books, audiobooks, DVDs, CDs, and more.

Plug into the energy and insights of other top-performing real estate agents, investors, and experts in the real estate community. Take your sales business to its highest level possible!